KATHLEEN D. RYAN
DANIEL K. OESTREICH

Driving Fear Out
of the Workplace

Creating the High-Trust,
High-Performance
Organization

SECOND EDITION

Jossey-Bass Publishers • San Francisco

Jossey-Bass books and products are available through most bookstores. To contact Jossey-Bass directly, call (888) 378-2537, fax to (800) 605-2665, or visit our website at www.josseybass.com.

Substantial discounts on bulk quantities of Jossey-Bass books are available to corporations, professional associations, and other organizations. For details and discount information, contact the special sales department at Jossey-Bass.

For sales outside the United States, please contact your local Simon & Schuster International Office.

Manufactured in the United States of America on Lyons Falls Turin Book. This paper is acid-free and 100 percent totally chlorine-free.

Library of Congress Cataloging-in-Publication Data
Ryan, Kathleen, date.
    Driving fear out of the workplace : creating the high-trust,
high-performance organization / Kathleen D. Ryan, Daniel K.
Oestreich. — 2nd ed.
       p.   cm. — (The Jossey-Bass business & management series)
    Includes bibliographical references and index.
    ISBN 0-7879-3968-4
    1. Organizational effectiveness. 2. Work environment. 3. Fear.
I. Oestreich, Daniel K., date. II. Title. III. Series.
HD58.9.R93   1998
658.5—dc21   97–49000

SECOND EDITION
PB Printing
10 9 8 7 6 5 4 3 2 1

THE JOSSEY-BASS
BUSINESS & MANAGEMENT
SERIES

C O N T E N T S

PART I
The Dynamics of Fear

1 The Experience of Fear

2 Cycles of Mistrust

3 Defining a Trust-Based Workplace

PART II
How Fear Operates in Organizations

PART III
Strategies for Building a High-Trust Workplace

PART IV

A Future of Trust

16 **People Are Ready for a Workplace Without Fear**   291

Whatever Happened to Paul? ■ Talking About the Future: Knowledge, Learning, and Trust ■ Leaders Must Find the Courage to Speak Up ■ The Smart Thing and the Right Thing ■ Challenges of the Path

FOREWORD

A few years ago I was making a presentation called "Managing Fear in the Workplace" to a group of executives in a multinational corporation. A young executive raised his hand and commented, "I don't think fear is an issue in this organization. Your presentation is interesting, but when are we going to discuss the real problems?" "What do you consider to be your real problems?" I asked. He replied, "We are losing the people we want to keep, we continue to downsize and we don't get any better, we have consistently missed our sales projections, we have too many meetings, we have not developed a new idea in months, we continue recycling old strategies, . . ." The list went on and on.

The level of energy in the room was high. The entire team engaged in the discussion as I captured everything on a flip chart as fast as I could. I wanted them to see the relationship between these issues and fear. This connection was not explicit to them. As with many leaders, managers, and workers, it was hard for them to immediately see that fear had a lot to do with the organization's "real problems" and the pent-up need to discuss them. When people are afraid to ask questions or tell the truth because they fear repercussions or don't believe anything will come of it, mistrust and negativity—and many of the problems the group mentioned—quickly follow. The questions I asked began to help people get past these invisible barriers.

Although fear is a universal aspect of everyday life, we only reluctantly acknowledge the inhibiting and destructive aspects of this emotion in the workplace. As W. Edwards Deming noted: "The fundamental problem in American business is that people are scared to discuss the problems of people" (Gitlow and Gitlow, 1987, p. 137). Fear is indeed a problem of people. It does exist in the workplace and works its destruction all the more successfully because we refuse to face it. Fear is a distracting force that robs employees and organizations of their potential. It can be to an organization what high blood pressure is to the human body—a silent killer! It can go unnoticed, but its effects are devastating nonetheless.

More than ever, this is a time when leaders need to be concerned about the effects of fear. Organizations are undergoing enormous change, and leaders need all the help they can get to make it through them successfully. Yet fears of all kinds afflict and impede organizations during such times—fear of speaking up, of conflict, and of failure, to name a few. I have seen how fear can prove to be highly destructive in the long run if it is allowed to undermine the social system of an organization. Many mistakenly believe that fear is good as a motivational tool. There is no such thing as healthy fear: the outcomes are usually negative! Fear can generate short-term bursts of performance, perhaps bigger efforts but never better results. When people experience fear, they focus on evading the threat. Indeed, fear of failure—which is often something in organizations we cannot talk about—is self-fulfilling. It becomes the springboard for failure.

In 1978, as a teenager at the circus, I watched Karl Wallenda, the tightrope aerialist, traversing a seventy-five-foot wire. It was a windy day and he looked tentative. After walking just a few steps, he was struggling. He was losing his balance and tried to get on his knees in an effort to hang onto the wire. He released the balancing pole and shortly after fell to his death. Afterward, Mrs. Wallenda, also an aerialist, discussed the incident with the press. She said: "All Karl thought about for three straight months prior to this walk was falling. For the first time in his life, it seemed to me that he put all his energies into not falling rather than walking the tightrope successfully."

It was a tragic moment—I still recall every second of it—but I learned an important lesson: our tendency to avoid failure opposes, dampens, and inhibits our ability to undertake achievement-oriented activities. Fear-based outcomes, in most cases, affect both personal and organizational effectiveness and performance. Fear doesn't motivate toward constructive action. On the contrary, it nourishes competition within an organization, fosters short-term thinking, destroys trust, erodes joy and pride in work, stifles innovation, and distorts communication. As Edmund Burke said, "No passion so effectively robs the mind of all its powers of acting and reasoning as fear." I think that for the most part, successful organizations have done well in spite of fear, not because of it.

Fear is an emotion we all know about—scholars, psychologists, managers, social workers—but we rarely talk about it and very little is written about it. When I embarked on the difficult task of conducting research in this area I was surprised to find a lack of resources, publications, and research efforts. That changed in 1991 with the publication of *Driving Fear Out of the Workplace* by Kathleen Ryan and Daniel Oestreich. This book put the issue on the table and offered an insightful and provocative view of fear at work.

Kathleen and Dan have done it again in 1998. In this revised edition they put continual improvement and learning into action. They have further refined and enhanced what was already a wonderful book.

This new edition takes direct aim at organizational fear and the importance of creating a climate of trust. It also contains a provocative new chapter on addressing fear during periods of rapid change. The book uncovers what often is known privately in most organizations but is ignored. Kathleen and Dan make the undiscussable discussable! They offer practical new directions for action and advice on where to begin and how to deal with this complex human emotion. This book encourages a spirit of trust and cooperation in human affairs. It is bountifully illustrated with examples and stories. It is sound, challenging, and thoughtful.

Kathleen and Dan's argument on the repercussions of fear in the workplace should be required reading for anyone who has an interest in bringing joy to our work environments.

February 1998   J. Gerald Suarez
                         Director, Presidential Quality Management
                         The White House
                         Washington, D.C.

P R E F A C E

Attempting to succeed amid the business realities of the 1990s, executives and managers have discovered many barriers. These go beyond the now-familiar challenges of global competition, shrinking resources, and the continued urgency to produce short-term profits while ensuring long-term success. The emerging dilemmas include the significant gap between workforce skills and business needs, the appropriate use of new technologies, the question of how to manage information and apply knowledge, constantly escalating customer demands, and the challenges of leading an increasingly diverse workforce during a period of enormous change.

Not very hidden within these barriers is the presence of fear. We see fear as an increasingly visible background phenomenon that undermines the commitment, motivation, and confidence of people at work. It is most easily observed as a reluctance to speak up about needed improvements or other important work issues because of fear of repercussions. To move forward into a new century, organizations must break through this barrier to create environments where trust, productivity, and innovation can flourish.

The problem, as a vice president of a Fortune 500 company told us, is that fear is at the root of "all the time people spend in meetings not saying what's really on their mind." These silences, built into organizations at all levels, plague most managers. They represent the absence of ideas or enthusiasm, suggestions that never go beyond the ordinary, reluctance to share information, conversations that circle the problem but never pin it down, and unfinished business that leads to poor follow-through and mediocre results. Behind these silences, at the root of fear, are ingrained negative beliefs about the motives of managers and employees. To help create a better environment, this book describes

- The impact fear has on individuals and organizations
- The reasons people do not speak up
- The issues people cannot talk about openly at work
- Practical methods leaders can use to encourage people to speak openly and turn patterns of fear into creativity and trust

Our work on this topic has been inspired primarily by personal consulting experiences over many years. Countless times, these efforts to help organizations create a spirit of openness and trust have revealed the pervasiveness of workplace fear. Even in relatively open environments, it is possible to observe the reluctance of talented employees and managers to speak up about key organizational issues and needed improvements. Inquiring about people's hesitation, we have often heard lines such as these:

"You've got to be careful on that subject."

"You can never be fully honest around here."

"You just never know how [boss's name] will react."

Ten years ago, these experiences confirmed the teachings of W. Edwards Deming and others involved with continuous quality improvement. Deming asserted in his fourteen obligations of management that quality was impossible where people are afraid to tell the truth. Scrap and breakage get hidden, numbers and schedules are misrepresented, and bad products are forwarded to customers because the quality assurance inspector knows better than to stop the line. Deming strongly admonished managers to drive out fear so that everyone can participate meaningfully in the organization. It is from his work that the title of this book is drawn.

Besides Deming, other voices strongly reinforce the need to understand the dynamics and effects of fear. Chris Argyris's extensive body of work clarifies how invisible and self-reinforcing miscommunication due to fear can be. Peter Senge's explorations of systems thinking illuminate its far-reaching effects. Both of these thinkers underscore the need to understand the negative assumptions about people that keep fear in place. Peter Block's works on empowerment and stewardship demand a wholesale rethinking of the concepts of management and leadership as a way to escape these destructive beliefs. Most recently, Thomas Stewart's examination of the rapidly emerging value of intellectual capital demands that even more attention be paid to reducing fear and building trust.

Finding Out About Fear

As we began to research the literature in the late 1980s, we found references to fear, trust, organizational climate, and the supervisor-subordinate relationship, but often what we read seemed to only lightly touch our primary interest. No one major work directly addressed the fears that keep people from speaking up at work. This was an impetus to learn more by talking directly to people. Although times have changed, and there are new voices, such as Gerald Suarez's, in the field, many gaps in knowledge still exist. In the Recommended Resources at the end of this book, we summarize some interrelated works that have provided a foundation for our own exploration and that serve as helpful reference points. You are encouraged to look over the Recommended Resources as you pursue other literature related to building trust and reducing fear.

In 1989 and 1990, with a third colleague, George Orr, we began extensive interviews around the country in which we asked about people's experiences with workplace fear. The three of us talked with 260 individuals in a broad spectrum of organizations—twenty-two altogether, evenly divided between service and manufacturing sectors with government included. Our geographic spread included the areas surrounding Atlanta; Chicago; St. Louis; Rochester, New York; San Francisco; Austin, Texas; and Seattle. We talked to people at all levels, from CEOs to mechanics.

We saw this work as a form of "reconnaissance," rather than science, that enabled us to learn by directly listening to people. Each sixty- to ninety-minute standardized interview was shaped by four basic questions:

1. What issues have you hesitated to talk about at work in the last five years of your job experience?

2. Why didn't you talk about them?

3. Did you hesitate to speak up on an issue because you feared some type of repercussion?

4. What were those threatening situations and what impact did they have?

From the answers to these questions, our definition of fear in the workplace emerged:

Fear is feeling threatened by possible repercussions as a result of speaking up about work-related concerns, ideas, and suggestions for improvement.

This definition focuses on the fear people may feel in talking about their experiences at work. Many things can cause people to feel tense, anxious, or scared, from the impending urgency of a business change to threats of disciplinary action. We assumed that many of these fears were a typical part of organizational life. For us, the bigger issue was whether people felt free to speak up about their worries, frustrations, and any other uncomfortable aspects of their work experiences to those who could do something to directly help. If people could not speak up, we wanted to know why and what impact this might have on their personal and organizational performance.

Our definition was not shared with study participants and no effort was made to channel the way people might respond to the interview questions. Individuals usually were selected as participants by someone inside the organization who served as an internal coordinator for the interviews. This was done in no particular manner and often simply depended on the schedules of study participants. We specifically asked that people *not* be selected because they might have some special experience related to fear. Other than that, there was no effort to control the makeup of our sample. The numbers fell into the categories shown in the Appendix.

As a result of this field study we have often been able to bring concepts to life through stories and vignettes drawn from what the participants shared. Although the details are modified—this sensitive information could not have been obtained without guaranteeing anonymity—each story is real.

The study has not been reverified through additional interviews for this revised edition. This choice is the result of continuing consulting experiences that confirm that the dynamics originally described remain on target. The study findings still serve their original and primary purpose: to be a catalyst for discussions with leaders about their own experiences and the experiences of others in their workplaces.

Fear Is a Challenging Topic

To examine the patterns of fear, it is necessary to look at a less positive side of organizations. In particular, many of the stories told in this book are about managers who *unconsciously* do things that cause their employees to be afraid to speak up. These descriptions of negative behaviors are offered as helpful examples of what *not* to do. While it may be painful to read some of these stories, we hope you will appreciate this method and the intention behind it, which has nothing to do with manager-bashing. Our years of working in every type of organization have taught us that the vast majority of managers are highly committed and dedicated to their jobs. We have great respect for the many very difficult aspects of their roles.

To turn around the patterns of fear, leaders must be willing to take the risks that come from making changes in their personal style at work. For example, some strategies require a genuine willingness to hear feedback about oneself as a leader or to learn about previously hidden aspects of relationships. Such actions are not always comfortable because they can test personal assumptions, long-established habits, and communication patterns. However, making these types of changes is an entirely doable challenge, one that is particularly important for leaders who see the inextricable links between personal and organizational improvement.

In spite of these challenges, we believe you will be greatly rewarded by learning about fear and initiating action to reduce it. When fear is reduced and trust enhanced, people naturally become more committed to their work and are more enthusiastic about their organization. They exercise their talents confidently and are more open to change. They support the enterprise because they feel that the enterprise supports them.

Leading changes of this kind is a powerful contribution, and often a deeply heartfelt one. Changing an organization by building trust is one of the best ways to fulfill the legacies of the quality movement and create a preferred future. It taps the long-term passion expressed so well by W. Edwards Deming: "We are here to make another kind of world." While this work is no panacea, it can provide hope and meaning, particularly in workplaces where the true potential of people has been forgotten or has become obscured by the day-to-day press for corporate survival.

Why a Second Edition?

A great deal has changed since the first publication of *Driving Fear Out of the Workplace* in early 1991. Against the backdrop of an ever more powerful global marketplace, we have seen vast structural changes in the economy, shifting demographics, and significant adjustments in the way people think about organizations. Some of the changes, such as widespread e-mail and the common use of the Internet, have had a significant impact on the way work is done and where it is done. Others, such as the increase in diversity, have changed the workplace as a social network. Some of these changes have added new layers of complexity and ambiguity or the challenge of new tasks. And some of them have more seriously destabilized the workplace, increasing people's fears and their concerns about speaking up. For example:

- Organizations have undergone a destabilizing period of reorganization, downsizing, and layoffs.

- Quality and reengineering efforts, in which many people were involved and on which some staked their careers, are now often viewed as fads past their prime.

- There is a growing belief that individuals themselves, not organizations, are responsible for personal well-being and career stability.

- Powerful efforts are being exerted to reinvent or simply reduce government.

- Technology has given people access to enormous amounts of information, which can be overwhelming, contributing to confusion in work environments because "everything is a priority."

These and other changes have created a deep need for people to have honest, ongoing conversations about the complexities, ambiguities, and fears they are experiencing. More than ever before, it is important to address uncomfortable data, give and receive feedback, and tackle issues that in the past might have been brushed under the rug. Today leaders cannot afford to lose information or creative ideas that may help their organization to face the future. They especially cannot afford to lose the energies and talents of employees to fear and low morale. In order to help their organizations accomplish needed changes and help people past their fears, leaders must create open workplaces where everyone can be candid about her or his experiences, concerns, ideas, and hopes. An open, trusting environment is the essential antidote to mixed-up times when old ways and old expectations no longer work. A revised edition of this book is one way to help with that prescription.

It is true that for some, perhaps many, the recent years have been a time of deepening anxiety. Popular cartoons that darkly celebrate a background culture of powerlessness and cynicism adorn many workplace walls. But this period of change has had positive effects, as well, particularly for organizations that have learned to help people speak up and to collaborate freely. Examples such as the creation of the Saturn automobile and the Boeing 777 aircraft show the way toward more genuinely participative and profitable workplaces. If this is a time of cynicism, it is also a time when people have a deep interest in finding out more about collaboration and trust and the barriers—like fear—to achieving these qualities.

In truth, today organizations are most often someplace on a continuum between trust and fear. Some work consciously, devotedly, toward building high-trust environments. Others, holding on to the past, are still trapped in older, hierarchical patterns of mistrust. Most are between these two extremes, looking for a way, in the moment, to move toward the trusting end.

We see this as an essentially hopeful time, full of opportunity and potential. If the current state is one of extraordinary flux and change, it also brings the problem of fear center stage and into the spotlight. In turn, this means that the possibilities for learning and progress are better than ever.

Our Audience

We think of you, our reader, as a leader. Perhaps you are responsible for initiating and overseeing others' work in a formal way, for guiding an organization or a part of it. You may be an executive, middle manager, first-line supervisor, project manager, or lead worker. As you read, you may feel that you are wearing two hats at once: supervisor and employee. You may find that what you are learning while wearing one hat helps you to see what you need to do while wearing the other one.

You may also be someone outside of line management who works with human resources, quality, learning, or organization development issues, as an adviser or practitioner of change.

In a broader sense, you might be a person who simply feels a strong personal investment in creating a better workplace.

Regardless of your exact leadership role, we picture you as a person who knows that things are changing and who wants to play a role in this transformation. You are likely to be someone who understands the current implications in the old saying: "If you always do what you have always done, you will always get what you have always got." You already know or suspect that the fear of speaking up is an impediment. And you are willing to address the challenges, recognizing full well that improvements may require some aspect of personal growth and development.

Our Approach and Structure

Accordingly, our approach highlights the practice of leadership: what leaders can do to create environments where people feel free to speak up. The focus is on the individual leader and work teams within a personal sphere of influence. Direct relationships down a reporting ladder are highlighted most often. We have deliberately chosen this emphasis because we believe it offers the place of greatest leverage for change and reverses a common dynamic of self-imposed helplessness and blaming of others, especially those higher up. This book is not about wishing that "those people" higher up would make a change. It is about the personal change *you* can make. Instead of shifting responsibility, we hope you will focus on what

you can do in relationships where your influence is the most immediate. This approach follows these beliefs of ours:

- Influencing relationships with direct reports is often easier
  and faster than with superiors.

- One of the best methods of influencing higher levels of the
  system is by creating success stories in other parts of the
  organization.

- Leaders have a responsibility to initiate efforts to reduce fear
  and build trust, whatever their position.

In addition to reporting data from the field study and describing a framework for understanding the dynamics of fear, we have
devoted over half of this book to practical strategies and methods.
We provide a wide range of optional approaches for reducing fear
and building trust that can be customized for many types of work
environments. These approaches have emerged from our day-to-
day consulting work with organizations committed to building
high-trust environments. Our aim is to offer the best of what these
consulting experiences have yielded in terms of practical, meaningful methods for producing change.

This second edition has been reorganized and reformatted to
make it as readable and useful as possible. We more directly emphasize the context of ongoing change and the value of working from a
positive vision. We have refined our suggestions to concentrate on
those we have personally found most useful, deleting some that
were in the first edition and adding or augmenting others. Finally,
we have added a section called "New Lessons and Reflections" at
the end of each chapter to highlight the lessons we have learned
since the first edition was published. The ideas in this section reflect
the emphasis our individual work has taken, with Kathy addressing
the broad issues of changing an organization's culture and Dan
focusing on the more personal aspects of leadership transformation.
We hope that you will use these ideas to stimulate additional reflections as you review the key points of each chapter and think about
the implications for your own leadership work.

The book is divided into four parts, structured to help you
to understand the problem of fear and then choose effective strategies to do something about it. Part One, "The Dynamics of Fear,"
sets the context by comparing the difficult realities of a workplace

characterized by cycles of mistrust to the vision of a high-trust organization. Part Two, "How Fear Operates in Organizations," directly explores the findings of our field study in order to more fully describe the negative effects of fear. This part discusses what people are not talking about (the "undiscussables"), why people are not talking about them, and how this directly affects productivity and innovation. Part Three, "Strategies for Building a High-Trust Workplace," offers seven categories of leadership action to help managers and their teams work toward a positive, trust-based vision. Each chapter provides a detailed array of specific steps, often right down to the words to say, to help leaders move forward with a sense of confidence. Part Four, "A Future of Trust," describes key points for dealing with fear during rapid organizational change and concludes the book by encouraging all leaders to take the risks necessary to move their organization forward.

Readers who want to learn more about speaking up, particularly about ways to influence people at higher levels, may find *The Courageous Messenger: How to Successfully Speak Up at Work,* a useful companion volume. This second book, written with our colleague, George Orr, focuses on helping people find the courage to speak up and shape their messages in the ways that are most likely to be heard and acted upon positively.

Acknowledgments

This book began with the gracious assistance of 260 people across the country who talked to us about their experiences with fear. Without their help, our work would lack candor and the vitality of real life. Each of their organizations had at least one person who served as a logistic contact. These people went out of their way to be of assistance. Their willingness to take risks and their practical help made our fieldwork possible.

While writing this book, we have been surrounded by supportive friends, colleagues, clients, and family members whose belief in us and enthusiasm for our work kept us on track. Many of these individuals, particularly among our clients, consistently demonstrated management practices based on trust and collaboration and a willingness to deal with fear in a straightforward, courageous way. We have learned much from them. In particular, we want to thank Jane Dailey of South Fulton Medical Center near Atlanta; Diane Soules at the University of Washington Medical Center; and Greg Simmons, CEO, and the MetaStar organization in Madison, Wisconsin. Each has offered a living model of commitment to personal and cultural change.

Many people helped us along the way. George Orr, Kathy's business partner and husband, conducted interviews, assisted with data analysis, did library research, and served as a third, less visible member of our team. His ever-present support was a critical resource to us. Howard Strickler created space and time for us to develop and finish our work for the first edition. Deborah Ray and the Ohio Quality and Productivity Forum created many opportunities to present and develop our ideas. Joshua Hammond brought new perspectives and connections and helped to expand the context for our work. Geoffrey Bellman opened many doors for us, one of which led to Ray Bard, who managed the production of the original book. Ray's knowledge of the publishing business and fine thinking sharpened our concepts and helped us make tangible the desire to write the book. Byron Schneider, our Jossey-Bass editor, has been an unfailing source of support and insight.

In a category of their own are our spouses, George Orr and Sarah Stiteler. Their unquestioned patience and loving commitment will be remembered and treasured. We have learned through them that book writing—at least our version of it—is truly a family affair.

February 1998   Kathleen D. Ryan
                                                    Issaquah, Washington

                                                    Daniel K. Oestreich
                                                    Redmond, Washington

The Dynamics
of Fear

1

The Experience of Fear

When people hear the word *fear* connected with the workplace, they think about it in many different ways: fear of change, fear of failure, and fear of the boss, to name only a few. When general fears like these are looked at in detail, they may involve more specific worries, such as

- Having one's credibility questioned
- Being left out of decision making
- Being criticized in front of others
- Not getting information necessary to succeed
- Having a key assignment given to someone else
- Having disagreements that might lead to damaged relationships
- Getting stuck in a dead-end job
- Not getting deserved recognition

- Not being seen as a team player
- Having suggestions ignored or misinterpreted as criticisms
- Receiving poor performance ratings
- Getting fired

Although ways of doing business are shifting, the background noise caused by these fears is likely to continue unless it is addressed directly. A little bit of fear, even if it is caused unconsciously, can go a long way. Small interactions, often based on the best of intentions, can take on greater, sometimes symbolic, proportions. Like pollution in water, their effect can spread fast and far.

Our goal in the first half of this book is to help you toward a deeper understanding of how fear operates by answering such questions as

- What issues does fear conceal in organizations?
- Why don't people speak up?
- What does this mean for results and morale?
- What behaviors trigger mistrust in relationships and how does this mistrust become ingrained in organizations?

By examining what people are reluctant to speak up about and why, we have an opportunity to see how fear prevents them from doing their best at work. This is not just a problem of a few unassertive souls who lack confidence. Virtually all of us, at one time or another, have hesitated to talk about certain specific work-related issues. When that hesitation is linked to concern about personal negative consequences, we become victims of fear. Consider the case of

- The manager who feels frustrated by, but unable to talk about, the direct power a CEO exerts over personnel selection in his division
- The front-line employee who quietly resents the fact that she is really doing her manager's job
- The human resources specialist who is scared to confront her supervisor's public negativity about changes and new initiatives
- The technical assistant who is reluctant to talk to a coworker who is not pulling his weight

■ The president of a subsidiary organization who resists, but does not openly address, ineffective practices mandated by the corporate office

■ The front-line manufacturing worker who hesitates to tell a new supervisor about practical ways to make the work go more smoothly

Reluctance to speak up in these scenarios creates negativity, anger, and frustration. When these emotions remain hidden—to be discussed only with trusted colleagues in the relative safety of a hallway or cafeteria, or after work—fear begins to take its toll. It depletes pride and undermines trust, productivity, and innovation.

Taking our lead from the teachings of Jack Gibb, we can imagine a continuum, shown in Figure 1.1. At one end are organizations that work diligently to create a new kind of workplace, characterized by trust and openness. At the other end are workplaces that are still locked into a style of operation characterized by fear, mistrust, and control. Today, most workplaces contain some combination of these qualities and would be located somewhere in the middle of the continuum. An assumption behind this image is that the more trust goes up, the more fear goes down.

A good place to begin thinking about how you want to use this book is by considering the connections between this continuum and your own organization. We will refer to this figure from time to time throughout this book as a way to orient our remarks.

Central Themes

The following set of core questions and explanations illustrates some important elements of the trust-fear continuum in more detail. Affirmative responses to the highlighted questions all draw a workplace toward the fear side of the continuum.

High-Trust Organizations	High-Fear Organizations

Figure 1.1. Trust-Fear Continuum.

Do a high proportion of people in your organization frequently hesitate to speak up about certain issues? The more people who experience moments of hesitation, the more pervasive the problem of fear is likely to be for an organization. In our study of 260 people in twenty-two organizations (described more fully in the Preface), at least 70 percent said they had hesitated to speak up once or more in the last few years because they feared some type of repercussion. This pattern fits with what we—and others—have observed time and time again: the problem of fear is a widespread phenomenon, not isolated to a few workplaces.

Fear operates as a set of limits that affect people *from time to time.* They may not be felt every day, but these limits are invisibly present and show up as a set of issues that people are careful in talking about, a list of "undiscussables." The more frequently people feel limits in what they can say, the more undiscussables there are, and the greater the problem of fear in the workplace.

Does a fear of speaking up exist at many levels in your organization? Our study revealed that fear of speaking up can be present at any level of the organization, from the CEO, through senior, middle, and first-line managers, to the level of lead, professional, and front-line employees. In fear-based organizations, the overall ethic is that the "boss" at each level of the hierarchy runs the show. As one seasoned retiree we know put it, in this kind of organization the job of an employee is to "find out what the old boy wants and give it to him." The supervisor, not the customer, is always right and sets the party line. And if the supervisor does not get what she or he wants, the employee pays. Managers hire "hands" to do a job. While common sense and rational thinking ability are important, employees are not expected to voice opinions or feelings about what they see happening in their organization. The predominant view is that the workplace is supposed to be systematic, efficient, and rational—a place not to be cluttered by outspoken people voicing their interests, concerns, ideas, or emotions.

Are people in your workplace associating managers and supervisors with the presence of fear? In interview after interview, the pattern was the same. The quality of the relationship people have with their direct supervisor is a key determinant of the fear—or lack of fear—

they experience at work. As one person succinctly told us, "It all depends on who you're working for." A marketing professional in a large telecommunications company told us, "My boss makes the difference. If I don't have someone I can trust, I get angry and scared and my work quality is lowered. People need a climate where they can grow." A district manager in the same organization said that he was lucky; he trusted and respected both his immediate manager and his manager's manager. Reflecting on past experiences, he allowed, "I'm more hesitant to give bad news to some than to others. Some just go critical, rather than going forward." Typically, people talked to us about their one-on-one relationships. But frequently, we would hear "us-versus-them" references that indicated that fear exists as a broad pattern between hierarchical levels.

Are leaders in your organization exhibiting behavior that causes employees to be afraid? While some managers consciously intimidate their employees, most do not. We are confident that most intimidating behaviors are committed *unconsciously* by managers who have no idea how their behaviors are affecting others. As one manager said, "No one tries to manage by fear. Our behavior is avoidance for the most part and people become afraid because of it." Another interpretation came from a dock worker who observed, "Some of the worst offenders in terms of fear are the ones who don't know they do it." If leaders are behaving in ways, consciously or unconsciously, that trigger fear, this can easily overwhelm other actions that are supportive and intended to build trust.

Are people reacting with strong emotions to a perceived environment of fear? The fantasy about organizational life is that people will behave in logical, unemotional, and well-organized ways. It is as though the boxes on the organization charts are designed to keep the messiness of reality, people, and emotions away from work. If anything, our interviews have confirmed that the messiness is largely inescapable. People are not objective about their jobs; they take their work very personally. Their feelings cannot be separated from their productivity and the quality of their work. When they cannot do the right thing or do a good job, it bothers them a great deal. And when a fear of repercussions is a barrier to quality work, their emotions are strong ones, as the following statements reveal:

"If you experience fear every day, it drags you down and you become cowardly."

—Hospital phlebotomist

"I'd rather go someplace else, make less money, and feel better about myself."

—Career manager, Fortune 100 company

"After my suggestions were ignored, the quality of my work was still there, but I wasn't."

—Internal consultant in a bank

"In retrospect, I felt like a battered wife. I wasn't allowed to talk with anyone."

—Personnel manager, major U.S. corporation

Is fear having an impact on work and how it is getting done? Sixty percent of our study participants' responses involved strong negative emotions about not speaking up and about the issues that were left unresolved. To many people, there was no question that these negative emotions had a destructive effect on the quality, amount, or efficiency of their work. People told us that they made mistakes, failed to bring up key issues, or could not be creative because of working in a fear-oriented environment. For many, this inability to do their best work was inseparable from the way they felt about themselves and their organization.

The Difficulty of Assessing Fear in Practice

If the answers to the foregoing questions are all "yes," the workplace is clearly fear-based. To summarize, in this type of organization:

- Many individuals, at many levels, feel they cannot be open.
- People associate this dynamic with the way management operates.
- Managers and supervisors are, in fact, acting in threatening ways, though unconsciously in many cases.
- The sense of threat causes people to be upset and demoralized.
- The feeling of threat affects, directly or indirectly, the work of the organization.

This assessment is deceptively simple because each of these points requires a *judgment* about what is being observed and the degree to which it is present. For each point, it is possible to ask: what has led to a conclusion that this is so, or not so? Making these judgments can be particularly hard because of the nature of fear itself and the variety of ways, some quite subtle, in which fear plays out in the language, perceptions, and behavior of people. It is no surprise that people from the same workplace may express very different views regarding how bad or how important the problem is within their organization.

In this section, we will demonstrate some of the ways in which fear may be present at work. This discussion highlights the need to sensitively read signs and symptoms when assessing fear's presence and to pay close attention to the means by which fear reveals and perpetuates itself. Most importantly, it illustrates why it is essential to carefully evaluate one's own judgments about the presence of fear. These categories are examples only, ones we have frequently encountered in our work.

Fear of Talking About Fear

The fear of talking about fear can directly influence the ability of people to accurately describe what is happening within their workplace. For example, in organizations where there is a great deal of fear, it is sometimes hard to publicly acknowledge the problem at all. Instead, people voice their denial that fear is a problem, or they may express disdain for a topic that is a "waste of time." Top managers in this situation may say quite honestly that they don't see any fear, but that is because no one has told them of its behind-the-scenes presence and its effects.

This dynamic of background perceptions can operate in many ways. For example, as consultants we are frequently asked to make a speech or give workshops about fear. One indication that the fear of talking about fear may be at work is a client organization's request that we change the title to something less threatening than "Driving Fear Out of the Workplace." People worry that using this title will be seen as criticism of their workplace or of management, itself sometimes an indication of fear's presence.

Another, slightly different, situation can be seen in organizations that have an officially stated culture of openness or truth-telling. In such a workplace it may be hard to talk about the real hesitations, however small they might be, because to do so violates the image of the organization that people have come to believe in. Openly discussing fear in this type of workplace might lead to stories about embarrassing contradictions with the preferred culture and self-image of the organization.

Including the fear of talking about fear as part of the assessment is one way to get a better handle on the levels of tension and denial in a workplace. Chris Argyris, the noted Harvard organizational theorist, has called environments where such defensiveness proliferates "self-sealing," because people cannot talk about what they cannot talk about (1986, p. 76). This makes personal and organizational learning particularly difficult.

"Acceptable" Amounts of Fear

As part of business culture today, people are frequently asked to benchmark their performance. For better or worse, fear sometimes ends up being treated the same way—as if it were an error rate or frequency of missed schedules. People sometimes ask questions about whether there is such a thing as an "acceptable" amount of fear, an amount that should be tolerated.

These questions obscure or help to deny the full extent of what people are experiencing at work. In some cases, they may even cause a few people to feel that they are off the hook for having to make improvements if they believe that the levels of fear in their organization are acceptable. Or these questions may just reflect a natural desire to be reassured that everything is normal, and that people are working in a "good" organization. Whatever is behind the questions about acceptable amounts of fear, the fact that they are asked is a clue that at least some fear is present.

When we are asked about acceptable levels of fear, we try to help people avoid these comparisons. It is really only the self-assessment that counts: whether the existing level of fear is having a negative impact and whether something is being done to bring about positive change. Wherever organizations are on the trust-fear continuum, the issue is *not* comparison with one another, but progress toward the goal.

A Focus on the Cost Benefits of Driving Out Fear

When people become overly focused on the immediate cost benefits of driving out fear, they may be reflecting an anxiety that what they do must always show a positive, immediately visible financial impact. When they feel that they must prove the short-term benefits of trust-building work, we have learned to ask them whether this is something that they personally need or that they *believe* others, who are often higher in the organization, are going to need. Most often, they care less about having the evidence personally than about the danger of losing credibility with the higher levels. This focus on short-term returns makes it harder to determine what fear is present and what might need to be done about it.

Additionally, if leaders such as middle managers focus too much on trying to prove these cost benefits, they may inadvertently create fear for those who see the managers' behavior either as compliance-based ("They are saying this because they have to") or as insensitive to the more human and value-based reasons for driving out fear.

It is fair to be concerned about the cost benefits, but perhaps the best way to think of these benefits is in terms of performance *potential*. Fear undermines the potential of any organization, no matter what the financial measures show. For example, a fear-based organization might be doing well financially because of its markets. Much as a person who smokes may not feel unhealthy, the organization may not notice the impending long-term effects. But when the crunch comes for the smoker—the required hike up the mountains—the weaknesses begin to appear. So, too, an organization facing major reorganization or a demand for innovation can suddenly and dramatically feel the effects of a fear-based background, as people "resist" or morale plummets.

The Impact of Positive Initiatives

The three previous categories demonstrate how the presence of fear can be underestimated. But it can also be exaggerated. The problem of fear has been ignored and suppressed for so long that it is natural in some environments, once the subject is opened up, for people to find elements of it around every corner. But this temptation needs to be resisted. Fear may be operating as a negative legacy, but other forces may be at work that simultaneously draw an organization toward a brighter future. It is not appropriate to *solely* focus on the problem of fear if other efforts to build trust are under way. This is an easy trap to fall into, but it leads to demoralization and cynicism and can unnecessarily magnify negativity.

In every workplace, some things do work well and these positive strengths need to be accounted for and acknowledged just as much as the problems that have been hidden. An organization's initiatives in continuous improvement or customer relations, communications, group development, or the learning organization may be taking the workplace toward a positive destination. People need to feel proud of their workplace, and focusing exclusively on fear and what's causing it can destroy this pride. If people are speaking up, helping one another, finding hope in improvements large and small—even if this is happening only in pockets of an organization—this, too, needs to be factored into the assessment.

The Importance of Balance

As the preceding section shows, identifying the connections between any one organization and the trust-fear continuum can be difficult because of the way fear plays itself out. It is easy to get snarled in interpretations and perceptions that lead to placing the emphasis on the fear side of the continuum. In turn, this can lead to focusing on fear simply as a problem to be solved. This is a remedial approach based on finding a "hole," determining why it is there, and then filling it up.

Just as important is understanding the trust side of the continuum, especially having a strong vision of what a trust-based workplace is like. A vision of trust can help people see the alternatives. It establishes a positive goal and is a guide to how the work of driving out fear might be done. In effect, the work of building a high-trust, high-performance organization requires a sensitive balance between noticing and correcting the dynamics of fear and staying focused on achieving the energizing goals of positive initiatives. This is realistic because eliminating all fear is probably not possible. But releasing extraordinary potential by reducing fear's destructive background presence is quite doable.

Without this balance, an effort to reduce fear can get sidetracked or can backfire. Because fear is a threatening topic, it can cause tension just by being put on the table. Without a well-articulated positive goal, people may push to reveal instances of fear and then consciously or unconsciously point fingers. Leaders who focus solely on the problem, rather than combining their concerns with a trust-based vision, risk driving fear in by trying to drive it out. They may end up taking all the blame, defending themselves, or shifting the blame to others. An extreme example of this approach is contained in the comic line: "If you can't drive out fear, by golly, we'll find somebody who can!" Of course, this is just the opposite of what is needed.

To achieve the right balance requires understanding of both the dynamics of fear and the dynamics of trust. In our experience, this awareness-building phase, done first and done well, can liberate leaders and their teams to focus on what they want to build together rather than to become mired in what's wrong. It frees them from quick fixes and the all-too-easy slide into blaming others for fear's presence, which can just perpetuate fear. Thus, the next two chapters of this book are dedicated to looking closely at the cycles of mistrust in which people can find themselves entangled and at a vision of a high-trust, high-performance workplace.

Although it is work, we know that it is very possible to turn the cycles of fear and mistrust around and to tap the underutilized potential of every organization. As many of our strategies suggest, beginning to personally reflect on and then talk about fear, acknowledging its presence and saying it out loud with understanding, can become a powerful way to move forward. This action can be a signal that something new is on the horizon, something that can counteract negative expectations of the past. Fear of speaking up has been around and ignored for so long that addressing it directly can be a dramatic and visible way for an organization or leader to break new ground.

In promoting a hopeful view of your organization's potential as a high-trust, high-performance enterprise, there is a call to action we hope you will hear. It is based on a deep optimism and faith in people and what all of us can create together. The work of leadership in driving out fear consists of releasing this vision from the shackles of the past—from doubt and cynicism—and helping people claim the possibilities for building a new kind of workplace community.

New Lessons and Reflections

Thoughts on Organizational Culture

To better understand the trust-fear continuum, think about the underlying assumptions, or mental models, that form the instinctive core of your organization's management philosophy. When the organization was formed, what did its key leaders truly believe about people? Could people be trusted, or not? Did they have the capability of performing at a high level, or not? Would they handle information appropriately, or not? Did they have valuable ideas, or not? Would they believe that meeting the customers' needs is just as important as meeting their own, or not? Now think about the current set of key leaders. How would they answer these questions? How would you answer them?

Depending on the answers to these questions, it will be easier—or harder—to successfully build trust and reduce fear in your organization. For example:

- *High probability of success:* Past and current key leaders believe that people are honorable and capable.

- *Reasonably high probability of success:* Current leaders hold this view in spite of a past where people were seen as untrustworthy.

- *Lower probability of success:* Current leaders do not see people as worthy of trust and respect, and this has historically been the case. In these situations, you need to be both strategic and effective at building the business case for increasing trust and reducing fear (see Chapters Seven and Sixteen and the Recommended Resources), so that key leaders are persuaded to shift their positions.

- *Very low probability of success:* Historically there has been no inclination to trust people, and current leaders do not believe there is a need to change this practice. If you disagree with these views, now would be a very good time to start looking for another job in an organization with a different philosophy.

Thoughts on Personal Leadership

In addition to looking at fear from an organizational perspective, think about your own attitudes as a leader who is interested in genuine growth and development. This part of the effort to assess fear's presence and impact is more personal, but it is also important in gaining perspective. You might ask yourself the following questions:

> *"How does the fact of fear's presence in my organization make me feel?"*

"To what extent am I truly hopeful that fear can be reduced and trust can be enhanced?"

"How do these feelings translate into biases about what to do about it or who should do it?"

"To what degree is fear a threatening topic to me, either because I am concerned that I might be causing it or because dealing with it is likely to place me in risky situations?"

It is worth reflecting on questions such as these. The more you are able to stop to consider your reactions, the more you will be able to learn about your leadership and your responsibility for building trust. Studying your own reactions may enable you to better empathize with the reactions of others and may give you insight into why many organizations have not moved faster in developing an environment of trust.

2

Cycles of Mistrust

At one end of the trust-fear continuum (Figure 1.1) is a vision of a trust-based, high-performance organization. To understand why organizations do not automatically or naturally achieve these possibilities, the dynamics behind the other end of the continuum must be understood.

This is hard work because these dynamics force a look at what keeps negativity in place, especially between managers and employees. But looking at this end is valuable because it provides a meaningful way to think about the complex mixture of behaviors and feelings that makes up the culture of a business enterprise. No workplace is totally at either extreme, although some seem to come close to one or the other at times. With the perspective gained from considering both ends, it is easier to see why conscious, persistent efforts are essential to driving out fear.

The work of leadership to create a high-trust workplace can, at times, feel like climbing a sand dune. Enormous energy may be expended to reach the great view at the top. But simultaneously there may also be a feeling that gravity is causing a slide backward and down. In times of exceptional change, the sand dune can feel particularly steep. Pushing too hard or holding on to the expectation that this ought to be quick or easy work can lead to exhaustion. Careful steps and a steady pace are more likely to be successful.

Why Does Fear Persist?

If fear's impact is so negative, why haven't people naturally discarded the practices that continue its presence? The answer lies in understanding how patterns of entrenched negative assumptions about people maintain a *cycle of mistrust*. It is just as important for managers to understand how this cycle works as it is to understand that a positive, trust-based vision must be founded on positive beliefs about people.

The most basic negative assumption that lies at the root of the problems described in this book is the assumption that supervisors and employees *cannot* trust one another. As a result:

1. Each side assumes that the other operates from a philosophy of self-interest.

2. Each side is expected to try to achieve its self-interest at the expense of the other party.

We know that this assumption does not control all workplace interactions. In practical terms, supervisors and employees must trust each other to some extent if the work is to get done. But trust is definitely a matter of degree. Even in an otherwise positive relationship, underlying doubts and cautions usually exist that surface easily in times of stress. The negative assumptions can be heard in such statements as these:

> "When the conflict occurred, this was the feeling we got from the top: 'Well, we have a problem here between a manager and an employee. Managers are hard to replace; the employee should probably go.'"
>
> —Human resources professional

> "They put out messages on the rumor mill that there are going to be layoffs. There probably won't be any layoffs.

They just put the rumors out there to get people to work harder."

—Administrative support employee

"There's a saying around here about retaliation by upper management: 'They may not get back to you right away, but they will get back to you.'"

—Financial analyst

"Our former supervisor—now our manager—doesn't like someone to show him up. He blows up at you; when it's his fault, he won't admit it. When he's around me, I'm nervous. I don't know what will happen if my current supervisor and I can't figure something out and we need to go to him."

—Assembly worker

Similarly, managers sometimes report manipulation and self-interest as a theme that ties together their views about employees. They say:

"All this emphasis on feedback for supervisors is just an opportunity to 'get your supervisor.' All it does is nurture the bad apples who want to get you back."

—Risk manager

"When people come in the door, it's almost like they lose their competence and become people who say, 'Just tell me what to do.'"

—Engineering supervisor

"After a while, I gave up on trying to treat people equally. Some people are what I call 'workers.' They're only interested in putting in eight hours a day and no more. Why should I treat them as though they are special?"

—Company owner

"When are these people going to grow up and stop whining?"

—Department director

At the core, these comments suggest that when two people have different levels of organizational power, they cannot fully trust one another. Employees worry that their managers will ultimately put personal self-interest ahead of the goals of the organization, fair treatment of customers, and the needs of employees. Supervisors likewise worry that employees will put their self-interest above the interests of the organization, the customers, quality, and productivity.

In an environment where comments such as these are heard, relationships between people are rightfully characterized by mistrust. The experience is similar to having a case of the flu but going to work anyway. The participants feel sick, yet they continue with the normal routine because they do not yet feel bad enough to do what is necessary to get better. As with coming to work sick, the illness only worsens with time. These relationships are susceptible, just waiting for a new policy, organizational change, or other initiative to create a new outbreak of fear.

Perpetuating Mistrust

The virus that causes this organizational flu starts with negative assumptions. These drive self-protective behaviors in a self-reinforcing pattern that repeatedly traps both managers and their employees. The cycle can start anywhere (see Figure 2.1). We have chosen arbitrarily to describe its seven steps beginning with a manager's negative assumptions:

1. *Negative assumptions:* A manager adopts negative beliefs about an employee's intentions, style, or behavior.

2. *Self-protective behavior:* The manager behaves in ways that are self-protective, acting to defend against the employee's potential to harm or hinder the manager.

3. *Observed aggressive, confusing, frustrating, or irritating behavior:* The employee sees the manager's self-protective behavior and interprets it as intended to harm or block the employee in some way.

4. *Negative assumptions:* Based on this interpretation, the employee adopts negative beliefs about the manager's intentions, style, or behavior.

5. *Self-protective behavior:* The employee acts in self-protective ways in order to defend against the manager's potential to harm or block the employee.

6. *Observed aggressive, confusing, frustrating, or irritating behavior:* The manager sees the employee's self-protective behavior

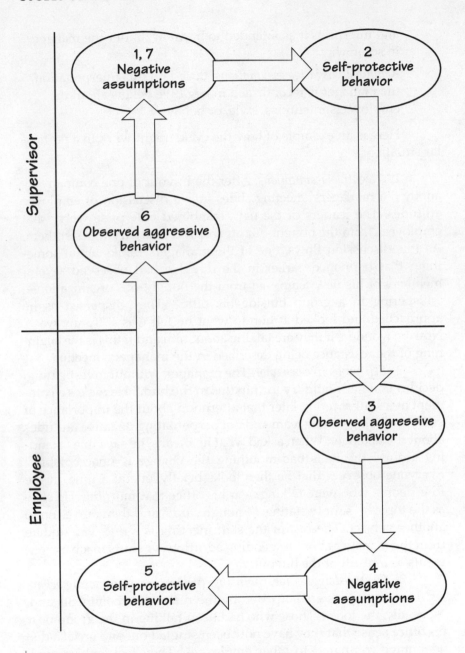

Figure 2.1. The Cycle of Mistrust.

and interprets it as intended to harm or hinder the manager in some way.

7. *Reinforced negative assumptions:* Based on this interpretation, the manager is reconfirmed in negative beliefs about the employee's intentions, style, or behavior.

Here is an example of how the cycle might work in a particular situation:

1. *Negative assumptions:* After the buyout of one company by another, a managers' meeting slides into a discussion of employee attitudes. The leaders of the new, combined enterprise worry that employees from the bought-out organization may try to resist them. As this discussion flows, one of the managers thinks about something that happened earlier in the day. He had observed several members of his new team—all from the bought-out organization—whispering in a group outside his office. They dispersed as he approached and looked at him in what he felt was a "funny way." Now he wonders if they are talking about him and if this is the beginning of the resistance being described in the managers' meeting.

2. *Self-protective behavior:* The manager, without investigating, decides that he should try to "nip this in the bud." He makes a comment at a staff meeting later that afternoon about the importance of everyone being on one team and not perpetuating negative attitudes about the takeover. When asked what he means, he says that "standing around the halls bad-mouthing the change is unacceptable." Everyone observes that he then looks briefly, one at a time, at the four people who were talking near his office that morning. He closes the topic by simply stating, "Enough said," and then moves on to another subject. The rest of the staff meeting is a one-way update from the manager about impending additions or shifts in job assignments as a result of the buyout.

3. *Observed aggressive, confusing, frustrating, or irritating behavior:* The employees are surprised by the manager's comments and, especially, the looks. Those who had been talking in the group near his office sense that they have now been singled out and are at a disadvantage compared to other employees. They feel embarrassed, confused, and misjudged.

4. *Negative assumptions:* The four employees talk together after the staff meeting. They decide that their new manager's behavior

shows that he is likely to be insensitive, overreacting, and controlling. They worry that their legitimate concerns and questions about the buyout will go unheard. They begin to believe that the environment will be less open and more compliance-oriented and wonder what they should do about it.

5. *Self-protective behavior:* During the following week, the four make a point of not talking to one another as a group. However, at the next staff meeting, a week later, the four enter the room together and sit on one side of the table. They say little during the meeting, but their body language and facial expressions suggest tension or dissatisfaction. During the meeting, one of the four sarcastically asks, "When will the new dress code be implemented?" This causes the other three to laugh, although no one else understands; it's an old in-joke about a failed management initiative that only those from the bought-out organization are familiar with. When the manager asks what the dress code issue is about, all four of the employees laugh again and try to pass it off as unimportant. One says, again with a sarcastic edge in her voice, "It can't be explained in the time available."

6. *Observed aggressive, confusing, frustrating, or irritating behavior:* The manager sees the behavior of the four as disruptive and irritating. In particular, the in-joke makes him feel that he is the intended target of a negative remark he can't respond to. The four employees seem to be operating together and he worries that the one who expressed herself sarcastically is "poisoning" the others with a negative attitude.

7. *Reinforced negative assumptions:* The manager feels reinforced in the belief that the employees from the bought-out organization will resist him as a new leader and will try to make life hard for him.

Cycles like this one can happen over and over in many different ways at all levels of an organization. Consider these possible examples:

- Department heads believe that the CEO will operate politically, make decisions behind the scenes, and react defensively to suggestions for change. What self-protective strategies will they adopt in response to these assumptions? How will their behavior look to the CEO, and how will he or she respond?

- A middle manager concludes that first-level supervisors are unwilling to take a big-picture view of their responsibilities.

How will the middle manager act? How will the supervisors see this behavior and how will they act in return?

■ Front-line staff and their supervisor are locked into a conflict over deadlines and staffing. The front-line workers believe that quality and safety problems will result from the pressure. The supervisor thinks that the employees are using their concerns as an excuse to make their lives easier. How will each side manage its assumptions and behavior?

As these instances show, the situations can vary considerably, but all involve making and acting upon negative assumptions. Cycles can form between levels of an organization, between divisions, between labor and management—literally between any two people or groups. The model may also describe staff-customer relationships that have grown tense. For example, patrons of a large public library system complained about disrespectful treatment from "government employees" who "don't care about taxpayers." This negativity was mirrored by assumptions on the part of many employees that patrons would do things, such as lie about whether they had paid fines, in order to "rip off the system."

Negative Assumptions, Self-Protective Strategies, and Reinforcing Perceptions

The flu of mistrust can become especially pervasive in an organization when managers and employees are ready to believe in traditional negative stereotypes of one another. These stereotypes are a collection of negative assumptions that drive patterns of self-protection. The stereotypes can be the hallmark of a low-key, smoldering war between levels of a hierarchy, a persistent set of skirmishes in a conflict that has too often become a fixture of organizational life. When they are taken for granted in this way, these stereotypes and their effects define a "default" position of mistrust to which people return in the face of ambiguity or stress. To make the stereotypes and their role in creating mistrust as vivid as possible, we have cataloged them according to the six central elements of the cycle just described.

We know that such lists can easily be glossed over rather than being read slowly and carefully. We encourage, however, careful consideration of each of the items presented here, which relate to the points on the cycle. As you read them, think about your experiences as a leader and as an employee. Which items have been part of your behavior or beliefs? To what degree have you contributed to or been trapped by the cycle of mistrust?

Negative Assumptions Managers Make About Employees (Point 1)

Employees

- Do not take accountability
- Do not really care about their work beyond getting their paycheck
- Are unwilling to look at a big-picture view
- Look for excuses
- Test policies and rules
- Need structure, control, and limits in order to stay focused
- Will not contribute unless they are forced to do so
- Do not understand political realities and budgetary pressures, and are unwilling to do so
- Focus on rights, benefits, money, and other "entitlements"
- Resist changes needed to help the organization be successful financially
- Are capable of dishonesty and sabotage

Self-Protective Strategies Adopted by Managers (Point 2)

Managers will therefore

- Micromanage employees' work
- Restrict participation in policy or other important workplace decisions
- Institute new performance standards that focus on commitment, attitude, and loyalty
- Emphasize a formal chain of command for handling employees' complaints or suggestions
- Develop tighter personnel rules
- Limit the information communicated to employees

- Transfer or reassign people
- Take, or attempt to take, disciplinary action with employees who appear to be causing trouble for management
- Restrict meetings to upper-management groups
- Nip dissent in the bud
- Come down hard on people who are screwing up as an example to others
- Criticize employees and hold them up to ridicule
- Focus on their "rights" as supervisors
- Try to dictate changes or attitudes about changes

How These Self-Protective Strategies Look to Employees (Point 3)

Employees see or hear

- Two sets of rules—one for managers, one for employees
- Employees being transferred, reassigned, or terminated without explanation or apparent rationale
- Rumors about possible changes in the work, layoffs, or reorganization without confirmation or denial by management
- Announcements of new rules that restrict behavior without input or explanation
- Closed-door meetings by managers
- Managers' actions that do not correspond with stated fair treatment policies on promotions, training, appraisals, equal employment opportunity matters, or other human resources issues
- Warnings by managers to employees not to take their complaints or suggestions higher in the organization
- The immediate supervisor being the only person allowed to take good ideas to higher levels of management
- Managers who think that ridiculing, harassing, or punishing employees is acceptable
- Forced changes without awareness of what they mean to people

Negative Assumptions Employees Make About Managers as a Result (Point 4)

Managers

- Are insensitive to the personal life and legitimate needs, rights, and interests of employees
- Are secretive about motives and decisions; operate behind the scenes
- Have as their biggest interest personal control and power; use organizational power to achieve private ends
- Operate as a privileged elite, a closed club that creates a "caste system" in the organization
- Continuously try to get more work out of employees with no additional rewards
- Play politics; are more interested in politically correct solutions than technically correct ones
- Show favoritism and bias
- Are defensive about ideas they did not generate themselves
- Ask for input as a sop to employees' emotions, but are never really influenced by employees' ideas or interests
- Are insecure and threatened by competent employees
- Will do whatever they need to do to promote their own careers
- Think that they are better than employees with less power
- Are dishonest and capable of hidden retaliation
- Are inept in leading change

Self-Protective Strategies Adopted by Employees (Point 5)

Employees will therefore

- Openly suggest that management or particular managers are incompetent
- Prevent information and data from flowing up the system
- Allow a manager to make mistakes in front of the manager's supervisors or peers

- Blame others or circumstances for performance problems
- Ask for more money or better working conditions
- Joke about or make fun of the manager with coworkers
- Challenge all management decisions
- Complain to vendors or competitors about the organization's problems
- Fail to contribute at meetings, but complain about them afterward
- Refuse to do overtime work required by an urgent issue or problem
- Seldom acknowledge their own contribution to a problem situation
- Fail to inform managers of pertinent stories on the rumor mill
- Send grievance petitions to high-ranking or influential people
- Form a union; focus on their "rights" as employees
- File a legal complaint or lawsuit
- Make demands for high levels of involvement in change processes

How These Self-Protective Strategies Look to Managers (Point 6)

Managers see or hear

- Excessive time spent resisting reasonable requests; a general lack of cooperation
- Excuses; people not taking responsibility for problems they have caused or could correct
- Employees who do not give the organization a reasonable chance to correct problems
- Requests for personal leave or other benefits that will slow down the work
- Considerable time spent with coworkers complaining and "whining"
- A lack of new ideas to improve the product or service
- Frequent requests for new benefits

- Petty complaints represented as serious organizational problems
- Statements that do not support the organization and its customers
- People who are not working up to their potential
- Aggressiveness
- People who are working the system for personal gain
- Lack of speed and cooperation in implementing changes

Reciprocal Self-Protective Strategies

The negative images managers and employees have of one another are often reciprocal; that is, they can be mirror images in which the self-protective strategies may be identical. Both sides engage in such activities as

- Blaming
- Making excuses
- Restricting the flow of information
- Restricting participation in important decisions
- Creating us-versus-them distinctions
- Reinforcing mandated structures, authority, and rights
- Discrediting others' competence and willingness to take responsibility
- Undermining or sabotaging others' efforts
- Expressing cynicism

These and other similar behaviors are both the cause and result of fear. They are typically read by the other side as offensive rather than defensive. The reciprocal quality of the conduct means that a continuous, usually low-key, struggle between managers and employees hides beneath the surface of events. This conflict is not talked about effectively and subtly influences emotions and behavior.

It is clear that some people feel the cycle of mistrust more strongly and deeply than others. Their actions implicitly express its assumptions and self-protective strategies. Once, for example, when we were presenting the cycle as part of a management training class, one of the participants commented that he thought the term "assumptions" was inaccurate. He told us that "facts" was the better word. His response highlights precisely the problem with the cycle of mistrust. When people believe that the stereotypical view of supervisors or employees is true, the conflict is certain to continue. This is sometimes the case even when the agreed-upon facts suggest other, more accurate interpretations.

This powerful lesson hit home for us while interviewing a supervisor who had terminated one of his employees. He explained:

"When I took over as boss, there was an older woman in my group who was not performing. I set forth expectations for her performance with clear statements of rewards and punishments. I was, however, never able to help her. She was afraid and became fatalistic. I worried that her two coworkers would be scared, and in fact one of the two was very worried. She and I talked for three hours one night. She wanted to know whether I was there to fix the problem or just set unrealistic goals."

We also had an opportunity to interview the coworker:

"I sympathized [with the woman who would later be terminated], but I also realized that improvements were necessary. I tried to be positive about her and help her implement the needed changes in her performance. There was a lot of stress and tension in our group. It made it hard to concentrate on my job. The quality of my work probably was reduced.

"While I felt the supervisor was correct in handling the situation, it was hard not to side with my coworker. The situation made me suspicious of my supervisor. He was new to our area and within nine months he had terminated my coworker. There was a question of whether the supervisor had come into our area with his mind made up to get rid of her or to work with her performance."

These two versions of the same event show how people's fears can intrude, even when the supervisor's actions are understood to be appropriate. The cycle of mistrust can be heard in the employee's question: did the supervisor have his mind made up to get rid of her? It was significant to us that both people identified this situation as something they could not currently talk about. They did not want to reopen the conversation and express their experiences and emotions. Thus, there was little chance to resolve these leftover frustrations and fears. It was clear to us that the supervisor felt ineffective with his employee. Conversely, the employee continued to worry about what her coworker's termination meant regarding her supervisor's methods.

In this situation the supervisor should have found a way to gently reopen the issue. If he had done this, he might have been able to demonstrate his willingness to hear his employee's fears about his motivation and respond nondefensively. The employee needed to know that the termination was not just an outcome of the assumptions that underlie the cycle of mistrust. In this way, the incident could have become an opportunity for building honesty and trust. Left undiscussed, matters of this kind can easily feed a belief that managers are secretive or insensitive and that employees are unable to see the big picture. The lesson is that leaders

- Need to do their best to avoid the fear-provoking behaviors described in this book
- Should stay away from making negative assumptions about their employees
- Should realize that workplace changes, no matter how justified, may cause the cycle to surface
- Should deal gently and persistently with employee reactions, listening carefully for feedback about the events or behaviors (some of which may be personal) that have triggered the cycle

We have found that when people understand the dynamics of the cycle and how it can influence behavior, they become both better able to let go of mistrust and more tolerant of feedback from others. It is very easy for anyone getting feedback in an environment of mistrust to take things personally and be offended by other people, alleging that they have some type of negative motive. But with a thorough understanding of the cycle, these tense situations can be viewed more objectively, and some of what might have gotten under someone's skin can be seen for what it is: a pattern of negative assumptions to be dealt with constructively. The trap can be avoided by seeing how the dynamics of the cycle work. When this understanding is coupled with an explicit vision of trust, a leader is in a strong place to begin turning around relationships that have become undermined by fear.

In the next chapter, the last in Part One, we share a view of a high-trust workplace. This vision can draw people naturally away from the cycle of mistrust toward a new set of possibilities for better workplace relationships.

New Lessons and Reflections

Thoughts on Organizational Culture

When people come to work, they bring the outside, larger community culture with them. The media, in particular, convey strong messages about whether or not management can be trusted and organizations can be healthy, creative places for people. Listen to and watch the way popular music, advertisements, and movies reinforce the cycle of mistrust. How often do you hear managers and organizations stereotyped as heartless, power-oriented, and dishonest? For years, one of our favorite examples of this pattern was a national advertising campaign for a company that produces beer. Playing frequently on a radio station that targeted eighteen- to twenty-five-year-olds was a sixty-second spot that had the tag line, "While you may never find honesty in the workplace, you can find honest refreshment. Drink XYZ beer." Messages such as these make it even more important for leaders to consistently behave in ways that inspire trust, since so many aspects of the national culture suggest that they cannot.

Thoughts on Personal Leadership

Breaking cycles of mistrust is one of the best ways to think about driving out fear. To notice these cycles in action is to have a systems perspective on fear and how it operates in organizations. Seeing how a particular cycle involving your own beliefs undermines work relationships can be a source of embarrassment—and opportunity.

Think about a relationship of mistrust between you and someone you know. See if it is possible to describe your relationship in terms of all parts of the cycle. Completing this exercise may provide you with insight about how persistent and destructive such cycles can be. It may also provide you with some clues about how to begin breaking cycles by eliminating negative assumptions and changing your behavior.

Many times, in our travels as consultants, members of an organization have felt that we must have some "inside information" or must have interviewed people in their organization to arrive at our view of the cycle of mistrust. If you feel this way, you are not alone. This is evidence of the pervasiveness of fear, but it also shows how common and predictable its dynamics really are.

3

Defining a Trust-Based Workplace

The vision of a high-trust workplace is something people already know. It is carried internally and waits to be expressed. It does not come from the views of experts or specialists and is not dictated by leadership. Rather, it comes from day-to-day experiences that people associate with trust. This chapter presents one possible vision of what a high-trust workplace is like and examines some of the key points that can help a trust-based vision flourish.

Over the years, we have asked hundreds of people in a variety of small-group settings to define their idea of a great working relationship. Since, for some, differences in organizational power seem to complicate this work, we often ask people to describe outstanding coworker relationships. This approach helps people to concentrate on the characteristics of the relationship rather than on differences in authority. The results are the raw data from which a vision begins to unfold.

People easily and spontaneously generate long lists of qualities they personally have experienced in satisfying work relationships. Within ten minutes, groups can list twenty or thirty
characteristics. Here are some commonly cited qualities:

- Mutual helpfulness and understanding
- Serving as a reality check for one another
- Providing feedback for one another, on strengths as well as
  areas that need improvement
- Influencing each other's ideas and decisions; willingness to
  be influenced
- Humor; enjoyment of each other's company
- Creative, synergistic problem solving where the results are
  greater than the sum of the parts
- Respect for different backgrounds and talents; reliance on
  one another's expertise to ensure the best results
- Willingness and ability to work through conflicts and dis-
  agreements
- Common commitment to the same goal; commitment to one
  another's success
- A high level of rapport and honesty with one another
- Straightforward communication

These qualities suggest interpersonal relationships that genuinely support the performance and success of others. They are *core
behaviors* because they describe partnership and teamwork at their
best: individuals doing high-quality work directed toward common
goals and achieving personal satisfaction at the same time. A trust-
based workplace may be defined as one in which core behaviors are
displayed frequently, whether or not power differences exist
between individuals.

Employees who enjoy this type of relationship with a supervisor may say, "Of course my boss has greater decision-making
authority than I do, and that's fine." A manager in this type of relationship may say, "Naturally, the front-line employees are more
familiar with the daily pressures of getting our products out the
door, and that's as it should be." Because people are tuned into their
common goals and their commitment to open communication and

one another's success, differences in power become a nonissue—except when they can be used to help others be more successful.

Day-to-Day Action

The exercise of asking people to describe core behaviors is simple and a good way to get started defining a vision of the future workplace. But to make the vision real and flesh it out requires another round of thoughtful reflection. For example, what do these core behaviors mean for day-to-day action, especially among people whose positions vary in power and scope? Here are some ways the core behaviors have been translated by people, regardless of their position.

They give credit for good work that is being done, instead of blaming each other. Managers and their employees publicly acknowledge each other's hard work, strengths, and original ideas. Employees are encouraged to express their ideas and be visible to top leadership. On the other hand, employees talk about how a manager's insight or technical skill helps them be successful. Both talk about how much they learn from working together and let one another know how much they—and their work—are appreciated.

They take responsibility rather than making excuses. Supervisors and employees alike admit when they make mistakes. They identify problems early so that others are warned of potential difficulties. They take the initiative in offering solutions, pulling people and other resources together to correct difficult situations. They believe that if people do not make mistakes, they never will improve. They support each other when mistakes are made and help each other to figure out how to do things differently in the future.

They openly share information. Information related to decisions, rumors, events, and technical developments is passed easily between employees and managers and back again. They all believe that accurate and timely information is essential to anyone doing quality work. They are committed to keeping each other informed. They know that not all information can or should be exchanged.

Both employees and managers trust each other to pass along information appropriately. If they do not get the information they need, they talk to each other and set plans in motion that will prevent problems in the future.

They collaborate on important issues. Managers and employees are sensitive to the way their decisions influence one another. They seek one another's opinions and expertise. When possible they work with the spirit of partners to design, organize, and complete work that needs to be done. When it is practical, decisions are made by consensus. People speak up and fully participate in offering their views. If decision making must be top-down, managers explain why this is so, share the reasoning behind the decision, and explain how employee input was used. By the same token, employees seek their managers' views and support on sensitive decisions that fall within their areas of responsibility.

They speak in terms of "we" rather than creating "us-and-them" distinctions. In spirit, people assume, "We're all in this together." They see success, failure, learning, and problem solving as issues of mutual concern. They think about how their own roles and behaviors affect others and the organization at large. Without regard for the power differences between them, bosses and subordinates believe that their job is to make sure all of them are successful.

They focus on the common purpose and do not get sidetracked by differences in the details. Employees and managers keep their collective mission in mind. They acknowledge their differences regarding details and figure out how to work with them. They recognize the real issue: "How do we move forward together to accomplish what we both believe is important?"

They respect organizational structures and roles and do not use them in undermining ways. Whatever the role, they mutually try to make sure that decisions are correct, information is exchanged, and conflicts are attended to constructively. People do not feel a need to talk about their "rights" or their turf. They decide together what is right in a particular situation.

They value each other's background and experience and do not discredit each other's competence. People seek each other's opinions because they have learned that "one plus one equals more than two." The synergistic effects of combining viewpoints and expertise lead to better-quality work. They ask each other questions like "What have I forgotten here?" or "How would you approach this problem?" Because people think and talk in terms of "we," they do not say or do things that would deliberately discredit anyone. They value diversity and speak positively of one another's contributions to others in the organization.

They openly voice concerns, criticisms, and conflicts. Neither employees nor managers act in ways that would undermine, manipulate, or sabotage each other's efforts. Because of their commitments to common goals, most disagreements and conflicts relate to methods of accomplishing work. When these arise, they are discussed openly. People say what they think and trust that the other person will hear the criticisms in the spirit of help in which they were intended. They give each other essential feedback that will help to improve individual and collective performance. They do not worry about "getting paid back" for suggesting different approaches or a different line of reasoning. If that concern should ever come up, it would be discussed directly. In response to the feedback, people listen carefully and do their best to respond to each other's concerns. They see their ability to disagree and manage their conflicts as a strength of their relationship.

They speak positively about their work, the organization, and the future. Cynicism does not get in the way. Dilemmas are identified and talked about in realistic ways that help people to move forward. Uncertainties and the impact of changes in industry, technology, and the environment are discussed openly and positively. People are encouraged to express their concerns, frustrations, discouragement, confusion, and anger. Acknowledgment of these feelings is considered an important step toward managing change. Positive feelings prevail because people target their actions to arenas that they can truly influence.

Together, the core behaviors and their translation into day-to-day action start to form a vision for the high-trust, high-performance organization. As this vision comes together, however, people sometimes become skeptical. They may accept the notion that it is possible to achieve the vision among peers or coworkers, but they may become more doubting when it comes to those with different authority levels. Their questions can usually be boiled down to this one: how can a manager and employee have the type of relationship described by the core behaviors when it is obvious that the manager has more organizational power?

This is a point well worth examining.

The Problem Is the Power Difference

Managers' organizational power is typically based upon their greater level of decision-making responsibility. This responsibility typically includes the ability to evaluate performance, hire, fire, promote, demote, and change employee assignments and roles. Managers at all levels have a larger scope than their employees. They typically have more responsibility for larger numbers of resources and oversee a greater number of functions. With closer access to the top of the organization, they usually get information from higher levels before their employees and have a greater opportunity to influence the direction of the organization. Employees have a smaller and more focused area of decision making. Whether they are workers on the shop floor or vice presidents in executive suites, they still have a smaller scope of decision-making authority than do their managers. And, obviously, they do not personally have the formal authority to hire, fire, promote, or demote their superiors.

The slippery point here is that differences in decision-making authority do not inevitably require supervisors and employees to give up on the high-trust vision we describe. Mistrust emerges at the point where supervisors and employees connect their differences in organizational authority with their potential to negatively affect one another's lives. This negative, power-oriented focus often causes both managers and employees to feel threatened. Fernando Bartolomé and André Laurent (1986) documented this dynamic with a study of over 100 executives. Although their work concentrated on people in midlevel and senior management positions, we believe the pattern holds true throughout the organizational hierarchy. They observed:

> Managers as superiors know how much they depend on their subordinates' performance and, therefore, how much

real power, as opposed to formal power, their subordinates have over them. But when bosses are subordinates, they often forget this reality of organizational life. They forget that their boss's performance depends heavily on how committed the subordinates are to their jobs and on the quality of their work. . . . They don't always recognize that they possess real power that they can use with their bosses to negotiate and obtain satisfaction for their legitimate needs and demands [p. 80].

When managers and employees talk about this relative balance of power, they will most often cite negative examples to prove their point. Employees will talk about how a manager can disrupt their lives with a sarcastic comment, an unwanted assignment, a critical comment, or a poor performance appraisal. Managers will tell stories about uncaring staff, operational information that was negligently delayed, and the unwillingness of employees to take the initiative to solve problems on the spot. It is clear that if the goal is to make another person's life miserable, each has the ability to be quite successful. It is like two boxers in a ring. One may weigh twenty pounds more than the other, but that is no guarantee that both will not be bloodied by the time the match is over.

Change begins when people consciously and jointly commit to building a high-trust, high-performance workplace. When they mutually operate with this goal in mind, while fully acknowledging the differences in their organizational roles and decision-making authority, they search for ways to make these differences complementary rather than adversarial. They focus on building each other's professional and operational strengths, rather than competing or playing on another person's weaknesses. When a manager and employee are able to relate to each other in this way, they make it easier for coworkers to experience this same high-trust, high-performance relationship.

Although it may be difficult, at first, to achieve this goal, sharing it creates a kind of interpersonal and professional glue. Once that glue is in place, there are few barriers to solving problems. The curtain of mistrust that separates managers and employees comes down. People become proud of their ability to give feedback openly and to accept it from others. They become excited about their ability to learn from one another and work together to accomplish a greater purpose.

If it is allowed to grow, the vision defines both the quality of the interaction between a manager and an employee and the quality of the work they produce together. Once these relationships have been established, they both require and reinforce trust, creativity, risk taking, and commitment. They become their own positive self-perpetuating cycle—a cycle that has no room for fear and no time for mistrust.

The Key Is Changing Assumptions

It is sometimes difficult for people to believe in a high-trust vision because it runs counter to the cycle of mistrust that keeps fear deeply embedded in organizations. The vision of core behaviors and action described here is based on *positive assumptions* about people. Mistrust and fear are based on distinctly negative ones. When people begin with the premise that they *can* trust one another, their vision of work relationships is free to open up and take on new dimensions. They are able to envision trust in behavioral terms and in full bloom. Becoming committed to the high-trust, high-performance workplace can force people to look at how their own deep assumptions about others—particularly others who have a different level of authority—may need to change.

People want high-trust relationships, but the world is full of organizational systems, practices, structures, and habits that are based on negative assumptions. Many people are so attuned to these barriers that even thinking about the positive possibilities can feel patently unrealistic or painful. This is especially true for people who have a more pessimistic view of human nature.

However, individuals can challenge the negative assumptions about employees and managers they may have inherited from a culture of hierarchy. Suppose, for example, that managers assume that employees

- Want to take responsibility for their work and want to do a good job

- Care about their work above and beyond the money they get paid to perform it

- Consider a big-picture view essential to performing their work

- Are willing to take responsibility for their mistakes

- Are capable of establishing their own structures in order to maintain focus
- Want to contribute freely
- Are fully capable of understanding budgetary and political realities
- Do not just focus on their entitlements and rights
- Are intrinsically honest and trustworthy

Next, consider what might happen if employees believe that managers

- Are sensitive to the personal issues and interests of employees
- Enjoy open, participative problem solving
- Want to use the power of their station to serve the organization well, and consider it unethical to use power to achieve private ends
- Want the workload to be fair and reasonable
- Work to find solutions that are both technically and politically sound
- Pride themselves on operating fairly and objectively
- Want employees' input on decisions
- Are willing to put the success of the organization, the welfare of the employees, and service to customers before private interests
- Do not think they are better than their employees
- Are honest and would consider retaliation a sign of serious weakness

These lists of positive assumptions are also a part of the vision of trust and are much closer to reality than many managers and employees believe. The problem is that people do not think that the other side is trying to behave this way, too. All too often, individuals make positive assumptions about themselves but negative ones about the others, whoever they are. This "good guys and bad guys" perspective is read by the other side as an unspoken but real set of negative assumptions that must be defended against. Each group believes that the other wants radically different things. Yet time after time in conflict management and team-building work, the answer comes back that people generally want the same things: respect, participation, a voice, clarity, fairness, understanding, common goals, a meaningful job, and the opportunity to achieve something worthwhile. Jerry Harvey makes this point in memorable fashion in *The Abilene Paradox* (1988, p. 15). He asserts that it is the inability to manage our agreements, not our disagreements, that gets us into trouble.

Reasons for Building a High-Trust Workplace

Part of these agreements—and again, another aspect of the vision itself—is a shared view of *why* creating a high-trust work environment is so important. Two kinds of reasons together create leverage for change: business necessity and human desire. Both of these reasons are important, give power to the vision, and propel organizations toward the trust end of the trust-fear continuum. Energy to achieve the vision may suffer without some of each. Simply put, these reasons speak to what is both the *smart* thing and the *right* thing to do.

The Business Reasons

Trust is important as a practical business issue *only* if organizational success depends on people working together in collaborative and interdependent ways. When work demands something more than quick handoffs of individual efforts, the ability to follow explicit directions, and rudimentary communication, then trust becomes a vital and very smart business strategy.

Our reading of contemporary business is that very few work environments only require people to do what they are told. While there were glimmers of the information age in 1989 and 1990, when we were doing our field study about the fear of speaking up, it is now plain that this age is fully upon us. And with it comes the knowledge-based economy where, as Thomas Stewart reminds us, success "depends on new skills and new kinds of organizations and management" (1997, p. 17). Adding to this conversation is Arie de Geus. In his study of what he calls "living companies," de Geus emphasizes the need for supporting "experiments and eccentricities" that stretch understanding. This enables organizations to successfully adapt to change, increasing their chance to go beyond the average current corporate "life expectancy," which is well below twenty years. He suggests that "companies die because their managers focus exclusively on producing goods and services and forget that the organization is a community of human beings that is in business—any business—to stay alive." Living companies are ones where "the essence of the underlying contract is trust. Individuals understand that in exchange for their effort and commitment, the company will help them develop their potential" (1997a, pp. 52–59).

The capacity to partner with others in order to innovate is rapidly becoming a critical success factor as formal hierarchies transform themselves into flatter organizations, self-organizing groups, and virtual teams in various parts of the world. In these new types of workplaces, people are expected to carry out their work in serving key customers, resolving differences with counterparts, and taking action to resolve problems on behalf of the organization without direction or inspection. More importantly, people are recognizing that they must be able to learn together and apply that knowledge creatively in order to maintain a competitive edge. All the recent efforts to pare down organizations and to empower people in this way depend on trusting and upon being trustworthy. People will not share information or their ideas if they do not feel safe to do so, regardless of how much the company needs their best work in order to survive.

It only makes sense from a business standpoint to help people shift toward high-trust environments as other business changes occur. And the key to this is being clear about what trust means, having an explicit vision of trusting relationships, and continuously working to achieve this goal.

The Human Reasons

People want work environments where they are valued as individuals, where they can learn and contribute, where they feel they can be most useful and will be treated as adults. They want to feel good about themselves and have the chance to be themselves by openly bringing their unique strengths, skills, and intelligence to their work. They want to be proud of what they do, where they work, and who they work for. Fear undermines all this, and in so doing, it leaves people feeling belittled, cynical, disenfranchised, and understandably self-protective. Fear makes people smaller—and less capable—than they really are.

In a democracy, the right thing to do is to build organizations on the principles of fairness, choice, and the open exchange of information and opinions. It is at least misguided, if not wrong, to do otherwise. When leaders consciously try to reduce fear and build trust, they extend the legacy and live the promise of those who struggled to overcome societal oppression of all sorts in the eighteenth, nineteenth, and twentieth centuries. And yet, in spite of the clear and hard-won philosophical underpinnings of democratic nations, intimidating hierarchies are found in every sector: from family firms to nonprofit community organizations, churches, labor unions, megacorporations, and government. When asked for his thoughts on the "challenges already taking shape for executives as they move into the next century," Charles Handy (1997) observed that one "of the great paradoxes of our time is that it is totalitarian, centrally planned organizations, owned by outsiders, that are providing the material wherewithal of the great democracies. Free people do not relish being the instruments of others. The best of them will, increasingly, either refuse to join such institutions or demand a high price for the sacrifice of their rights" (pp. 27–28).

Trusting people so they can grow and genuinely participate in the life of their organization reflects the deepest values of a democratic society. This position is neither naive nor simpleminded. It is good business and it is good for all of us as people. It is both the right—and the smart—thing to do.

A vision of a high-trust workplace is a cornerstone for all efforts to drive out fear. We hope it is clear that this vision is not the same as a vision "statement" that does little more than hang on the wall and inspire more silence and cynicism. A genuine vision is about hope and finds a way to live in the real day-to-day interactions of people.

One way to think about where the vision must be strongest is to consider how each person participates in a variety of relationships that radiate outward—to an immediate superior, to immediate peers, perhaps to reports—and more distantly to others outside this inner circle of immediate contacts. This immediate circle is the place where trust is most directly felt. Each person is at the heart of a social network where trust is either a reality or not. This is the ground where a vision needs to take hold and have an impact.

At the core of this vision is an understanding that the human connections in a workplace are potentially much more powerful than organizational ones. In the long run, things get done well because of the quality of the relationships between people, not because job descriptions are well thought out and explicit. It is not that organizational roles and structures are unimportant or that organizations should forgo formal human resources systems. In some form, they are essential and can either increase or reduce fear. It is just that they can never be a substitute for energizing, trust-based relationships at the heart of an organization that is meeting the challenge of the new era.

The subject of the four chapters that make up Part Two will be the patterns of fear that interfere with an organization's ability to move ahead. The results of our field study will be described in detail, revealing the triggers, symptoms, and costs of fear.

New Lessons and Reflections

Thoughts on Organizational Culture

Vision is extremely important. But it will only be powerful if it guides visible action on a consistent basis. To do that, it must be firmly established inside of people, as an internal set of concepts and principles. This is more likely to happen if you engage others in the development of collaboratively created statements of vision (what you are trying to make happen), mission (what you do and for whom you do it), and values (what fundamental beliefs underlie the delivery of your product or service). This work can be done, if desired, at every level: organization-wide to the smallest of work units.

The risk involved with creating these guiding philosophical documents comes after they have been published, framed, and posted. To mean anything, they must be used as a daily reference point for all sorts of decisions—from how money gets spent to who gets sent to a conference. The individual behavior of leaders and the organization's policies, practices, systems, and structures are key leverage points in the organization's cultural infrastructure. If these elements do not clearly reflect the organization's vision, mission, and values, people will see the documents as a sham. Instead of serving as an important tool to increase trust, they will become the source of increased cynicism and suspicion.

Thoughts on Personal Leadership

Developing a vision of a trust-based workplace can take a long time. Leaders may need to directly help their teams verbalize their hopes for a workplace where people can talk openly and develop trust in an environment of mutual learning. People often need the leader to initiate conversations of this kind, helping them to articulate and feel secure in expressing the type of workplace *they* want to be part of. The result of these conversations can be thought of as a group understanding and agreement. At its best, this agreement is a deeply felt personal commitment to create a high-trust workplace that does not need to be made into a wall plaque.

When such an understanding is in place, people welcome opportunities for development and growth. They *choose* to take some risks in their relationships on behalf of the organization and in response to their own desire for growth. As this occurs, a natural sense of community emerges. What ties people together is their shared promise to one another.

How Fear Operates in Organizations

4

Patterns of Threat, Triggers of Mistrust

An initial result of our field research interviews was a framework for viewing how fear manifested itself as a sense of threat in the stories of study participants. This framework is a kind of lens through which the dynamics of fear can be viewed. Through the framework, it is possible to gain perspective and objectivity on material that might otherwise appear to be wholly subjective or emotional.

Patterns of Threat

Threat comes in five ways:

1. Actual experience in the present or in a past situation—
   what has happened directly to the person and what has
   been directly observed

2. Stories about others' experiences, especially those who are liked or trusted

3. Negative assumptions about others' behavior and intentions, based on private interpretations about what has happened

4. Negative, culturally based stereotypes about those with different levels of organizational power

5. Externally imposed change

These sources of threat, in various combinations, are present in most accounts of organizational mistrust and fear. The following story illustrates the five patterns at work. It was told to us by Shakeem, a well-paid fiscal manager in a large service organization. To better convey the emotional realities of fear-based stories, it is told at length and in the first person. At the time of the story, Shakeem had worked for her organization for over ten years.

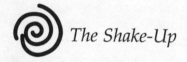 *The Shake-Up*

Ever since the reorganization, rumors had been flying about what might happen to Jackie and all of us in Administrative Services. When the board appointed Bill as the new CEO, there was a wave of panic all through our division. He had been the head of the Planning Office and he and Jackie had disagreed plenty of times about the direction of the company. She'd stood up to him as head of our division but now he was her boss.

I worked directly for Jackie and I was upset about the changes. Jackie had worked hard to create a solid management team. We had our problems, but people were beginning to build more trust with one another, and I didn't want to lose any of this. While Jackie hadn't always achieved the things she had aimed for, I appreciated what she was trying to do. We were able to talk about our differences and be honest with one another.

A week before Christmas, Jackie said she'd heard some serious rumors that she would be replaced by Brian, a friend of Bill's from the Planning Office, who would take over her job. This sounded incredible because Brian had virtually no management experience and people thought of him as a cold fish and a suck-up to Bill. Jackie told me that she e-mailed Bill right away about his plans, but he never got back to her. At an employee meeting just after the board appointed him, he said that he planned "no wholesale changes," but he also made a point of saying that he would be looking to keep "only the best of the best." This left a big question in people's minds about what this meant. I was scared for Jackie.

Two weeks after her e-mail, Jackie cornered Bill and asked him point-blank about the rumors that Brian would take over her job. Bill said this was true. Jackie told me he made one of those apologies, "Oh, I guess I forgot to tell you." That's when Jackie found out that she was the only senior manager asked to step down from an executive role. Bill didn't try to explain the reasons—it was just a fact and she had to accept it. He told her she should announce the change herself to her staff. Jackie was furious inside, but she did what she was told. She told me she was afraid that anything she did to resist Bill's direction at this point might get her in more trouble. If she accepted her demotion quietly, perhaps there wouldn't be any further punishment of her or people in the division.

So everybody knew what was going on but there wasn't any official confirmation of who our leader would be. You could feel the mistrust building, of Bill and of Brian, who had not even arrived on the scene. Things got worse. Bill started making big demands for information about how the division was operated. At the same time, Jackie was being pressed to move out of her old job into a new one, where she didn't get paid benefits and nobody reported to her anymore.

By the time Brian officially accepted the job and took over, morale was at an all-time low. During his first meeting with the team, he seemed to be anticipating a hostile reception, and what he did seemed aimed at provoking exactly that kind of reaction from us. He had a flip tone in his voice. "I'm not much for meetings" he said. "I prefer e-mail." He said that he didn't want to meet with us one-on-one because he found this to be "divisive." He said he would meet now and then with the group as a whole.

Somebody finally asked him, "Don't you like anything?" He just smirked at us. "I like food and vacations" was all he said. This was the first time people had met Brian and the whole thing only lasted fifteen minutes. People left feeling there would be no way to please him.

I wanted things to change. I mean, what could we do to improve this? It was just such a mess and there were so many bad feelings. I thought we needed to do something to help Brian understand what was happening, so I took a chance. I went to him privately; I told him he ought to talk to the managers one-on-one to get their views of all these changes and how we should be working in the future. I figured this would be a way for people to talk about their true feelings and get things back on a positive track. For what it's worth, he did what I asked and set up the conversations. In mine, I told him the truth about how I saw what was going on.

These conversations just backfired. After he finished talking to everybody, I asked him what he had learned. First he laughed nervously and then he got stern. "The whole process just pissed me off," he said. "Why?" I asked him. "Because you are a very disobedient group." That's what he actually said. I commented that from my view the job of a management group was to lead and make decisions, not be obedient. But it was clear the conversation, as far as he was concerned, was over.

I don't think Brian had a clue what kind of damage he'd done with that comment, that word "disobedient." I felt insulted personally and for the whole team. It said a lot to me about his inexperience and what was coming as far as his management style was concerned.

It was at that point that I started to see where this all would lead. I thought about the way Jackie had been treated, the way the whole team had been treated by Bill. I was disappointed and angry and upset. It was clear this was no longer going to be a place where trust or speaking up would be valued, or where people would be respected for their honest views and their past accomplishments. After that comment from Brian, I realized I needed to look for another job.

This story illustrates how the five sources of threat are interwoven and reinforce one another. Thinking about them separately and together in the form of questions can make it easier to take a step back and understand the mistrust and pain represented by Shakeem's experience.

What actual events are being described? Shakeem is describing what she personally has seen happen to her manager, her peers, and herself. She observed Jackie's relationship with Bill before and after reorganization. She saw team members' behaviors and heard their comments. She directly observed and interacted with Brian. She was the immediate recipient of Brian's comment about disobedience, which she felt as a personal and group insult. She feels threatened by what has happened to her directly.

What stories about others' experiences add to the tension? Shakeem heard from Jackie how Jackie had learned about her demotion— through the rumor mill and finally from Bill, but only after pressing the matter. The fact that Shakeem respects Jackie makes her story that much more likely to trigger anxiety. Shakeem feels threatened because of the teller's credibility and the events she describes.

What negative assumptions are people making about one another? Many people in Shakeem's story seem influenced by their negative interpretations of others' behavior and motives. Shakeem mistrusts Bill's intentions and relates an anecdote about the mixed messages he sends at an employee meeting ("no wholesale changes" versus keeping "only the best of the best"), apparent evidence of a private agenda being worked out. Similarly, Brian comes to his new assignment with the reputation of being "a cold fish and a suck-up to Bill." The team's initial reactions to Brian are another example of negative assumptions at work, as well as the group's concluding assumption after a fifteen-minute staff meeting that nothing would ever please him.

The point about these assumptions is that they operate as great sources of potential threat, regardless of whether they ultimately turn out to be true. As we pointed out in Chapter Two, these negative assumptions operate at a hidden level in the cycle of mistrust to produce the very thing people are afraid might happen. An example of this could be Brian's mindset during the first staff meeting. Shakeem believes that he is anticipating a hostile reaction and behaves in a way that is likely to get one. She feels threatened by the hidden motives and intentions that she believes are behind the events.

What cultural stereotypes about managers and employees are involved? Shakeem and the managers developed an us-versus-them mindset when Bill started asking for information while Jackie was being treated in a way that felt unfair. This taps into the view of Bill as insensitive and power-based in his actions, a common stereotype for upper-level managers. On the other side of the coin, Brian's comment about a "disobedient group" may reflect a negative stereotype of rebellion by people at a lower level in a hierarchy. Shakeem feels threatened to the extent to which she buys into these us-versus-them dynamics.

How much externally imposed change is going on? The story is all about changes facing the group, starting with the reorganization and Bill's appointment as CEO, where the group had little information and almost no control over how things might turn out. Shakeem is threatened to the extent that she feels she has no power to influence what happens to her.

The mutually reinforcing effects of events, stories, assumptions, cultural stereotypes, and imposed change make fear at work powerful. It does not really matter where the feelings of threat start, or whether they are based on fact, fancy, or some combination of the two. What is important is that they exist and that they keep people from taking initiative and being fully productive. In Shakeem's situation, because all five elements of threat are involved in some way, the situation is very tense and it is little wonder that she feels she needs to leave.

Using the framework can bring three important insights:

1. *When people are afraid, there is nearly always more than one side to each story.* Stepping back, one can ask, "So what's really going on here?" before drawing further conclusions. New questions come to mind, including these:

- Why, really, was Jackie demoted?
- Is Bill truly as deceptive and retaliatory as he sounds?
- What are Bill's and Brian's good points? Is there any positive rationale for their behavior?
- How did Brian genuinely feel about his new assignment?
- Are there other possible interpretations of the "disobedient" remark?
- How did the group's behavior feed the problems?
- How reasonable are the assumptions Shakeem makes in deciding to leave?

The views of others add to, shape, or contradict Shakeem's perceptions. There will be different "realities" for each person involved, with overlapping interpretations and emphases, depending on who is speaking.

As just one example of this, here is an additional detail of Shakeem's story. When she talked with Brian during her one-on-one meeting, Brian confided: "I was really nervous about that first staff meeting. There were so many of you. All I could think of was 'These are Jackie's loyal people. They must hate me.'" The point is that there's a person with vulnerable feelings behind the mask that appears in Shakeem's story. Unless that person's realities are understood, it becomes all too easy to see the situation—and the fears involved—in a way that reinforces the perspective of the person telling the story. This in turn can lead to the creation of villains, instead of to a three-dimensional view of the situation where everyone may be anxious in some way and may play a role in perpetuating the difficulty.

2. *The dynamics of fear often seem to have a life of their own.* Once the ball gets rolling, situations can feel unstoppable and overwhelming, with few choices and many risks for those involved, and significant disappointment if efforts to change the dynamics fail. Because the sense of threat may come from many things that act in a mutually reinforcing way, a sense of helplessness can easily set in. Jackie worries about getting in more trouble. People conclude that they won't ever be able to please their new manager. And when Shakeem's efforts to "take a chance" with Brian backfire, it isn't long before she decides to leave. This life-of-their-own quality of events means that fear can quickly become taken for granted as part of an organization's culture.

3. *Resolution comes from learning about others' perspectives, not finding "the truth."* Through the framework we can also see how total objectivity is likely to be impossible. Efforts to find an absolute truth may end up mired in the differing recollections and defensiveness of those involved. Yet bringing people together to share their many sides of the story has enormous value. Helping one another consider the multiple factors that have created a sense of threat can make a powerful difference. The goal is not to step back from a situation to find an absolute truth, but to step forward to learn what people do, say, and feel that gets in the way—or leads to a solution. Slowing down to listen to others and sort out the reasons behind their reactions is a way to understand their world. When this is done, the ball that seemed unstoppable may well come to a halt.

Triggers of Mistrust

What people learn about when they slow down is a range of behaviors and beliefs that cause mistrust to surface and keep it going. Through our field study we were able to categorize the most frequent of these triggers of mistrust. The stories we heard led us to conclude there are three major categories:

1. Abrasive and abusive conduct by managers and supervisors
2. Ambiguous behavior by managers and supervisors
3. Perceptions about the culture of the organization—"how we do things here"—with special emphasis on how human

resources (HR) systems operate and on the conduct of top management

Going back to Shakeem's story, it is possible to see some of these behaviors and beliefs at work. Through words, actions, unexplained events, and the assumptions that followed, her workplace became complex and emotional. The more familiar you can be with these triggers, the better able you will be to understand what sets a repeating cycle of mistrust in motion and the changes required to arrest it.

The balance of this chapter describes these three triggers and how each contributes to fear and mistrust. Abrasive and ambiguous behaviors are the more immediate causes of fear, so they are described in detail. These are the behaviors that most stimulate and reinforce the cycle of mistrust on a moment-to-moment basis. They are also addressed in Chapters Nine and Eleven.

As noted above, poorly operating personnel systems also stimulate negativity and anxiety. These formal systems send strong messages about the value of people to the organization and how employees can expect to be treated. In turn, these may be reinforced by informal views of how upper management appears to operate. People at the top who demonstrate abrasive or ambiguous behavior, who appear insensitive to others, or who do not seem to collaborate with one another reinforce a general sense of mistrust.

Abrasive and ambiguous conduct by managers, coupled with poorly handled personnel matters and coldness from the top, can create tremendous barriers. Much of the time only one or two of these factors are operating, but even so, this smaller amount of fear still goes a long way.

By dividing triggers of mistrust into these categories, we hope to make them more visible. As with the sources of threat discussed earlier in this chapter, it is important to remember that they overlap and reinforce one another and, in actual practice, are often combined. An example of how multiple triggers can be combined would be

An upper-level manager who repeatedly delays (ambiguous behavior)

or dismisses (coldness from the top)

a meeting with an employee to discuss a performance appraisal (HR system)

that was felt to be unfairly critical or blaming (abrasive behavior)

Abrasive and Abusive Conduct Exhibited by Leaders

Abrasive interpersonal behavior is aggressive and intimidating. When the behavior is gross or intentional, it is abusive. Intentionally or unintentionally, these behaviors cause people to feel bullied, humiliated, isolated, insulted, and threatened. Descriptions we heard from study participants included these:

> "My manager is someone who leads by intimidation. She yells at staff, talks down to people. She makes blatantly discriminatory comments in front of gay employees. She has no time for people. When you approach her, all you get are short, sharp answers."
>
> —Secretary

> "Our supervisor crucifies people. She told one employee she was a 'fat slob.' In another situation she screamed at a person whose father had just died for not calling in every day. Then, when the person came in to pick up her paycheck, our boss offered the person her performance evaluation. She is formidable, unpredictable, and volatile. She will say things like 'You'll be in my office at eight o'clock and if you are not here you'll be considered insubordinate.' If you show you are the least bit intimidated, she'll have a field day—crumbling is a sign of weakness."
>
> —Health care professional

> "Normally, my boss and I would get along well. But if I surprised him with a problem and he had to make a quick decision, he would get red in the face. You could see it creep up his neck. Suddenly, there would be a lot of tension in the air. He'd lose his temper and start shouting."
>
> —Middle manager

Such behaviors immediately destroy trust and end communication. They create a thick wall of antagonism and resentment. It is easy to see how a person who repeatedly puts others down or loses control of his or her temper might create hesitation and worry in others.

Our interviews with study participants, many of whom were managers, convinced us that much of this behavior is the result of defensiveness and lack of awareness. While a few supervisors certainly will use these techniques in a conscious way, *we believe that most managers do not actually mean to hurt or punish anyone.* "I do things I wish I didn't do," one manufacturing manager told us. "Managers are not perfect."

Whether the behaviors are intentional or unintentional, however, the impact is largely the same: people are very careful around managers who behave in this way. Their abrasive or abusive patterns create tricky situations for employees. One person told us of his experience with an abrasive supervisor: "I was advised, 'To handle him, yell back.' But this is not something you experiment with. If you are wrong, you are dead wrong."

These working conditions require great stamina and courage from the employee. Because they are potentially explosive or damaging, it is hard to know what to do to stop the patterns. As a result, the problem frequently goes uncorrected and the manager's style becomes undiscussable. People learn to make do in a fearful environment, never knowing when or where the next abrasive interaction will take place.

There is a range of these behaviors and some are more damaging than others. The "gray scale" shown in Figure 4.1 explores the scope of this conduct. The numbers 1 to 11 on the scale describe the various types of behaviors. These are generally arranged in order of increasing impact. *Abrasive* behaviors are near the light-gray end; those at the dark-gray end are more *abusive.*

The horizontal intensity dimension (letters A to E) places each fear-causing behavior on a continuum of subtlety, generality, frequency, and exposure. This is simply an aid to help you think about the wide variety of ways in which behaviors can be fear-provoking. For example, insults and innuendoes can be delivered in many different ways. They may be more like an innuendo at point A, or they may happen infrequently. By comparison, at point E, the insults would come across as frequent and direct personal attacks made in a more public way. A behavior on the A side is not always less damaging. Subtle, manipulative forms of aggression are very destructive.

Here, in more detail, is a description of the types of gray-scale behaviors that emerged during our study. As you read through them, we encourage you to think about how each leads to negative assumptions, about individuals and about managers in general.

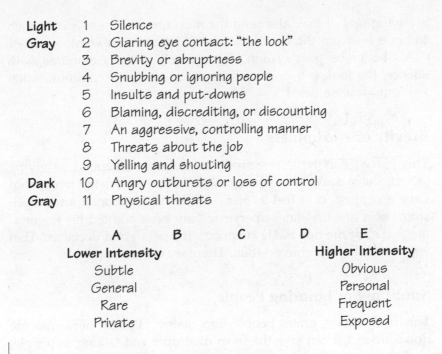

Light	1	Silence
Gray	2	Glaring eye contact: "the look"
	3	Brevity or abruptness
	4	Snubbing or ignoring people
	5	Insults and put-downs
	6	Blaming, discrediting, or discounting
	7	An aggressive, controlling manner
	8	Threats about the job
	9	Yelling and shouting
Dark	10	Angry outbursts or loss of control
Gray	11	Physical threats

A	B	C	D	E
Lower Intensity				**Higher Intensity**
Subtle				Obvious
General				Personal
Rare				Frequent
Private				Exposed

Figure 4.1. What Leaders Do to Threaten Employees.

Silence

Silence can be a useful and appropriate tool to elicit communication from others. However, pausing and allowing that pause to continue, especially if it is accompanied by direct, deadpan, or cool eye contact, can be extremely intimidating. It is interpreted as questioning the speaker's judgment. People fumble inside trying to figure out what to say next.

Glaring Eye Contact: "The Look"

Some people can look at others with sufficient power to wither the brightest flowers of confidence. This is more than just eye contact. The look is a testing, evaluative glare. Vaguely irritated or on the verge of criticism, it is often filled with parental messages such as "What did you do this time?" or "You and I both know you are screwing up." It may also send the message that there is not much to hope for from the speaker, as in "What do you want now?" or "This better be good. I don't have much time." Combined with silence, the look is a powerful way to shut down communication without saying a word.

Brevity or Abruptness

This behavior is what one study participant described as giving "short, sharp answers" to questions or comments, using words that have a clipped, cold feel to them. "When I questioned a top decision," said one first-line supervisor, "my boss pointed his finger at me and shut me down. He snapped: 'It was a good decision.' That was the end of the conversation. There was no reason."

Snubbing or Ignoring People

This behavior separates people into castes: "I'm up here. You are down there." It can take the form of simply not talking to people, leaving them out of meetings important to their job, or reminding them of their "place." A manager described his observations of this phenomenon as "the male dominance ritual: in-crowd conversation, sitting in the power seats, turning one's back on someone at the meeting. In general, making sure everyone knows these people consider themselves very, very important."

Insults and Put-Downs

These include a wide variety of cutting remarks, direct or implied, that attack a person's credibility, competence, or integrity. They often take the form of labeling, making jokes at someone's expense, ridicule or sarcasm, and racist, sexist, and other discriminatory remarks of all kinds. These comments elicit a combination of fear and anger, permanently engraving the remarks in people's memories. For example, a supervisor told one of his employees, "You're not as good as the other clerk. You don't understand computers; you don't have a mind for math." We also heard this story from a senior manager for a service organization of about two thousand people:

> "My boss was an abrasive guy. One day in a staff meeting
> he looked at me and said, 'You know, you are about as

important as the hole left in water after you pull your hand out.' This kind of comment was typical. He took a parental approach even though all of us working for him were about the same age. One day he took me by the arm and pulled me into his office with the phrase, 'Step into my office, son.' He pursed his lips, sat up in his seat, and looked down at me like a child. 'This is just like raising children,' he said."

Another study participant told us about her supervisor, who became irritated when her phone line kept buzzing. "Who's the idiot who's ringing my line?" she snapped. The study participant, who was in charge of the phones, told the supervisor that she wasn't doing it. "No?" loudly replied the boss, "Then who is the other idiot?"

These are not just instances of people having a bad day. This type of behavior was described by employees as habitual, something that happened routinely. We were impressed with the clarity with which people recalled these events. A single remark would last a long time.

Blaming, Discrediting, or Discounting

These behaviors place responsibility for a problem on someone else. The process is one of labeling or fixing blame in a way that traps or targets the other person.

For example, an office coordinator discussed morale problems caused by a coworker with the coworker's manager. She reported that her discussion resulted in her being blamed for the problem. The manager was a "'finger pointer'—you really had to document things up to your neck. He'll twist things, dump blame on people. You really have to cover your behind."

In another scenario, a change in management led to major personnel changes. When an employee, a buyer for the company, received her performance evaluation, she found that she had been criticized for her "lack of organization and follow-through"—areas that she said were actually her strengths. At a later meeting, one of the managers made the public comment: "We are not going to be promoting any more secretaries to buyer around here." She was the only secretary in the company who had been promoted in this way. These discrediting remarks about her performance preceded her transfer to another part of the organization and eventual layoff.

An Aggressive, Controlling Manner

People described this autocratic behavior as demanding, intense, "my way or the highway." A secretary reported that the head of the operation called, looking for her manager. She explained that he was at the barbershop. "Barbershop!" he exclaimed. "What barbershop? Go find him. Get him to me." In another case, a boss was described as "banging her fist on the table. She wanted people jumping and under pressure." This type of behavior easily blends with a micro-managing, high-surveillance approach to controlling people, such as requiring time logs for every task.

If behavior of this kind is calculated and manipulative, it crosses into being abusive. A high-level program manager described working for a vice president with a reputation for yelling at people. The manager reported that the first time this happened to him, he confronted the vice president. "I told him he wouldn't treat me that way in the future. He smiled at me when I got done, and he never yelled at me again." But then the story continued:

> "Not long after that confrontation, I was in a meeting with him and some of his chief managers. He publicly dressed one of them down—up one side and down the other. And then he did something that told me it was all an act—it was just for the pleasure of exercising his power. In the middle of yelling at this guy in front of the others, he turned to me and winked."

Threats About the Job

Comments like "I'll remember this. You're undermining me" and "I can replace you" put the employee's job security on the line. Threats can be either implied or direct. Performance criticisms related to a particular project can include an unstated threat of job loss. When someone higher says, "I'll get somebody else," as one top manager heard, it raises the question: "For what?" A variation is to make the threat public. A market analyst reported an angry office scene in which a higher-level manager threatened to terminate the analyst's supervisor. "I'm going to fire you!" he shouted. After that the analyst reported that he "was shaking." He and others were "not willing to share true feelings or opinions. We were all waiting for management direction. It made us slaves. We felt we were not free to make statements. We really had no power or say."

Yelling and Shouting

Next to put-downs and insults, this category was the most frequently cited interpersonal behavior that triggers fear. It is all about loud voices and loud arguments. Sometimes, people said, someone's voice could be heard "all the way down the hall" or "all over the building," as if the venting was intended to widely publicize a failure and to humiliate the employee. One person commented that her manager seemed to "like the adrenaline rush" of loud arguments. A supervisor remembers hearing his manager say during one of these sessions, "Bob's been pouncing on me, so now you are going to get it, too." It is not unusual for obscenities, threats, and insults to be thrown into the bargain.

Angry Outbursts or Loss of Control

This behavior represents an explosion. It is the point at which people throw things in their offices or resort to exaggerations. For example, a group of employees tried to give their supervisor feedback about her style. As the group talked to her, she started to cry and turned their statements around. She accused the team of "ruining her career" and going to higher management behind her back. She threatened to hold them "directly responsible." In another company, the CEO had a reputation for blowing his stack when he was brought bad news. He would get so angry that he would stamp his feet, causing his pant legs to hike up slightly. There was an underground rating system among the managers about whether a particular episode was a "one-leg" or "two-leg" tantrum.

Physical Threats

Physical threats are only one step away from patently criminal behavior. In the following story, the threat for a young professional woman is not spoken, but it is surely felt.

> I did not think my boss was technically competent. Our conversations would get adamant and personal. He would twist my words, so that I felt

"damned if I did and damned if I didn't." I did a lot of rear-end covering. All our conversations degenerated into his yelling at me and my leaving. He violated my personal space, and I felt trapped and became afraid he would assault me.

At the end of one workday, after many others had left, he followed me into my cubicle. He whispered harshly, "You will do this!" I backed up to a corner. His fists were clenching and unclenching. He was breathing rapidly and his shoulders were heaving up and down. He had a wild look in his eyes. I thought he was going to hit me. At that point my values kicked in. "You're harassing me," I said to him. My boss defused at that point and walked away. Nobody was there to help.

I fell apart. It was hell. I went home and called the employee relations representative. I was afraid to go back to work. As far as I know, he was never reprimanded. He wasn't fired. I had a real fear for a long time afterward about working at night. It was a feeling of terror.

Ambiguous Behavior Displayed by Leaders

Next to abrasive behaviors, ambiguous behaviors appear to cause the most tension for employees. These behaviors are difficult to read. They cause people to "wonder what the rules are." They leave people confused. And, in so doing, they also set off the cycle of mistrust as people assume a negative intent associated with an absence of needed information or involvement. Six types of ambiguous behavior surfaced repeatedly in our interviews. The order in which we present them reflects the frequency with which they were mentioned to us. They are secretive decision making, lack of or indirect communication, lack of responsiveness to input or suggestions, inconsistency or mixed messages, uninviting behaviors, and unethical conduct.

Secretive Decision Making

This area emerged most often. Related issues, such as indecision and failure to explain decisions once they have been made, were also identified. Closed-door, behind-the-scenes decision making causes anxiety for several reasons. First, it is regarded as a put-down. Not being included sends the messages: "You don't know enough" or "Your judgment isn't valued." Second, not knowing the rationale for decisions makes them especially difficult to implement, thus raising performance fears. Third, if people are not involved in or informed of decisions, their work life becomes unpredictable and open to a range of possibilities beyond their influence. They do not know what to expect. These reasons leave people feeling tentative and on edge. This is especially so for those who have a hard time managing ambiguous situations.

In one instance, an HR staff person described her manager as "very closed-door, secretive."

> "She'd close the door with the assistant director. They kept the door closed literally for hours. 'We are in here making plans for the department' was the sense of it. She didn't make decisions. Rather, she seemed to hide behind procedures. She said she was big on teamwork, but it was a joke. There she'd go again into her room with her door closed."

In another organization, a group of our interviewees talked about "the unknown," meaning upper management. According to them, "We didn't have a clue where upper management was coming from. We only got the end of it. They are so secretive. Why don't they ask for our advice? Maybe we could help."

This is a serious problem area for many organizations because decision making is such a vital and frequent activity. Chapter Thirteen provides specific advice on how to break down the barriers to effective decision making.

Lack of or Indirect Communication

Indirect or insufficient communication pertains to information that is necessary to do a good job. This includes feedback on performance. Key concerns are how much information to share, who to share it with, and how to make sure it gets to people in an accurate, timely, and consistent manner.

An example of poor information flow comes from one of our consulting experiences. The manager of a branch unit and her chief assistant had developed a serious conflict around who was to have particular information. The manager felt that her assistant did not need certain budget reports and would not pass them along. In return, he failed to give her information about customer complaints. This mutual undermining of the relationship caused anxiety and embarrassment for both sides and exacerbated their long-term conflict. Each had a private interpretation of the other's intent based on this limited flow of information, but neither had expressed these feelings openly. The conflict, while minor, was a symptom of distorted communication that influenced virtually everyone in the organization.

Lack of Responsiveness to Input or Suggestions

When people do not hear back about their suggestions, the door is left open to negative conclusions. They ask themselves questions that reflect confusion and a disquieting combination of mistrust and powerlessness:

- Was the idea dismissed?
- Did upper management find it offensive?
- Is it worth it to try to improve things around here?
- Should I ask what happened to my idea?
- What will they think if I make too big a deal about this?

These questions lead to doubts and to disappointment that nothing has happened with their ideas. In the absence of other information, people often assume the worst. This worst-case thinking typically promotes both fear and a sense of powerlessness. People worry that because there has been no response to their suggestions, their credibility is being questioned. They hesitate to ask what happened to their ideas for fear of being labeled the "squeaky-wheel troublemaker." They also see the lack of response as more evidence that nothing will change and that there is no use trying to make a difference. We touch on solutions to these problems in two later strategy chapters. In Chapter Ten, we outline actions that encourage people to bring their ideas forward and describe ways to respond appropriately. In Chapter Fourteen, we explore the phenomenon of worst-case thinking in detail and recommend ways to help overcome it.

Inconsistency or Mixed Messages

When a manager sends a double message or confused signals, people worry or become cynical. In one case, an administrative support worker discussed how her supervisor gave feedback by talking about the performance or conduct of other employees. For example, the supervisor told the worker that she would not have to worry about her calls being monitored to ensure that they were all business-oriented, "unlike someone else in the office." The employee interpreted this to mean that in fact her calls were being monitored or were in immediate jeopardy of being monitored. Her interpretation was confirmed by a coworker who had experienced a similar problem with the supervisor. This type of behavior can be extremely intimidating because it leads to a paranoid questioning of all the supervisor's comments: "Is she really talking about me?" "What does she really mean?"

Many employees also talked to us about "two sets of rules" for managers and employees, as when a decision made by an employee according to policy is overturned at a higher level. These apparent inconsistencies lead people to question their own judgment and feel unclear about how to proceed without losing favor.

Another example of this type of behavior takes the form of inconsistent reasoning behind decisions. A professional who questioned the hiring decision of a white manager was told that her white appointee had more experience than a competitor from a different racial background. However, in a second selection procedure, the manager argued that another white appointee had been selected because she was not "overqualified," like a second candidate who was a person of color. The two stories increased rather than resolved the employee's concerns about the presence of racism, mixed messages, and double standards.

Uninviting Behaviors

These are behaviors that are not clearly abrasive but are generally cold or aloof. They reflect inattention to the small, but significant and expected, pleasantries and manners associated with human interaction. A number of those interviewed commented on the fact that their managers rarely acknowledged them when they passed in the hall. This lack of common courtesy was taken as the sign of a caste system.

When a manager behaves in a way that can be interpreted as impolite or deliberately distant, the message sets off a line of thinking that goes something like this: "This person does not care about people. Which means that this person probably does not care about me. Which means that I may be in trouble."

For example, even though a manager was highly regarded for his "people management" decisions, his cold, "computer-like" intelligence intimidated and confused people. Part of the problem was simply a lack of personal disclosure. Employees said they did not know "who he was." Another manager talked and acted fast. Her impatience communicated the message: "How come this isn't done? I told you to do it!" Even though employees recognized that she was simply being impatient and not abrasive or aggressive, the behavior startled and intimidated those who reported to her.

Unethical Conduct

This behavior pattern was not frequently mentioned, but people did identify behaviors such as outright stealing or embezzling from the company, lying, bragging about drug abuse, and requiring employees to do the boss's personal work on company time. Along with these more extreme examples, we heard about less obvious unethical behavior by managers, such as claiming an employee's idea as the manager's own, playing favorites, or asking employees not to give complete information to customers.

Such behaviors leave employees juggling and sometimes caught between three sets of rules: the company's, their manager's, and their own. The threat of repercussions can hover over their heads from any source—not the least of which is an employee's own personal sense of integrity.

The Culture of the Organization

In addition to abrasive or ambiguous behavior, the perceptions of the HR staff and top management can trigger fear responses. Both relate to the culture of an organization. By *culture*, we mean the way things routinely operate, what people can take for granted about their organizational life, and how people can expect to be treated. How HR systems function and how senior leaders behave are frequently read as two central clues about the nature of an organization's culture and whether that culture is based on trust or fear.

When major personnel management issues surface, people watch closely. These can be defining moments for both the reputation of Human Resources as a function and the leadership of senior management. The following story illustrates this point.

 *The Layoffs*

A company making a shift to a more entrepreneurial business focus initiated a broad round of layoffs. Human Resources and top decision makers came under tough criticism for the following—all of which caused great anxiety for people:

■ The reasons for the reduction in force (RIF) seemed to relate solely to short-term profits at the expense of the welfare of the organization and its long-term customers.

■ There was a lack of useful, reassuring follow-up with the survivors.

■ The RIF was carried out with an air of secrecy.

■ Those who were selected to be laid off were often long-time, well-respected employees.

■ The RIF was staggered through departments, so that people were unsure what part of the organization would be hit next and when the RIF would end.

■ People were given no warning; they were notified and given almost no time to adjust before being asked to leave.

■ There was no obvious effort to place laid-off employees in other positions.

■ The names of people to be let go leaked out before they had been officially notified.

How the RIF was carried out was interpreted as an enormous message about how people were valued by the organization. Given the negativity of the perceptions, it is no wonder that many people concluded that management no longer cared about them.

Almost symbolically, the company president's conduct became a lightning rod for these fear-provoking elements of the RIF. People said that

■ He seemed reluctant to answer questions; his responses felt "prompted."

■ He did not have the image of a "people person"; he used videotape and memos to communicate about the RIF, more than actual meetings. He didn't seem as easy to talk to as the previous president, who was someone "you could joke with In the elevator."

■ His motives were rumored to be purely ones of financial self-interest; he was attempting to set the company up for a takeover.

These behind-the-scenes beliefs and perceptions reinforced the negative views of what to expect from the company. As one survivor put it, "The president is the one person I want to trust, but I don't." It's easy to see the cycle of mistrust spinning through these comments about the layoffs and the president's demeanor and motives.

Human Resources

Views of Human Resources reflect stable, ongoing perceptions that are accepted as part of the work environment. In the end it boils down to the question, "Can the people in Human Resources be trusted or not?" For example, the HR department may be thought of as simply an enforcement mechanism or a conduit back to line management, causing employees to worry that seeking advice or counsel will only lead to repercussions. For those with legitimate concerns who need assistance from HR specialists, this results in a feeling of being trapped and fearful or alone. One study participant told us about her organization: "Human Resources is a totally Theory X organization [an organization based on negative beliefs about people]. If you went there, the word would get back to your boss before you got back to your work station."

People pick up on the nature of the policies and HR practices within which they are expected to operate. If these practices make negative assumptions about the intentions of employees, they create confusion and trigger the cycle of mistrust. An example comes from a company with numerous plants and a practice of rotating career-track managers between these locations. An unstated but unbreakable rule was that no assistant plant manager would ever advance to the plant manager position in the same location. The reasoning behind this rule was that it would prevent the assistant manager from trying to undermine the top manager in an effort to get his or her job. This rule communicated the belief that middle managers might do this undermining if they had the chance. Yet no one could give an example of this ever having happened nor remember exactly when the rule was formed.

The Personnel or Human Resources director or vice president is a symbol for management. If this person is cold, abrasive, or ambiguous in her or his leadership of the function, people will worry. Poor handling of performance, equal employment opportunity, or career development problems inside the HR department is a signal to everyone else in the organization that they should expect no real help if they seek the assistance of someone in the department. These perceptions will always spread to other areas of the organization via the rumor mill.

These perceptions of Human Resources are the reference points that teach people how to negotiate the work environment. They reflect embedded beliefs and assumptions that continuously seed the cycle of mistrust. An organization development manager pointed out to us that with employee orientation, there are always two versions: the official personnel department orientation for the organization and the real orientation given by one's peers. The latter is made up of the "Three B's": the benefits of working in the organization, the location of the bathrooms, and what (and whom) to beware of.

Top Management

Even at the entry level, people have a perception of and are concerned about what is happening at the top of their organization.

In circumstances far less dramatic than layoffs, we often found that people possessed a characterization of those at the top. We saw consistent themes from interview to interview. In one organization, upper management was considered to be "inconsistent"; in another, "indecisive"; in a third, "arbitrary"; in a fourth, "overly competitive" and "incompetent." Generally, these opinions were backed up with specific stories that had traveled freely through the organization's grapevine. Clearly, the words and actions of people at the top set the tone—or undertone—for the way business is to be done.

In one organization, a first vice president was reported to have said, "Perception is reality." A lower-level manager assured us that this phrase was a well-known indication of how the vice president expected people to operate. The manager said: "People lived by that quote. It meant, 'If I think it is, it is.' In other words, if something came to his attention, it was true. There would be no investigation. If they heard the bad news at the top, then they would fix blame."

In another organization we heard the comment: "Top managers are competing with one another to build monuments to their areas or to themselves. It's a game of one-upmanship. They are competing for resources." Needless to say, when top executives have a reputation for being abrasive, this behavior sends shock waves of mistrust throughout the organization. People worry about what will happen to them, or to their managers, if they step out of line. In a few organizations we visited, stories of angry reactions, put-downs, and threats by the CEO surfaced loudly. Interviewees saw these behaviors as a revealing demonstration of the core values and operating standards of their organization.

Perhaps the most troubling theme that surfaced as we listened to these stories of abrasive, abusive, and ambiguous content, as well as to stories of negative background cultures, was the sense that talking about these issues was unacceptable. These triggers of mistrust could not be addressed openly or positively. Along with a wide variety of other important issues, they, too, were hidden under a veil of undiscussability. In the next two chapters we explore the range of what is under this veil and why it exists. We then conclude Part Two by exploring the costs of the negativity and fear.

New Lessons and Reflections

Thoughts on Organizational Culture

If your organization is one where people cynically point out that those of you in leadership "do not walk the talk," here's what you need to do to change that perception. Think about the assumptions that underlie your company's vision, mission, and values. Typically, these documents assume the best about the intentions and capabilities of both customers and employees. Next, take a look at the policies, practices, systems, and structures of the organization. Very frequently these are based upon negative assumptions. They assume that people will lie about sick-leave absences, abuse telephones or copy machines with extensive personal use, put themselves rather than the customer first when they control their own scheduling, or produce low-quality products or service unless they are supervised. It is this misalignment that causes people to believe that their leaders say one thing but truly believe something else. Instead of the trust, respect, and creativity talked about in the public documents, people see an organizational culture characterized by mistrust, bias, and control.

To correct this situation, conduct a review of your policies, practices, systems, and structures. Decide which of these most affect the daily experience of employees. Whenever possible, get rid of or reshape any that make negative assumptions about the intentions of employees. Recognize that there are very few policies, practices, systems, or structures that absolutely need to be in place to protect the organization in case of lawsuits. In those cases, ask yourself, "Is there another way we can protect ourselves?" Remember that leaders, not lawyers, are the ones who guide organizations to success. This work can be tedious, but it has tremendous payoffs, especially if teams of employees are involved in the review and revision of the misaligned elements.

Thoughts on Personal Leadership

This chapter has focused on behaviors that keep fear in place. It is very easy to react emotionally to these behaviors. Reading about them can trigger memories of events and past experiences where they were present. Reactions to behavior can naturally lead to an effort to *explain* the experiences—for example, to explain the abrasive behavior of a boss in terms of her or his "insecurity," or to explain the reasons behind a mixed message you may have sent to your work team. These explanations are worth exploring, because they highlight how easily negative assumptions about others become entrenched and how defensive assumptions about oneself may prevent a hard look at the actual impact of personal behavior.

For the purposes of this book, however, asking *why* certain behaviors are present in you or others is less important than being aware of their effects and making a commitment to improve. Answering the "why" can go deeply into personal psychology as well as into the roots of organizational culture. But ultimately, change needs to occur at a behavioral level and this does not require a final answer to the "why" for any one of us. When coupled with a positive assumption that people naturally want trust-based relationships and can see their business value, the focus on behavior is the high road to rapid change.

CHAPTER

5

Undiscussables: Secrets That Everyone Knows

In this chapter, we explore some of the undiscussable issues that were raised in our interviews. This exploration is about the types of problems that remain sealed by the hesitation of people to speak up and work through them. These are the problems that fear makes inaccessible. The following vignette is typical.

A new manager who worked for a well-respected manufacturing firm was aware that several of his employees had complaints about how the operation had been going. He knew this because they had talked to him individually about their concerns. He made a point of bringing up these complaints at a staff meeting, believing that people would appreciate the chance to discuss and resolve some of them. To his great surprise, when he raised the issues, there was dead silence. People would not talk openly about what they had expressed privately. The manager and his group had run into a brick wall of undiscussable issues.

The result was predictable. The manager, unaware of how mistrust influenced relationships in his group, was frustrated and mystified by the staff members' reactions. Resolution of problems in the operation

77

was delayed because people would not talk about them. Those who worried about the problems continued to be troubled with operational difficulties. Unsolved problems continued to waste time and money.

What Is an Undiscussable?

Our use of the term "undiscussables" comes from the work of Harvard educator Chris Argyris (Argyris, 1986; Argyris, Putnam, and Smith, 1985). In our usage:

> An undiscussable is a problem or issue that someone hesitates to talk about with those who are essential to its resolution.

As illustrated by the vignette opening this chapter, by their nature, undiscussables create barriers to productivity. They prevent quality work and erode working relationships.

Undiscussables are not talked about in the settings where they could be explored, explained, and resolved. They are the secrets that almost everyone knows. The longer they remain undiscussed in the appropriate forums, the more they contribute to a climate of fear within the work environment. And the longer they remain undiscussed, the harder it becomes to talk about them. They are at the same time both a cause and a result of fear.

In spite of what our definition might imply, people do talk about undiscussables. Sometimes a lot. They are discussed privately, in the halls and restrooms, over lunch or after work, during breaks at meetings, and on the job when other work should be attended to. They are discussed between friends, family members, coworkers, and others in the workplace who are trusted but not directly involved. Rumor mills exist almost solely to accommodate undiscussable issues. To give you an idea about how undiscussables can come into being and relate to specific situations, we include two short stories.

> A small southeastern company was bought out by a larger corporation. With the new ownership came new people, including a new CEO. As part of the purchase agreement, the previous CEO was to remain in the purchased company, but in a less influential job. Before this shift could be implemented, however, the previous CEO confronted his replacement about several uncomfortable aspects of the transition. The exchange was heated and public. This disagreement was remembered by virtually everyone who remained in the organization.

Even though the official reasons given for the shift in top leadership had to do with the superior technical skills of the incoming executive, the public disagreement became the standard explanation for his predecessor's demotion. People linked this early confrontation to the change, and it became an emblem for what the new environment would be like. As a consequence, a variety of fear-related beliefs were established, among them the belief that people could not speak up to the new owners without fear of retribution. Undiscussables multiplied, along with tremendous amounts of mistrust and misperception. Conflict became rampant. Even fairly straightforward problem solving became mired in arguments.

It was not until five years later, when we were asked to consult, that many of the background issues came to light. At that point, the undiscussables—what people could not work on directly without anxiety and anger—included

■ How people genuinely felt about the new company and many of its technical methods and procedures

■ The management style of the current CEO

■ Office politics, played out on a daily basis, regarding the slow-burning power struggle between the old and new CEOs

■ The tendency of people in the organization to take sides with the "old way" and the "new way"

■ Contradictory standards for handling customer complaints

■ The wide range of inefficiencies and problems that were driven by mistrust

A manufacturing company places enormous emphasis on meeting customers' requirements. This holds true not only for direct service operations but also for the staff departments that provide service to operational field units. The talk about commitment to customers and delivery dates is very strong. A common question asked of a staff department manager who is making a commitment to deliver a service at a particular time is "Will you stake your job on it?" While this question is typically raised in a joking manner, it nonetheless worries people. They know there is a serious side to the statement.

Many believe that in this organization, it is not acceptable to say that a schedule is unworkable. As a consequence it is impossible to say, "This won't work" until it's too late, "even when people on the team have known about it for a long time." It is not uncommon for delivery dates to be postponed, but not until the eleventh hour. One person commented, "This really is one of those places where there is never enough time to do it right, but always enough time to do it over. People here won't listen to a lesser level when we ask for more time up front."

Predictably, some of the undiscussables in this organization are

- Impossible schedules and unrealistic service promises
- The real reasons driving customer complaints
- Problems, delays, errors—anything that might slow the work down
- Having to fix and redo orders instead of doing quality work the first time
- Cynical views about the company
- Not being able to voice concerns

As these two examples show, the outcomes of undiscussable issues can be a significant but unseen waste of time and energy. Problems do not get solved and change is resisted. Innovation does not occur. Customers are dissatisfied and morale is low.

What People Are Not Talking About

Undiscussables are an important window on the dynamics of fear in the workplace. In our field study, we wanted to know what issues people were most likely to be hesitant to talk about. From the stories shared by study participants, undiscussables were tabulated according to the frequency with which they were mentioned. Figure 5.1 summarizes the results.

Management performance comprises by far the largest category of undiscussables. It includes a variety of subsets related to how managers behave: study participants made comments in general or overall terms about poor managerial performance; they expressed disappointment in the technical competence of their superiors; they were critical of the ways in which higher-level leaders managed people. Skill in "people management" was the shortcoming in management performance most often mentioned as undiscussable. This area directly pertains to the way managers interact with and provide leadership to their employees and is heavily influenced by perceptions of interpersonal communication skills. In effect, the largest single category of undiscussable issues was the immediate manager's interpersonal style.

Category	Percentage of Responses
Management performance, competence, and interpersonal style	49
Coworker performance	10
Compensation and benefits	6
Equal employment opportunity practices	6
Change	4
Personnel systems other than pay	4
Individual feelings	2
Performance feedback to respondent	2
Bad news	2
Conflicts	2
Personal problems	2
Suggestions for improvement	2
Other	9

Figure 5.1. Undiscussable Issues.

Other aspects of management practice that were identified as undiscussable are

- Decision making—how decisions get made and the quality of decisions
- Favoritism
- The boss's role in promotions, assignments, and terminations
- Information flow that does not relate to decision making
- Too heavy a workload
- Ethics
- Assumptions about management motives
- Corporate politics

Coworker performance, at 10 percent, represents the second largest cluster of responses. It includes how well peers do the technical aspects of their jobs, as well as their personal conduct and interaction in the work environment.

Compensation and benefits includes concerns about pay equity and benefits as well as the way such systems are administered.

Equal employment opportunity practices combines any references to affirmative action, equal employment, or related aspects of workplace harassment or discrimination.

Change is a small category, but one that primarily reflects the concerns we heard about specific changes that had been implemented in various organizations we visited. People also talked to us about their perception of how much things in general seemed to be changing around them. (Given the rapid changes affecting workplaces since the original publication of this book, this category might be cited more frequently if our study was repeated today.)

Personnel systems other than pay includes organizational systems other than those that relate to compensation or benefits, such as hiring, promotion, termination or transfer, and employee development.

Individual feelings includes the personal emotions people have that relate to their work or work environment.

Performance feedback to respondent reflects a lack of comment—positive or negative—about someone's performance.

Bad news refers to negative or critical messages or observations about individuals' or the organization's performance.

Conflicts are actual or potential interpersonal disagreements that escalate to a higher level of open conflict.

Personal problems includes various types of trouble a person experiences that are not related to work—divorce, illness in the family, financial troubles, drug and alcohol problems, or interpersonal difficulties.

Suggestions for improvements consists of ideas or suggestions about doing something differently and better.

Other undiscussables were a mixed bag of issues and individual concerns that fit no common pattern.

Themes and Observations

During our interviews, four themes representing the most important undiscussed and unresolved workplace issues began to emerge.

Management practice was a clear focus for undiscussables. People find it very difficult to speak up to others at higher levels in an organization about management style, actions, or competence. Undiscussables that fell into this category outnumbered any other category at least four to one.

It seems clear from these data that undiscussables related to mistrust of management are the most common of all. This is a vital point. As you initiate efforts to drive out fear and deal with undiscussed issues, you need to be prepared for mistrust of leadership and specific leaders, perhaps including yourself, to surface. In order to build trust, it is wise to take a nondefensive approach to hearing this perspective. Another way of saying all this is that the cycle of mistrust not only causes undiscussables; it is itself an undiscussable, perhaps the biggest one. The fact of mistrust, its triggers, and its damaging effects are the essence of what people cannot talk about.

Given the legacy of hierarchy, it is no surprise that problems with coworkers were much less frequently reported than those with higher-level managers. Nevertheless, they are an important area for concern—the second highest in frequency. It is possible that as the trend toward flatter structures and a philosophy of self-management continues, aspects of peer relations and performance may more frequently be the source of undiscussables. Undiscussables among members of teams or networks can certainly be as debilitating as undiscussables with higher-level leaders.

Our findings did not reveal any basic differences from one level of the organization to the next in the types of undiscussables or people's willingness to speak up. We sense that factors such as the level of trust with a manager, financial obligations, interpersonal skills, and experience have a bigger role in determining whether a person speaks up than her or his level in the organization.

Human resources issues had a significant impact. Items related to HR issues and systems totaled 16 percent of undiscussables. How individuals are recruited and hired, paid, evaluated, developed, and promoted—or fired—says a lot about what the organization believes about people. Perceived inequities, discrimination, and other forms of unfairness in these areas dramatically concern people. Once again, negative views of management and of Human Resources seem tied together and are hard to talk about.

People very carefully voiced worries about race, gender, age, or other harassment or discrimination. Although virtually all types of discrimination surfaced in our interviews, the most difficult for people to talk about were issues of sexual orientation. Discrimination of all kinds warrants continued attention. The educational efforts of the 1980s and 1990s have not put these issues to rest. Due to the focus of this book, we do not directly recommend approaches that deal with these specific, sensitive concerns; however, we heartily endorse further work that enables issues of discrimination and harassment to surface more easily and to be addressed constructively.

People rarely said that they were unable to speak up about necessary improvements or innovations. This was a most interesting observation to us. When we started working on this topic, we believed—and still do—that fear causes people to remain silent about ideas they have for improvements or innovations. And yet, when we asked people to name the topics they hesitated to talk about, only 28 out of 925 responses indicated that people could not talk about a different approach or suggestions for improvement. This lopsided response seems contrary to some of the very stories we heard while doing our research. For example, the second and third stories that open this chapter involve work systems, not just managers' behaviors.

The answer lies in how people think and talk about the problems they face, and about fear. Looking again at these stories, it is clear that people are talking about work systems *as part of* a culture of mistrust. The focus is on the mistrust and what has caused it: a long-term conflict caused by a buyout and a dysfunctional demand for customer service.

Most work systems involve some element of management ownership. They are often inextricably connected to management practice issues in a way that makes it difficult, if not impossible, to talk about them without also including actual criticism of leadership or risking that the leaders will hear the conversation *as* criticism. We believe that if people think that by surfacing system problems they will offend or anger managers, the undiscussable is less likely to be termed a suggestion for a work system improvement. It will more likely be stated as an issue of management practice, such as poor decisions by higher-level leaders, ineptness, or lack of respect for people.

This is a slippery point and it has big implications. For example, to obtain some of the potentially big work system gains and improvements resulting from driving out fear, you must be willing to deal openly with issues of mistrust that do not seem to be about work systems at all. Thinking again about the third story in this chapter, leaders needed to sensitively hear how the service commitment—something they strongly believed in—was actually working to the detriment of the company. This could be a moment of surprise and embarrassment for the leaders. And it could be very much a moment of fear for those speaking out about the negative effects of the service commitment, because of concerns about how defensive or demanding the leaders might become.

Through our consulting practices, we have facilitated trust-building work within many management and employee teams that wanted to address their undiscussables. We have often found that issues of mistrust in a given group are a mixture of leadership, peer relationship, and work system problems all tangled up together. One cannot be dealt with without the others.

An Illustration of Undiscussables

A final story illustrates how easy it is for undiscussables to arise and how severe their damage can be. The story shows how undiscussables can create a powerful and negative self-perpetuating cycle all their own.

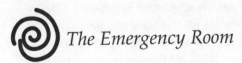 *The Emergency Room*

Over the previous five years, a hospital had made a concerted effort to be designated as a regional trauma center. Management, physicians, and the nursing staff had worked hard to streamline their procedures, augment their equipment, and build a solid reputation with the paramedics and firefighters who represented a primary segment of their customers. However, when problems arose in the emergency room (ER), many staff began to feel that their efforts to accomplish this important goal might be put at risk.

The nurse manager for the emergency room had hired a new assistant nurse manager from out of state to run the ER operations. Very quickly, the assistant manager began changing procedures and insisting that her way was the only right way. Upon observing her interaction with patients, the nurses worried that she was providing outdated and, in some cases, unsafe patient care. When the nursing staff would suggest alternatives or try to explain why their current practices worked, she abrasively ignored their advice. This reinforced the belief of many on the nursing staff that her nursing skills were deficient.

After six weeks, the nurse manager brought the nursing staff together because she was concerned that they were not adequately supporting the new assistant. When the staff expressed their concerns about the assistant's dogmatic approach, the nurse manager told them that if she heard of anyone making things hard for the assistant, she would "deal with that person on an individual basis." As a result, the staff nurses decided to "back off and do things our own way as much as we could. Even so, we tried to help [the assistant], but she wouldn't listen. Finally, a group of us couldn't take it anymore and started looking for other options."

After six months, one-third of the ER nursing staff, mostly veteran nurses, had found other jobs. Their plan was to leave all at once, to protest what they saw as both incompetent management and poor clinical practice. Two physicians who were equally upset with the tactics of the assistant nurse manager said that they also would leave if the nurses left. When she heard what was about to happen, the nurse manager finally began to listen to and believe the staff nurses. She talked with each one individually. Within a week, the assistant resigned. The staff nurses were highly involved in the selection of the next assistant manager, and things began to work well again.

Both the actual and the potential costs of this episode were significant. As one nurse said, "All of our spare time was spent dealing with this situation instead of doing something productive. Many of us used lots of sick time because we just couldn't handle coming to work if she was there." Another commented: "This almost destroyed the ER. I could see why the paramedics would have gone to other hospitals. Why should they come here to get their heads ripped off by the assistant? She didn't treat anybody with respect. She didn't seem to understand that they don't have to bring patients here."

The front-line nurse who told us this story found herself apologizing to the paramedics and "then feeling terrible for it. Why should I have had to do that? I'd spend part of my shift smoothing the feathers of other R.N.'s and M.D.'s. I took it on myself because I didn't want to see our reputation being destroyed. I'm very proud of my work and where I work. Yet people were being hurt and I couldn't stand that."

On the surface, this incident sounds extreme. And yet, from our experience, it is not uncommon. What separates it from countless other front-line experiences is that a sizable portion of the key staff were not just thinking about, talking about, or threatening to quit. They had a specific, unified plan that they were ready to put into action.

The nurses were ready to do this because the nurse manager failed to acknowledge that there might be something to their concerns about the way the assistant manager was running the ER. She discounted the nurses' concerns and wrote them off to resistance. Her threat to deal with resistant staff members individually triggered the fear that they would be harmed by further complaints. The staff members sensed the possibility of repercussions; this led directly to the perception that the assistant manager's behavior was undiscussable. In turn, this exerted a strong, negative influence on their work, with potentially major implications for their careers.

In response to this undiscussable, the ER nurses consolidated their opinion that the only way to respond was through self-protection and retaliation according to the only real power they perceived themselves to have. By quitting, they would paralyze operations, embarrass the nursing manager, and, they hoped, awaken her to the truth about her assistant's questionable skills.

When we put ourselves in the shoes of the nurse manager, we view a different set of circumstances, including

- The nurse manager wanting to support her new assistant's authority in a new job
- Staff nurses who may be stuck in their ways and resistant to new leadership
- Possible uncooperative attitudes and nonsupportive behavior on the part of staff nurses
- An assistant nurse manager who is doing her best in a tough, high-visibility situation

From this perspective, events triggered the nurse manager's mistrust of the nurses' intentions. On both sides, undiscussable negative assumptions operated as an invisible, unspeakable glue to keep this dangerous cycle of mistrust in place. Because the staff nurses perceived that their concerns were unwelcome, their frustration was driven underground and led to an extreme plan of action. Because the nurse manager thought that the staff nurses were being resistant, she did not fully observe and understand the impact of her assistant's management style.

From a long-term perspective, it is lucky that one-third of the nursing staff and two physicians were ready to quit. Without this dramatic threat to the operations, steps might never have been taken to correct the heavy-handed practices of the assistant nurse manager. We can speculate that, without this action having been taken, any nurse willing to openly express anger or resentment could easily have been branded as uncooperative and as harmful to the ER leadership. Fortunately, in fact, just the opposite was true. The staff nurses' views and concerns were listened to. Their involvement in the selection of a new assistant manager was an important demonstration of this change.

What people cannot talk about can hurt the organization in a big way. We believe that understanding and identifying undiscussables is the fastest way to figure out what people are afraid of in an organization. Getting rid of undiscussables is a primary step in reducing the presence and impact of fear on organizational success. With an understanding of *what* people are reluctant to talk about, the next step is to explore *why* people do not speak up. Chapter Six is about the answers to that question.

New Lessons and Reflections

Thoughts on Organizational Culture

One of the ways you will know that trust is on the rise in your organization is when something big happens and the rumor mill stays relatively quiet. Sudden departures of key individuals, downturns in business, bad press in the local papers or business journals, and the possibility of a merger are the types of events that, in fear-based organizations, whip the rumor mill into high gear. As trust increases, people will rely on established, official forums to raise their concerns, ask their questions, and find meaning in events. Gossip and second-guessing will diminish as people sidestep the cycle of mistrust. Instead they will rely on straightforward communication or on trust that the issues that cannot be talked about in public are being handled with professionalism and respect for confidentiality.

Thoughts on Personal Leadership

Over time, in our consulting practices, we have encountered a great many teams and a great many undiscussable issues. As people begin to think about addressing their undiscussables, they simultaneously desire to learn more and to avoid discomfort. For example, one Fortune 500 executive group asked us to facilitate a retreat in which their undiscussables might be identified, but no particular effort would be made to explore them. They simply wanted "the list." After some discussion about the value of this exercise, and careful framing with the group, we agreed to help. The first undiscussable that arose was "senior management performance."

The lesson is that the concept of undiscussables can be extraordinarily powerful in quickly bringing to the surface issues that people are not sure how to handle. The undiscussables may well be topics for which current problem-solving formulas do not work well or comfortably. The issues may have a strong emotional component, for the leader and everyone else. Just thinking about how to put them on the table can temporarily heighten rather than reduce the sense of fear. As a consequence, it is smart to go slowly, building on the understanding that unless the undiscussables are dealt with effectively, progress toward business goals will be hampered.

A breakthrough can occur if you, as the leader, are willing to openly and personally acknowledge the dilemmas that undiscussables represent and the negativity of their impact. Being able to name the undiscussables—up to and including those having to do with your own leadership skills—can help to break down the barriers to dealing with what is most sensitive. If you can model a confident, nondefensive attitude and ask for feedback, it will encourage others to also be "durable" in the discussion of tough issues and to deal with their own part of the problem. For example, if you can accept information about your involvement in a missed deadline or customer complaint, you will then be in a position to help others accept their share of the responsibility as well. If you deny or dismiss your responsibilities, however minimal, others are likely to feel justified in making their own denials.

CHAPTER

6

The Repercussions of Speaking Up

Although the individuals we interviewed expressed a variety of explanations for not speaking up, fear of repercussions clearly stood out as number one. At least 70 percent of all the people we talked with said that one of the reasons they had not spoken up in past situations was because they feared some type of repercussion.

Whether we were talking with executives, blue-collar employees, professionals, middle managers, or any other category in our sample, we heard similar responses. They told us about an incredible range of anxieties—everything from fear of being cut out of high-level discussions to worries that they would be "reorganized" or harassed out of a job. They also told us that the starting point for these potential repercussions was often a subtle loss of credibility and reputation. Given today's rapid pace of organizational change through downsizing, reengineering, or restructuring, people are more, not less, afraid of losing their jobs. Thus, protecting one's credibility becomes more important than ever.

This chapter examines how these anxieties powerfully shape people's behavior at work. It also highlights some of the interconnected themes that run through people's experience at work.

What People Are Afraid to Lose

When people told us that they did not speak up because of fear of some repercussion, we asked the question, "What are you afraid will happen?" Their answers are summarized in Figure 6.1.

Loss of credibility or reputation includes being seen as a troublemaker, a boat rocker, an agitator, or not a team player, or being given other labels that mark the individual as a problem to the organization; this category also includes fear of losing influence or of being seen as not possessing good judgment or acting in an unprofessional way.

Loss of career or financial advancement relates to losing one's chances for promotion, being rated down on performance appraisals, and losing pay increases, bonuses, or other discretionary perks.

Possible damage to relationship with supervisor is connected with antagonizing or upsetting the person to whom the individual reports, engaging in a confrontation or criticism that could lead to difficulties

Repercussion	Percentage of Responses
Loss of credibility or reputation	27
Loss of career or financial advancement	16
Possible damage to relationship with supervisor	13
Loss of employment	11
Interpersonal rejection	9
Change in job role	6
Embarrassment or loss of self-esteem	5
Job transfer or demotion	4
Other	9

Figure 6.1. Major Fears of Employees.

or long-term tensions, having fears about the manager or supervisor "making life unlivable at work," and other similar concerns.

Loss of employment is the fear of being fired, but almost always through a less direct approach, such as being laid off during a downsizing or reorganization, having job tasks pulled away until no assignments are left, or being harassed until one quits.

Interpersonal rejection consists of being disliked as a result of speaking up, being seen as not fitting in the organization, not having the right image, or being isolated or shunned by others.

Change in job role expresses the fear that small changes in assignments will take place, such as the individual's no longer being able to participate in certain meetings; that choice assignments will be given to others and less desirable assignments will be given to the employee; or that subtle changes will be made in the role and importance of the employee's work.

Embarrassment or loss of self-esteem includes being embarrassed or humiliated in front of others, particularly one's peers or powerful people in the organization, and fear of looking ignorant or unskillful.

Job transfer or demotion refers to being sent to another part of the company or being given a job with less status or money.

Loss of Credibility and the Power of Labels

The loss of credibility and reputation is most commonly expressed as a fear of being labeled. Words like "troublemaker," "whiner," "boat rocker," and "unprofessional" worry people. They convey poor judgment, last a long time, and lead to other, more tangible repercussions. These words imply that an individual is acting in bad faith, just complaining, or operating against the interests of the organization. They connote being an outsider. Many see that being labeled "not a team player" is the beginning of a downward cycle where duties start to change and performance ratings decline. These events, in turn, influence career opportunities and compensation and can lead to layoffs or transfers. In many organizations, the concept of the "hit list" represents the extreme outcome of fears about being labeled.

For example, in some organizations, transfer seemed to be the preferred method for dealing with those who had lost their credibility. In one corporation, comments included the phrase: "No one ever gets fired—just sent away on the inside." In this organization, people worried about their job responsibilities being changed, in effect creating a "nothing job." In another organization, we were told that the CEO openly bragged during a management training session about how many top people he had sent off to some organizational Siberia.

Labels can begin this process of shunning. They are signals of disfavor that quietly operate in the minds of managers and supervisors. People often believe that over time these psychological sorting bins control the ultimate success or failure of individuals in the organization. Once a loss of credibility has occurred, other incremental repercussions begin to accumulate, and the first subtle manifestations of change in stature occur. The person may be cut out of an important information loop, lose a key tie to decision makers, or lose the respect of those he or she most admires. The individual may no longer be seen as an important contributor. The ultimate message is this: "You may be good enough to stay, but don't expect to be recognized or important, to have influence, or to get the support you want."

Loss of credibility and reputation is experienced as being much larger than a question of job performance. It is felt in the broad realm of ego and self-esteem, not just in the local geography of tasks and specific skills. A vice president of a service firm defined credibility as "your boss's trust in your judgment." Other members of our sample described it as "people's faith in you," "trust of your motives," and "your validity as a person." These definitions are about one's core integrity as a human being. Labeling, they are saying, is felt as an attack on the person, not just on the performer. As one thirty-year veteran of a large corporation put it, "When your judgment is in question, it is very, very serious. Judgment is everything."

What makes the issue of credibility so complex, controlling, and frightening for people is that the labels are usually believed to be hidden. Many are convinced that management's subtle, derogatory conclusions about someone's credibility translate into negative consequences. But they also believe that the connections between the two will be obscured by time and false explanations. They will be dimmed by the decision makers' own lack of awareness that they are using these conclusions to make critical choices. Hence the concern to avoid, as a bank employee told us, any "slight, negative background feeling." Better to stick with the party line. Better not to rock the boat by speaking up.

People fear that a loss of credibility is final, silent, and absolute. One small group of interviewees repeatedly referred to "the memory bank of the organization." Another talked about "the area under the curve," meaning management's accounting of a person's total reputation and accomplishments, which includes both positive and negative events. The consensus in that group was that one "Aw, shit!" wiped out all previous achievements under the curve. Another interviewee observed, "When your career is hurt because your credibility has been questioned, you're never involved in the discussion and you'll never be able to prove it."

Two Types of Repercussions

The repercussions people fear fall into two categories: indirect, subtle ones and direct, abrasive ones. Indirect repercussions take place behind the scenes to damage an individual and his or her future. Direct repercussions are obvious attacks—for example, constant and public criticism of one's work, capricious demands for overtime work, or sarcastic comments and verbal assaults on one's character, competence, or credibility. Both types of repercussions cause fear and may or may not be present in the same situation.

Subtle, Indirect Repercussions

Over half the stories we heard about repercussions were about the background consequences of speaking up. Characteristically, these stories involved situations where the person was seriously affected but the repercussions were unpredictable, untraceable, and incontestable. They created a sense of danger and helplessness. A program analyst said:

> "I was asked to put together some figures and make a presentation to a senior manager of the company. The figures were not favorable to the company, but they were true. When I presented them, my VP and boss didn't support me. My boss said, 'Yes, Margaret, you had better redo those numbers.' I was never again invited to a senior management meeting."

In another situation, a fourth-level manager for a major corporation was demoted many months after he criticized a marketing program. Speaking of the vice president he offended, he told us:

"He never came to me. He carried out the demotion in the classic large-organization way, by assassinating my reputation and career without my knowing where it came from. 'Why are you moving the job to Omaha?' I asked my boss. He said, 'That's just the way we are going to do it.'"

These examples are about people who, with good intentions, spoke up. Yet, in attempting to help their organizations by sharing their views, they wound up hurt. Their stories reinforce the belief that behind-the-scenes repercussions can happen at any time to people who take too much liberty in expressing what they believe is right. A corporation attorney told us:

"I'm where I want to be now. Will they force me to transfer back to headquarters? There is the danger that if there is a downsizing, you want to be close enough to old Jack so that he doesn't send you back there. It's not even a conscious thing."

Subtle, indirect repercussions are what people constantly watch out for. This "watching out" is a source of background stress, what one study participant called the "long-enduring mental anxiety." People become continuously on guard for negative consequences of their behavior, no matter how well intended it was. A senior deputy of a large government service operation explained to us how he had to be careful about bringing up certain topics with the head of the agency: "It will come back on other issues—unpredictably, unrecognizably." And a technical worker summarized the feeling of long-term stress: "People are not afraid of what will happen to them tomorrow. They worry about what will happen down the road in six months or so."

These examples all demonstrate the double bind created for employees who want to help and contribute their best, but who must also be watchful and smart about not offending key people. Moreover, these dynamics are themselves very difficult to confront and talk about. Bringing them up may only lead to further negative consequences. Thus, the fear of subtle, indirect repercussions can become a form of victimization in a perceived environment of covert bullying and control. Where stories of indirect, subtle repercussions are frequently shared, the cycle of mistrust will have a strong foothold.

Immediate, Direct Repercussions

This second type of repercussions consists of fear of the boss and of what she or he can do directly and publicly. Unlike subtle, indirect repercussions, this part of fear has to do with supervisors as potential sources of immediate discomfort and pain. People are particularly afraid of being trapped in a stressful relationship where they work for someone who insults them and is abrasive, critical, and autocratic—a visible bully.

Fears of indirect and direct repercussions can combine and play off one another in an extremely volatile way, creating experiences of enormous stress. A highly experienced clerical employee told the following story about her job in a manufacturing firm.

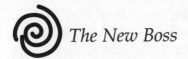 *The New Boss*

I got a new boss. She didn't want anybody in the department who had worked there longer than she had. She was very insecure. She wanted everybody to learn her way. She would choose a particular part of the department for critiquing. From then on, nothing good could come out of that area. People who had been there for years were suddenly "inept" and were let go. They were always let go on Friday night. This happened four times. Then I knew it was my turn.

She was a barracuda. I went over her head to protect my job. I worked there for two more years. It was misery. Every day was like walking on dynamite. My productivity went down because I was watching every word. I called it "ulcer gulch." There was constant dread, and in fact I developed ulcers.

I went to the CEO. He said he couldn't perceive this person doing these things. They take the attitude that if you complain it must be a vendetta. I think he dismissed it as a woman-versus-woman conflict.

It was a nightmare. She criticized people openly. Made obscene comments to a coworker. Humiliated people. I thought about the situation twenty-four hours a day, playing over the incidents that might happen. In some cases these things actually did happen.

I stayed because of pride. I knew I was right. It would have been an admission of defeat if I had quit. It was a question of self-esteem. I took the attitude: "You can't make me go away feeling like I didn't do a good job."

While such situations are not common, we did hear a number of similar stories. Most people do not run across the "ogre boss" in their careers, but there are enough abrasive supervisors and managers to keep the threat of their presence abundant. We are convinced that stories about abrasive supervisors spread far and wide within organizations, even if the relative number of such people is small. Insofar as companies tolerate their abrasive behavior, they risk strengthening the fear that repercussions—subtle or otherwise—are a way of life at work. This tolerance also sends a message to employees that the organization condones or even supports this style of management.

Interpersonal Rejection and Embarrassment

Study participants also called out interpersonal rejection and embarrassment or loss of self-esteem as repercussions they feared. Interpersonal rejection reflects the degree to which people believe that they may be pushed out of an organization because they do not "fit" its image. They feel that they must win approval as being the right "type." Interpersonal rejection results in ostracism, and as one interview participant expressed it, "Very few people come back from being shunned."

This dynamic was particularly evident in one organization with a flat structure and unusually high levels of employee participation. The company had a reputation for being cutting-edge in its industry and prided itself on an environment of debate and individual initiative. However, people expressed many private worries in interviews that they would not be seen as fitting "the XYZ Company way." A human resources person explained to us: "People have to prove they can operate in loose structures. People who want a lot of structure become performance problems here."

She continued that a person who was labeled as a performance problem would certainly get the message through the strained nature of his or her relationships with colleagues. Thus, although fear of the hierarchy was much less present than in other organizations, fear in peer relationships was higher. This is an important consideration for organizations engaged in flattening their structures. Flatter structures do not necessarily result in less fear. The fear may simply have been transferred to what happens among people in the less-formal, less-structured world of peer connections, where shunning is powerful.

Embarrassment and loss of self-esteem are primarily self-inflicted repercussions. A fear of "looking like an idiot," for example, can be very effective in stopping a person from speaking up. Self-inflicted repercussions of this kind can become sizable barriers for reflective people who want to see themselves as consistently confident, competent, and knowledgeable. In the long term, they undermine their own capacity to contribute, which may have a direct or indirect negative impact on their achievements, opportunities, and careers.

How Real Are the Repercussions?

This discussion of repercussions raises the question of how realistic these fears are. Do these repercussions really occur? When time permitted in our interviews, we asked people to tell us more about the way in which they became afraid. Could they point to actual events where obvious repercussions had taken place? Or was there some other dynamic at work? These discussions helped us to understand the continuum shown in Figure 6.2.

We know that many people have had actual experiences in which they suffered repercussions from speaking up. The most obvious situations involve abrasive or abusive bosses who are usually well known for extracting some type of payment from people who challenge their way of doing things. We believe, however, that the percentage of actual repercussions is far less than the percentage that is perceived or imagined.

Actual Repercussions	Perceived Repercussions	Imagined Repercussions

Figure 6.2. Experiences with Repercussions.

Perceived repercussions are those where people believe they have been harmed and there is a plausible, but not certain, connection to management behavior. Imagined repercussions are identical, except that the connection to management behavior is tenuous. In organizations where managers—at whatever level—are mistrusted and viewed with suspicion, a small number of actual repercussions is usually magnified many times. This sets in motion a pattern that causes people to perceive threats when none are intended. It encourages others to imagine all sorts of horrible things that "might happen" because "you never know what the boss might decide to do." The mix of reality and unexplained or ambiguous situations sets in motion a wave of perceptions that contain both truth and possibility.

As we have said before, fear is not a rational topic. People's fears are real, if not all their facts. It does not matter if the perception or imagination is grounded in truth. The issue is the fact that individuals hesitate to speak up because they fear some type of harm if they do. A senior-level engineer told us that he worries about possible repercussions. When we asked if he knew of actual cases of repercussions, he immediately answered, "Oh, yes." When we asked for details, he vividly recalled an event that had taken place eight years earlier.

We know that people believe very strongly in the *possibility* of repercussions. This is often the case even when they cannot name a specific situation or tell a distinct story verifying that repercussions have occurred. As one person neatly summarized: "If you get to the point where you should speak up, you look at how your boss has treated you over the past few months. Were you put down in front of coworkers? Was your pride or dignity insulted? Did the choice assignments go someplace else?" If the answer to these questions is yes, or *if people believe the answer could be yes*, the response is frequently the same: silence.

The Other Reasons for Not Speaking Up

While fear of repercussions was the reason most commonly cited for not addressing undiscussable issues, other reasons were also mentioned. We have chosen to concentrate on the fear of repercussions because it is such a strong and central theme. Figure 6.3 provides a breakdown of how people responded to questions about why they do not speak up.

Reason	Percentage of Responses
Fear of repercussions	44
Nothing will change	17
Avoidance of conflict	7
Don't want to cause trouble for others	5
Other	27

Figure 6.3. Why People Do Not Speak Up.

When we asked people about their reasons for staying silent on issues of concern, we collected 415 different responses. Forty-four percent of this total pool of responses involved anxiety about repercussions. However, we also noticed that most individuals gave more than one reason for not speaking up. When we looked at the data in this way, we found that fully seven out of ten people had specifically mentioned repercussions as one of their personal reasons. When these two figures—44 percent of the responses and 70 percent of the people—are considered together, they create compelling documentation for fear in the workplace.

Nothing Will Change

Next in importance to fear of repercussions, *Nothing will change* responses stood out. These responses were often characterized by a sense of futility, a feeling of certainty that speaking up would come to nothing:

"I'm a peon; management is powerful."

—Internal auditor

"Management turns its back."

—Lead assembler

"My boss says, 'Uh huh, uh huh,' but doesn't do anything about the problem."

—Clerical employee

These comments all reflect the belief that options have been cut off and there is simply no point in trying anything further. One accounting professional, for example, talked about his belief that his manager simply "doesn't value input" and gives the impression that "he's better than you are." The employee felt "helpless, stymied." This sort of experience can lead to the firm conclusion that speaking up is a waste of time. As another employee, also convinced that he had nothing to gain, put it: "Why bust my pick?"

These responses seemed to divide themselves into two groups: first, employees who had tried to speak up and had gotten nowhere, and second, employees who had not tried very hard to open an issue but who nevertheless were convinced that nothing would come of it if they did. These responses are like other aspects of mistrust. They are muddied by negative expectations and interpretations. We are convinced that, like fear of repercussions, powerlessness is real and is also expanded by perceptions, feelings, and past experiences.

Other Responses

The categories *Avoidance of conflict* and *Don't want to cause trouble for others* both reflect an interest in maintaining harmony and are flip sides of the same coin. Some people do not wish to bring up sensitive issues in order to prevent themselves or others from getting hurt. Like the fear of repercussions and powerlessness, these two responses also stabilize and control behavior. Such responses probably reflect a fear of disturbing relationships that might be difficult to restore. For people with these worries, the fear of participating in an open argument could be as much a barrier to speaking up as any other type of repercussion.

Last, the *Other* category reflects a wide array of miscellaneous explanations and personal interpretations. It includes responses such as these:

"It would cause an awkward conversation."

"It would violate my sense of propriety about who should take the message forward."

"Maybe it's only a personal perception of the problem."

People also reported that they do not speak up because they do not see it as part of their role or job, they lack the confidence to "even know what to say," or they do not want to get involved or expose how they really feel about an issue.

Powerlessness, Fear, and Cynicism

Reviewing the data about the two main reasons why people don't speak up leads to intriguing questions. What might be the connections between fear of repercussions and a sense of powerlessness? A middle manager reported to us that her fear of repercussions from a new boss eventually led to a long-term sense of frustration. "Now," she says, "it is more that I feel speaking up is hopeless." Another person made it clear that he feels it is easier to feel powerless than fearful. "I won't allow myself to even consider the fear." Another suggested that she never even gets to a point of worry about repercussions since she seldom speaks out, because she is so convinced that it will do no good.

It is apparent that a sense of powerlessness is often deeply intertwined with fear and can magnify its negative effects. When the two combine, it is an easy slide into cynicism and complaints. The dark humor of contemporary comic strips reflects this cynical mood all too well. The strips picture a workplace that is both unchangeable and absurd, where it is smart to be cynical as a way to cope. In this cartoon world, taking genuine interpersonal risks by acting on one's values—doing anything constructive to improve things—is considered hopelessly naive, "clueless," and therefore doomed to failure.

When it is openly voiced, this cynicism convinces managers that employees are either "whining" or just plain resistant to change. The managers wonder why efforts to delegate or empower people seem to take so long. At the same time, employees see management's effort to share power as one more insincere rollout of the "flavor of the month" management fad.

Cynicism can obscure the depths of fear that are present in a workplace. After all, it is safer to express cynicism than to express fear and other aspects of vulnerability. As a form of defense and denial, cynicism has a broad constituency. It is a passive rebellion against the way things are that keeps people from investing their time and talents in ways that would lead to positive change. This cynical viewpoint ensures a tremendous loss of energy in people and organizations and becomes a self-fulfilling prophecy about an organization's capacity to change. Until the underlying fears are dealt with constructively, efforts to build a high-trust organization are likely to be impeded by suspicion and negativity.

The fears, negative beliefs, and other reasons for not speaking up expressed through our field study represent invisible barriers to participation and contribution that are rarely addressed in a direct way. Yet they make the grade steeper and the way less clear. Fear saps the energy people need to perform. As we explore in the next chapter, the impact of not speaking up can be enormous.

New Lessons and Reflections

Thoughts on Organizational Culture

Many people hesitate to speak up because they do not want to cause trouble for others or want to avoid the trouble that open conflict might cause for themselves. At the base of this is a competence issue: most people do not know how to constructively engage in the exploration or resolution of differences. Interpersonal conflict scares them. They believe that a disagreement over something will lead to a situation that may "get out of control." They worry that direct or indirect repercussions will result.

Yet, increasingly, organizations are asking people to work quickly in teams to solve problems and create breakthroughs. Such work cannot be done without the meshing of different styles, perspectives, values, and ideas, all of which can be the source of disagreement and interpersonal conflict. Added to this, of course, is the increasingly diverse workforce from which these teams are drawn. This workforce is, in most places, multiracial, multiethnic, and multilingual, with a wide span of ages. In such settings, differences are an obvious part of the organizational fabric, but they are reluctantly acknowledged and explored.

To build the high-trust, high-performance workplace, organizations must provide support for people at all levels to learn how to constructively engage in talking about, appreciating, and resolving their differences. This should include a strong emphasis on interpersonal communication skills, including giving and receiving negative feedback, delivering tough messages, and participating in conflict resolution. Also important are facilitation and teamwork skills, both of which are important for groups that must quickly collaborate to achieve desired results. In addition to skills development, individuals and work groups should be encouraged, and perhaps held accountable, for respectfully and constructively sticking with points of disagreement until meaning is clear and resolution, if necessary, is reached. See Chapter Nine for ideas on building and reinforcing constructive group norms.

Thoughts on Personal Leadership

Fear of repercussions is sometimes hard for leaders to understand. They do not see in their own behavior evidence of retaliation or negative consequences. They may focus on their own sense of constraints in dealing with annoying or aggressive behavior by others. We have often heard statements such as "How can people worry about repercussions? Nobody ever gets fired around here!"

This aspect of fear's invisibility demands attention to the power of subtle losses—to credibility, competence, relationships, and security—not to the grosser outcomes like dismissal. People notice these underlying forces at work in their relationships. They measure their safety and their ability to contribute through behavioral signals that tell them whether losses could occur and are imminent. The fact, for example, that a leader complains about not understanding why people would be afraid can itself trigger a negative reaction. The leader's complaint could easily cause people to feel, "You are not noticing what we are actually experiencing here. If you don't understand, who knows what we are in for!"

All of this can be a considerable source of undiscussables. You may find that patience is required to open a discussion about what people's experiences really have been. Any given work group may have significant disagreement about the pervasiveness of repercussions, so you may do well to listen carefully during one-on-one conversations and gently help people to surface their concerns in a safe environment. The "baggage" about repercussions that people carry can be an incredible source of learning about private perspectives. Talking individually with people can then eventually lead to a more comfortable group discussion. The ultimate goal of this process would be to identify and eliminate all behaviors, by anyone in the group, that *are* repercussions or could be *misinterpreted* as repercussions, and to separate these from other actions, such as appropriately administered discipline or discussions of performance, that may be uncomfortable but are not unfair or retaliatory.

7

The High Cost of Fear

One manager we interviewed believed that topics like fear were not talked about because executives had a low tolerance for ambiguity. "Either it burns more fuel or less; they want to know the right answer," he told us. Putting aside his negative assumption about the executives, he is entirely right about assessing the results of a fear-based work environment. Measuring the impact of fear in the workplace is neither simple nor exact. It doesn't show up in a way that translates clearly or easily to a balance sheet.

Fear's cost largely comes down to figuring the influence of negative emotions on people's work and how it affects the potential of individuals and the organization as a whole. As we interviewed people, we asked individuals to identify how fear affected their quality of work, productivity, relationships, and feelings. While their answers were highly negative, they—and we—almost always found it difficult to translate the responses into concrete costs. It was like trying to calculate the dollar impact of a dissatisfied customer.

The responses of the study participants, however, do provide a broad and provocative picture of the intangible costs of fear. This is a picture of a *silent organization* made up of people who do not speak up about their concerns or their ideas for improvements and innovations. These patterns, discussed in some detail, are the focus of this chapter. Before describing what people told us, we would like to reference three other research studies that we have found useful in answering questions like these:

"What difference does the presence of fear really make on the bottom line?"

"Why should I make the investment that would be necessary to reduce fear and build trust when there are so many other things I could spend money on to increase our competitiveness?"

These studies did not directly examine the high cost of fear on organizational success. They do, however, create an impressive context for those who want data to justify the effort needed to overcome the patterns of fear by building a trust-based workplace. They also serve as a framework for what we have learned about the everyday impact of fear on people at work.

Fear and the Bottom Line

John Kotter and James Heskett, both professors at the Harvard Business School, studied the impact of organizational culture on long-term economic performance (Kotter and Heskett, 1992). They found that organizations significantly outperformed others when they were committed to and consistently reinforced a philosophy focused on two elements:

1. The needs and interests of employees, as well as those of customers and stockholders

2. Development and support of effective leadership among all levels of management, with important leadership characteristics that include openness, a strong power base, seeing the need for change, articulating the vision and strategy, and motivating large groups of people to make things happen

Kotter and Heskett believed that these two elements enabled organizations to be adaptive to their business environments, shifting strategies as necessary to maintain high performance.

Two Stanford Business School faculty members have worked on similar research issues. James Collins and Jerry Porras (1994) studied and compared what they called "visionary companies"— those rare organizations that are widely known as being premier within their industries (including profitability), have made an undeniable imprint on the world, and have been in existence at least since the 1940s. The companies in their study had these essential ingredients, among others:

- An unfailing commitment to a core ideology that goes beyond making money

- A drive for progress "to explore, to create, to discover, to achieve, to change, to improve" (p. 82)

- The steady building of an aligned organization that has the capacity to accomplish great things over time, without being dependent on one great idea or one charismatic leader

The third study, conducted by Royal Dutch/Shell, actually took place in 1983 but its findings and implications have only recently been made public. Arie de Geus (1997b) describes this work, which examined in detail twenty-seven companies worldwide that were larger in size (over $100 billion a year) and older (founded before 1890) than Royal Dutch/Shell. The charge was to learn how these companies had successfully weathered the changes they had faced in their lifetimes. The result is an exploration of a "living company" whose purpose, de Geus sees, is similar to that of all living organisms: to survive and thrive in order to "fulfill its potential and to become as great as it can be" (p. 11). As did Kotter and Heskett and Collins and Porras, de Geus cites a short list of common characteristics of organizations, which include

- Sensitivity to the environment so that the organization can learn and adapt to change

- Cohesion and identity so the company builds a community and a persona for itself

- Tolerance to enable the organization to build constructive relationships with other entities

■ Conservative financing to enhance the company's ability to govern its own growth and development (pp. 9–11)

To us, the crossover points of these three studies reveal five key elements within companies that show remarkable long-term financial success (not to mention their contribution to individual lives and communities). These companies

1. Develop and sustain a powerful identity that is felt and appreciated by members of the organization and the community at large

2. Respect and value employees as much as customers and stockholders

3. Willingly and enthusiastically look for improvements and new opportunities

4. Have leadership that models, supports, inspires, and facilitates widespread ownership of core values

5. Have leadership with the capacity to make change and create progress

As we look at the way these three studies intersect, we are pulled back to the trust-fear continuum presented in Chapter One. It is not possible to build organizations based on principles such as these in a climate of fear, autocratic control, and cynicism. De Geus (1997b) captures this point when he writes:

[The] idea of a living company isn't just a semantic or academic issue. It has enormous practical, day-to-day implications for managers. It means that, in a world that changes massively, many times, during the course of your career, you need to involve people in the continued development of the company. The amount that people care, trust, and engage themselves at work has not only a direct effect on the bottom line, but the most direct effect, of any factor, on your company's expected lifespan. The fact that many managers ignore this imperative is one of the great tragedies of our times [p. 10].

As you read the next few pages and digest what people told us about the negative impact of fear-based management, ask yourself this question: *How does the presence of fear inhibit an organization's capacity to be consistently profitable over a long period of time?*

The Impact of Not Speaking Up

Responses to our questions about the impact of fear reveal what it is like to be part of the silent organization. Figure 7.1 reports this impact as broad categories. We explore these categories through their subthemes, which we discuss in the order of the frequency of their mention by study participants, beginning with the most frequent.

Negative Feelings About the Organization

Many people reported negative emotions directed toward their organization as a result of situations they felt to be undiscussable. This was expressed in many ways, including the following:

Loss of Trust or Pride

The largest set of responses had to do with a loss of trust or pride in the organization. People said that they became less dedicated or committed. As one long-term, very loyal employee of a bank stated: "I need to be proud of where I work." Undiscussables and fear of repercussions undermine the ability to experience this pride.

Impact	Percentage of Responses
Negative feelings about the organization	29
Negative impact on quality or productivity	27
Negative feelings about oneself	19
Negative emotions	12
Other negative effects	11
Positive effects	2

Figure 7.1. The Impact of Fear.

Increase in Political or Self-Protective Behavior

Others, adapting to their loss of faith in the company, look for alternative routes to success or survival. A senior manager described this as a process in which people learned that "connections" are what is important. The end result, he said, was the creation of "Teflon™ people," to whom nothing can stick.

Contemplated or Real Job Transfers

In a number of cases, people said that, as the result of not being able to resolve their undiscussables, they thought increasingly about leaving the company or transferring out of the work unit. In one case we were told by a front-line employee that he was confidentially looking for a position outside the organization as a "safety net" in case things went wrong. Much more frequently, we heard about situations in which people left their jobs out of disillusionment and frustration. As one senior manager put it, "Why should I be loyal to them if they are not loyal to me?"

Petty Revenge or Sabotage

Occasionally we would also hear comments about petty revenge or sabotage. For example, one twenty-year employee commented that she would let her boss "stew and sweat" over issues that had become undiscussable. "I become less communicative—the thing he likes the least," she said. "I won't jump in and pick up the pieces. I take the attitude, 'I'm not going to help you out.'"

These responses indicate how people withdraw their support and distance themselves from the organization. They show the effects of a widening gap between the perceived interests of the organization and the interests of the individual. When people feel insulted and afraid, they withdraw their allegiance to the company and their leaders. We are reminded of a manager in our acquaintance who was once fond of saying, "I expect everything but loyalty. I *demand* loyalty." However, this is just the reverse of what we found to be possible. Loyalty is perhaps the one thing that cannot be demanded.

Negative Impact on Quality or Productivity

In many cases, it was evident that undiscussable issues and the fear of speaking up had influenced the work of individuals and teams directly. Study participants' stories revealed pivotal changes in their behavior.

Lack of Any Extra Effort

Many people described a retreat into doing what they were told as a result of fear. They were no longer interested in going beyond routine expectations or working to their full potential. They came up to the line of a particular performance standard but did not surpass it. In its simplest form, this pattern was often expressed as resentment. A store clerk who worked for a critical, manipulative manager related that she had said to a coworker, "You want thirty rivets? Count them yourself."

Making and Hiding Mistakes or Failing to Meet Deadlines and Budgets

In other cases, stressful relationships caused people to make errors in their work or be unable to finish it on time. Several people told us stories about getting caught between supervisors and managers who did not get along. One secretary described a situation where she worked for three managers who were "caught in a three-way spitting contest." She said her efficiency went down, along with her health. "I would check my letters six times. I made stupid mistakes. They get you scared, but they make you inefficient."

People not only can make more mistakes but also spend time hiding them. One of our interviewees recalled problems with broken semiconductors in an assembly operation. The company took what was perceived to be a punitive approach to reducing the number of broken components. The result was more broken parts, but fewer found. People focused on avoiding the punishment, and the stress actually had caused the problem to increase.

Loss of Effective Problem Solving, Work on Wrong Priorities, or Poor Methods

Another loss in productivity and quality can come from dysfunctional problem-solving efforts, a theme highlighted previously in the work of Zand (1972) and Argyris (1986). An example of a loss of problem-solving capability was reported by a deputy director of a large county agency; he described an executive who expressed his frustration by unpredictably leaving weekly management meetings. This created a feeling of tentativeness and undermined all genuine problem solving. The deputy director said, "People don't know what to expect from Stan. We are now trying to deal with our need to participate, not just sit there and grunt."

Loss of Creativity, Motivation, and Risk Taking

A midlevel manager for a West Coast service firm summed up these effects nicely:

> "Where there is a lot of fear of screwing up, people don't change behaviors or work systems. Creativity is inhibited. People work one day at a time, rather than looking to the future. High-fear environments just create 'knee-jerking.' You spend all your time putting out fires."

Negative Feelings About Oneself

Along with the foregoing effects, individuals often reported mild-to-serious losses of self-esteem. Comments such as the following were common:

> "Your value as a person is definitely in question."
>
> "I was a total mess."
>
> "I had a feeling of stress, self-doubts, a trapped feeling."
>
> "I take it out on those I can affect—the 'kick the dog' syndrome."

Individuals sometimes criticized themselves unmercifully. In turn, this influenced coworker and family relationships. A tone of self-criticism is evident in this statement from a division manager:

> "There was criticism from customers. Backlogs. Other divisions felt very frustrated about our performance. We were on the verge of breaking up—totally reorganizing the unit. I felt I should be able to handle it. I wanted to be competent. I didn't want to fail. I felt my boss would side against me if I talked to him about it. I was afraid of what his reaction might be. I spent one whole day cleaning out my office. There were a lot of sleepless nights. I made requests for extra people, but he sat on them. I was angry

at the other divisions for not supporting me. I was pounding on my people to improve. Finally, I had to let him know we were in trouble."

For most, loss of self-esteem may not be as crippling as in this example, but it definitely undermines performance. When people do not feel good about themselves, they move toward a state of ongoing negativity about their work, their relationships, and their workplace.

Negative Emotions and Other Negative Effects

Even if there is no visible decline in commitment, productivity, or self-esteem, people often experience an array of very negative emotions. Working through these feelings takes time and energy that could be better spent. A health care professional felt intimidated by her boss and unable to work out a conflict about how she should research a presentation. She reported:

> "I didn't do the research I felt I needed to do. I wasn't as prepared as I should have been. I was internally angry, but externally I acquiesced. I felt impotent and inadequate. I had a feeling of distance from others. I was frustrated and confused and felt very unsupported. I commiserated with a lot of other people."

Typical emotions people expressed were anger, frustration, depression, disappointment, disillusionment, and tension. "It was like tears choking me inside," a parking attendant told us. "If they didn't want me to work there, they should just say so." As a result of these emotions, and as evidence of their energy-sapping qualities, people sometimes also reported physical effects such as sleeplessness, fatigue, crying, illness, and weight or blood pressure problems. Many people reported time off task at work as they talked about or thought about negative events. They mentally rehearsed how they might handle the future and played back their memories of what had already occurred.

In Chapter Six we described the debilitating effects of cynicism on people and organizations. When cynicism is deeply entrenched, people become passive and self-protective. Personal productivity, initiative, and innovation are no longer that important. As one person commented, "I know that I'm here because I've learned to play the game. It doesn't matter whether you are good or bad."

There were many other miscellaneous negative effects. For example, some people talked about lawsuits against the company, contemplated or real. One individual recounted a story of how a union was brought in to protect employees, even though the initiators of this action did not personally want one. Significantly, some people described losing their personal commitment to change efforts within the organization. This is a price few organizations can afford to pay.

The Hidden Cost of Fear: Unnecessary Management

The costs of fear may be more qualitative than quantitative, but this does not mean that they are insignificant. To understand them requires the ability to get inside another's world and see and feel what it is like, then to begin to deduce the logical outcomes of these experiences. Consider, for example, the following vignette.

> An employee received positive performance appraisals for years but was not promoted in favor of a junior colleague. The reasons for this were unclear to him and, he felt, undiscussable with management. As a consequence, he began to suspect that there was an unknown "hidden totem" for promotions: "I asked myself, why would I do extra work? Why would I come in on Saturday? Why not play golf? I felt relegated to a job with the attitude of management that 'it's good enough for you.' I felt very expendable despite the fact that I'd received good feedback about my performance. I decided that all I needed to do from then on was eight hours a day. I lost initiative. I let time take care of problems, rather than addressing them directly. I felt hurt. I discounted what the boss said."

To understand the costs to the organization, it is important to think about the shift in attitude being described by this employee. Whether the emotional reactions are right or wrong is not the issue. The point is that the employee believed his problem to be undiscussable, and this magnified the disappointment and transformed it into bitterness and resentment that went unaddressed—except, perhaps, on the company rumor mill.

We can easily visualize how this employee may leak his negative feelings into everyday situations exactly at the times when his intelligence, energy, and dedication are most needed. Perhaps in a meeting his energy is low and he says nothing about the ideas that could resolve a key dilemma facing the team. Others regard him as "checked out," and in the hall his negative emotions rub off on others who have their own stories to tell. Where he might have stood out and added value to the discussion, instead he cynically retreats. His strengths and special talents are withdrawn.

The effects of this are bound to place a greater demand on his supervisor, who must become more attentive, active, and directive, leading in turn to even less initiative on the employee's part and the creation of a self-reinforcing negative cycle. Perhaps the greatest costs of all are then generated: the costs in unnecessary management time and energy. These include the need for increased direct intervention by managers and supervisors to compensate for the lack of energy and alignment displayed by employees. Leaders end up doing more, solving more, controlling more. They feel less able to delegate and to trust others with tough assignments and high stakes. Instead, they make more decisions for people and become central to more approvals; this in turn builds a more expensive hierarchy and bureaucracy.

These patterns around the need for more intervention surface in the following vignette.

> After a long period of mounting tension, a manager attempted to talk about a sensitive product cost issue and was abrasively cut off by his immediate manager. This was the straw that broke the camel's back. As a result of this occurrence and the long-term tensions, he reported: "I lost interest in doing the things I knew I was supposed to do, like pushing my group to do a better job and lower costs. 'Why bother?' was my watchword. Nobody else cared, so why should I? Why not take the easy way out? It was easy to just let things flow. I found myself getting more tentative with people. I didn't communicate much. I stayed in my office more. Relationships were restrained, unsatisfying. This lasted about six months."

Here again, the situation is a setup for problems. The lack of communication described by the manager is risky—for himself and for the organization. His lack of interest in "a better job" and "lower costs" means that somebody else, undoubtedly somebody higher in the organization, will need to get directly involved. We heard many reactions from study participants that would result in managers' doing more of the work—all in response to unresolved undiscussables and the behaviors that had caused them. For example:

"I didn't give a damn anymore."

"It's not worth an ulcer. I no longer strive for excellence."

"I had a long-term attitude of not caring. I just did the basics to survive in the job."

Because of these attitudes, hours of leadership time that could be devoted to other, more appropriate, tasks will be needed instead in direct management of people and problems. In one comparatively small instance, a senior manager calculated that he had spent 80 hours of his own time, and 145 hours had been spent by other top staff, to resolve an issue that should have been handled by managers closer to the front line. Ironically, he took on the problem personally because he feared potential repercussions from the top executive. Where undiscussables prevail, the workload of management just gets bigger—at every level.

In another company we heard the following story relating to management costs.

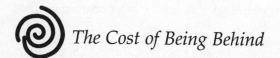 *The Cost of Being Behind*

Managers at an electronics manufacturing firm were constantly under the gun from senior leadership to deliver on time and within budget. Sometimes that was just not possible and so managers in the firm learned the practice of hiding actual schedules and costs. At any given time, there was a predictable 20 to 30 percent difference between the "official" estimates of project costs and schedules and the actual costs and production dates. People had learned by experiencing repercussions firsthand that bringing up the difference between official and actual numbers would get them in trouble.

One result of these discrepancies was that from time to time the company would be in trouble with its customers due to delayed deliveries and unexpected costs. This would lead to a redoubling of the pressure on middle managers. One solution, feared by those who did the production and delivery work, came in the form of a top-management intervention. A demanding, abrasive senior manager would be inserted on a temporary basis into the part of the organization that was falling behind. He used "verbal slaps in the face" and vulgar language to embarrass and intimidate employees and managers alike. The typical result was a short-term spike in production. People theorized that this leader had been "kept around to get us out of trouble when we were three months behind schedule and had to deliver in three weeks. Veteran managers up the system looked the other way."

Short-term gains in production were offset by serious morale problems. People complained to Human Resources about the abrasive manager's style, but little improved. The "solution" of autocratic pressure, combined with a lack of response to employee complaints, reinforced the belief that the environment was not open and that people would be made to pay.

After one and one-half years of concerted efforts by several managers, the abrasive leader was finally moved to "individual contributor" status. It took an enormous amount of time and energy by the managers to accomplish this change. The unspoken scheduling and cost issues remained unresolved.

In this case, the management costs in time and trouble are large, and these costs do not include the effects in long-term reduced productivity. The interventions of the abrasive manager caused serious morale problems. To correct them, in turn, other managers needed to become involved. And yet what caused the original discrepancies between real and actual schedules and costs was never addressed. Had those issues been allowed to surface, a constructive, systems-oriented solution might have been found.

Where fear is present, the potential evaporates for people to help solve their own and their organization's problems, to help bring change and adapt to new ways of doing business. The cost of this failure is the need for the leaders themselves to work ever harder to compensate for what people seem unable to do. The negative cost cycle shown in Figure 7.2 shows this.

As the preceding story amply illustrates, if management action to intervene and solve problems is abrasive or ambiguous, the negative cost cycle is completed and becomes self-reinforcing. It becomes a variation of the cycle of mistrust discussed in Chapter Two. The effect will be an increase in undiscussables, with more management time and energy required to address the resulting problems.

However, if the management action is trust-based and supportive, directly addressing and helping to resolve undiscussables, the negative cost cycle is broken. As the process of addressing undiscussables becomes more open and collaborative, people begin to

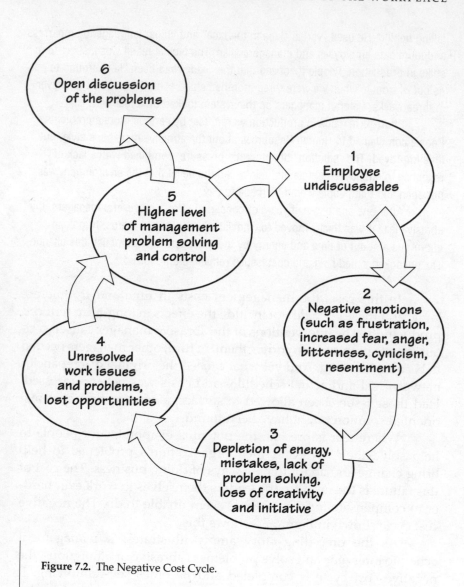

Figure 7.2. The Negative Cost Cycle.

share responsibility for resolving problems and building trust. This, in turn, breaks down the cycle of mistrust and supports the long-term success of the organization. The five principles, cited earlier in this chapter, that characterize organizational longevity have a fertile place to take root.

Can Fear Be a Positive Motivator?

In about half our interviews, we had time to ask people if they thought that fear could ever be a positive motivator for people. Given the negative cost cycle just described, it is no surprise that over half of the responses were a resounding "No way!" Fear was considered a *de*-motivator of the worst kind. Many people simply did not respect its use as an effective management approach. Typical comments included the following:

> "People who think they have to frighten someone must have a personality problem or low self-esteem, if fear is the only tool they have to feel more powerful and produce results."

> "Those who manage by fear are weak, not confident enough to be open."

> "Fear is one of the most despicable methods. There are many other ways to approach people. I generally think it is used indiscriminately and I don't like that. I'm realistic enough to know that it is used, yet naive enough to hope it isn't. In the long run, it's much more productive to use other means. Why use something that doesn't work the best?"

> "There are better ways to motivate people. Good bosses can do it."

> "Fear can get you to stop doing something counterproductive, but it cannot motivate you to do your best."

The remaining responses indicated that fear did have some place as a motivator, but only under restricted conditions. Slightly over 10 percent of the responses suggested that fear can be a positive stimulus, but only if it is self-imposed. That is, when a person takes on a risk as a personal or professional stretch, fear may be a successful *self*-motivator. Another group of responses reflected the idea that fear could work in the short term but not the long term. And even here there were deficits. As one manager said: "Fear is a constructive motivator only in rare circumstances, and then you pay the price of people resenting you forever."

A handful of people said that at some point, their fear of repercussions had been good for them. For example, a few people thought that fear-oriented environments caused them to "work my tail off." One professional-level employee felt that the fears that go with competition among peers "kept people sharp" and that the cost "didn't outweigh the benefits." Another professional thought that "paranoia is positive because it causes people to think."

Most responses in this category, however, were coupled with a reservation or two:

"I wouldn't call it a growth experience, but it did force me to cope."

"I have grown a lot. It would be nice to think you should-n't have to go through this type of negative situation in order for personal improvement to happen."

"I am working on not letting fear motivate me."

"Quality improved—what I had control over. I withdrew from the group, was labeled as 'surly, not a team player.' I lost respect for coworkers. I felt helpless and hopeless. There were blowups at home and on the job. I escaped into my work."

For this small group, such experiences helped them to get a grip on some of the details of their job, develop self-discipline, or put work in perspective with the rest of their life. However, the overall pattern unequivocally was the belief that externally imposed fear is a negative force with destructive long-term consequences.

Looking back over the evidence, it is apparent that fear is a successful motivator *only* if the desire is to have people do as they are told. However, in a world that demands rapid innovation, flexibility, and the best use of intellectual capital, few organizations can afford this costly compliance approach.

The Cumulative Impact of Fear

One story, in particular, dramatically illustrates how fear and undiscussables not only waste people but also can have a direct impact on the business success of an organization.

⟲ *The Software Company*

A small midwestern company described itself as a "Cadillac provider" of mainframe software. The CEO was a man frequently described as a "tyrant" by employees and managers. People felt that he had created a pervasive climate of fear by exhibiting a variety of destructive behaviors. These included

- Yelling and swearing at people
- Publicly criticizing others
- Not communicating with top staff
- Setting arbitrary deadlines
- Expecting sixty to eighty hours a week from people throughout the organization
- Deliberately pitting vice presidents against one another

The negative climate that resulted from these behaviors was so strong that it eventually resulted in the release of a faulty software package—a package originally intended to be the "jewel in the crown" of the company's product lines.

One incident, observed by many people, indicated exactly how the release of a faulty product could happen. During a top-management meeting, a bright young staff person criticized the process used to develop the key software package. The CEO stopped the meeting when the staff member voiced her concerns. A vice president who observed this noted: "She was escorted from the room and fired within the hour by a VP who was tight with the CEO."

As it turned out, the software package the staff member criticized was pulled off the market within two years of its release. Another management team observer concluded, "The program was a disaster. The software wouldn't do what we said it would do. There was no ownership, no pride in the product. People were not asked for their input. More energy and time was spent covering your butt than on the quality of the program."

Eventually, the CEO was removed. The company's actual losses as a result were six million dollars. It is likely that many other, less visible costs were also involved, including

- Opportunity costs caused by the company having created an inherently faulty package instead of the right product

- Damage to the long-term reputation of the firm
- The HR costs in demoralization and turnover

Because of the CEO's undiscussable behaviors, fear had been "mirrored all the way down the organization," according to the HR manager. "It was almost as if the goal was to diminish the individual." The CEO's successor described the company's employees in the following way:

> "People were scared here. They were like starved children. Their security was threatened. Their self-esteem was damaged. They had lost their belief in themselves and their ability to do quality work. Some people will never really get over that kind of experience, no matter how different I am."

We seldom came across a situation so explicit in its total company impact and management costs to repair. It is plain to see that in this case the damage is deep and will take years to fully heal. History of this kind represents a failure of leadership that people will not forget easily. In many ways, the only reasonable approach is to start over, to reinvent the company's identity and vision for the future.

Usually fear's influence accumulates in smaller, less visible ways. Declines in morale and dedication and loss of self-esteem usually happen in small increments, in turn affecting the capacity of the organization. In fact, fear is often damaging precisely because of this hidden, incremental quality. It can be taken for granted, like the scrap in a manufacturing process or the inherent waste in many paperwork operations.

As one front-line employee pointed out, ours is a result-oriented culture. People do not look at how; they only look at what and when and how much. This approach is felt to be a sign of toughness and impatience with bureaucracy and excuses. However, when a leader concentrates on short-term outcomes and the immediate bottom line, it is easy to overlook the negative cost cycle of repeated management interventions and their longer-term losses. As with the earlier story of harsh management brought in to handle unrealistic schedules, the issues and their solutions can remain undiscussable for a long time. The very effort to solve a problem—if it is done through exhortations, pressure, and control rather than through collaboration, openness, and mutual problem solving—will lead to creating greater silence and frustration between employees and their leaders. A destructive and costly cycle then begins to spiral through the organization, blocking the ability of the organization to act in ways that will produce long-term success.

New Lessons and Reflections

Thoughts on Organizational Culture

One of our favorite clients talks about the "power of the *n* of 1." What she means by this is that occasionally a well-documented story of one person's experience can make a powerful point. Sometimes such stories can be used effectively in helping others in your leadership circle to better understand the value of reducing fear and building trust. To do so, you might consider creating something akin to an old-fashioned math story problem about a recent situation that involved the fear of speaking up.

Use the details of our field study findings mentioned in this chapter to highlight fear's negative impact on feelings about the organization and on quality or productivity. Identify a recent situation that may have involved one or more of these aspects. Then assemble the data, looking primarily at the cost of time lost and any direct recovery costs related to unhappy customers. Some points to consider include these: Who was involved? What is their hourly rate of pay (plus benefits)? What kind of time was wasted or spent on rework or inspection? Were others affected in a secondary way? If so, how much cost might be connected to the negative impact on them? What was the end result of the situation on customers? Were there any direct or indirect costs that could be identified? How much management time was needed to correct or recover from the situation?

If you calculate, then share, the cost of fear for a situation that is easily acknowledged as an everyday occurrence, others will begin to understand the enormous expense involved in the silent organization.

Thoughts on Personal Leadership

The cost of mistrust to leaders can include intangibles that outweigh the dollars lost and time wasted. When leaders feel that they must constantly inspect others' work or frequently intervene to make decisions, another powerful loss can be at work: the loss of the inherent joy of leadership. When a person in an executive, management, or supervisory role feels that there is no choice but to solve others' problems for them, fix things that have gone wrong, correct people, and motivate them, the role of leadership can lose its intrinsic sense of contribution and value. Leaders, like anyone else, can experience demoralization in their roles.

If you feel this way, you will need to find a support base for changing the dynamics you are experiencing. This may include colleagues or a supervisor who can empathize with your situation and offer constructive feedback. More to the point would be a thorough review of the history and practices that keep the negative cost cycle in place, as well as a review of your own leadership skills. If you need to ask for help in breaking the cycle, do so. Nothing is worse than letting a difficult situation continue when you know in your heart that it needs to be addressed openly and constructively. One of the most important potential costs could be to your own sense of confidence in your skills.

PART

III

Strategies
for Building
a High-Trust
Workplace

8

Acknowledge
the Presence
of Fear

As with any process of change, people are likely to go through a series of stages in their understanding of fear and their commitment to reversing its negative patterns. These can be diagramed as shown in Figure 8.1. This chapter is specifically focused around the first three steps of the scale. It highlights the importance of early work that builds awareness and overcomes denial. Like other workplace changes, making a course correction with fear requires that people understand the problem and see it happening around them. Once fear's presence has been acknowledged, planning for and implementing a new course of action can begin.

We present four primary strategies in this chapter that will help you to begin to reverse the patterns of fear. Grid 8.1 summarizes them and their impact.

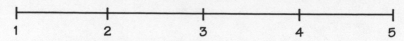

1   Lacking awareness or denial
2   Seeking information and listening
3   Recognizing the problem in one's own environment
4   Developing a plan of action
5   Carrying out that plan

Figure 8.1. Points of Awareness and Action.

Learn About Workplace Fears

Fear cannot be changed into trust unless organizational leaders consciously decide to behave in ways that will turn around the negative patterns. To do this, we recommend that you start with yourself. As you increase your personal understanding of fear and its impact, two things will happen. First, you will be better positioned to help others build that same awareness. Second, your proactive leadership in acknowledging fear's presence will serve as a model for others in the organization.

Learn from your own experiences with workplace fears. Patterns discovered by reflecting on personal experience can be powerful teachers. To see some of your own patterns:

1. Make a list of five times you wanted to speak about something but hesitated to do so.

2. For each situation, ask yourself these questions:

 "How recent was the situation?"

 "What factors contributed to my hesitation?"

 "In the end, did I speak up?"

 "What reasoning guided my decision?"

 "What risks did I weigh?"

"What difference did my position, my level of influence, or my confidence make in what I finally decided to do?"

"What benefit or loss resulted from my decision?"

3. After reviewing your experiences, look for common threads. What do these reminders or insights suggest to you about how others around you might experience fear, or trust, or vulnerability, or commitment?

4. Think about how these points might influence the way you go about exploring these same issues with others.

Be willing to discuss the sensitive subjects connected to fear in the workplace. When leaders show that they care about building trust and are open to talking about the reasons why people hesitate to speak up, many people are willing to participate. To get these conversations under way:

Strategy	What This Should Accomplish
Learn about workplace fears	Increased understanding of your personal experiences with fear Observations about leadership behaviors and their impact on others
Introduce the subject of fear in an informal way	Increased awareness of the issues without threatening others The issues of fear and trust become discussable and a part of normal workplace interactions
Enlist the support of other managers who report to you	Greater energy and a broader base of support for building trust and reducing fear More effective approaches to change due to greater input
Overcome denial	Increased recognition and support for addressing the negative impact of fear in the workplace

Grid 8.1. How to Acknowledge the Presence of Fear.

1. Express your interest in knowing what other people have experienced.

2. Ask thoughtful, open-ended questions that help to clarify what they are saying.

3. Be willing to share some of your own experiences.

4. Let people know why you want to reverse the patterns of fear and what you think needs to be done to help that change occur.

5. Be an open-minded listener when people share strong emotions or complex stories that are told from what you would see as a biased point of view.

6. When asked for your opinion, avoid making judgmental comments that might later be misinterpreted by others.

7. Encourage others to be less judgmental about past wrongs and more open to an honest exchange of views and caring feedback.

Discussions about sensitive experiences can be difficult. People may tell you things that you would rather not hear. Because of your leadership role, some may expect you to respond to their anger or cynicism. Others may want you to agree with their point of view, even if it runs contrary to your own. If the conversations get tough, remember that an important first step is doing exactly what you are doing—opening up the conversation and working to understand the situation. This lets others know that you are willing to hear them out and acknowledge the presence of fear. Your purpose in this moment is not to reach a point of resolution.

Resist getting caught in the cycle of mistrust. In conversations about workplace fears, you may encounter anger, cynicism, complaining, labeling, and apparent resistance to moving forward in what you see as a constructive way. At these moments:

1. Freeze your own negative assumptions about those who are speaking. Notice them as they come to mind and consciously bypass them in favor of a more objective view where you respond with such words as these:

   "It's obvious to me that you've got strong feelings about these experiences. Tell me what you've done in the past to try to get things on the right track."

> *"I can see that from your point of view, it must seem that no one in management cares about your ideas that have disappeared into the black hole. Let me tell you what I think we might do next, after this conversation—if you'll agree."*
>
> *"If you could replay this scenario, how would you like to have had things happen? Is there anything we can do now to help you move forward and be more positive in your feelings?"*

2. To prepare yourself for such conversations, review Chapter Two, where we describe the cycle of mistrust.

Seek feedback about your style and your performance. Of all the things leaders can do to help them reverse the patterns of fear, asking for, understanding, and responding to feedback are among the most powerful. Throughout many of the suggestions we make in this and the remaining chapters, you will find encouragement to gather others' perspectives about the impact of both *what* you do and *how* you do it. As you work with issues related to fear and trust, you will discover opportunities to learn about the way others see you. Sometimes this may come in a subtle reference or casual observation. Or you may hear it more directly in a request for you to do something in a new way. Staying open and tuned in to these moments will make it easier for you to gain a greater understanding about how your leadership is perceived. In Chapter Ten, we address this vitally important aspect in some detail.

Introduce the Subject of Fear in an Informal Way

Getting everybody into the pool usually requires someone to test the water first. Your role as a leader is one of encouragement, of saying to others, "Hey, the water's fine, let's get in." This does not mean that you must be a technical expert on either water quality or swimming. With workplace fears, an early goal is to get others to talk about them. To do so, begin by voicing your own concerns about fear and its effects. Model the level of openness about this topic that you would like to achieve with others. Do not feel you need to have all the answers. You may wish to include the following techniques.

Focus initially on the fear of speaking up. Here are some simple ways to do this:

1. Share a newspaper article about employee involvement or other workplace innovations as a catalyst for discussion.

2. Generate a conversation about the barriers companies face in getting people to identify needed improvements.

3. If it does not automatically surface, add the fear of repercussions to the list of barriers and ask people to describe their related experiences.

Show them this book. Sometimes a book can help to make subjects legitimate and therefore easier to discuss.

1. Share the definitions, some conclusions, or a particular quotation you find provocative from this book.

2. Ask people questions such as these:

   "How might we apply these concepts here in our work group?"

   "What impact would they have on our work in general? Our relationships? Our customers? A particular current project?"

   "Are there any special steps we need to take in light of this discussion?"

3. Listen and respond to points made in a light and easy way, not making too much of any one response, but noting the patterns and implications.

Tell stories from your own experience, preferably stories from other organizations. This will let people know that you will be able to empathize with them because of your own experiences.

1. To draw them out, say:

   "I remember times when I wanted to say something, to offer what I thought was a better way. But I hesitated because I didn't want to create a big deal. I never felt good about it afterward."

   "I once worked for somebody who had the habit of talking down to employees. It sure was annoying, and it scared the heck out of people who didn't know him well."

2. Ask if anybody else has had a similar experience.

3. Set a personal direction and ask for their help, by saying:

"I want to avoid making others afraid to talk to me. I hope you will tell me if I ever come across that way."

"Please let me know if I do things that cause you to think I don't want to hear your ideas."

Turn awkward moments into opportunities for deeper levels of honest conversation. If your introduction of the topic goes flat, it is possible that some of your own past behaviors are involved. There is usually something about most managers' conduct and performance that has been intimidating to others at some point in the past. Suppose, for example, that you mention a fear-causing behavior such as making secretive decisions and the room goes silent. People give each other meaningful glances but avoid eye contact with you. In the awkwardness of the moment, recognize that you have just stumbled across an important opportunity. To take advantage of it:

1. Make an observation to the group, such as

   "Looks like I've stepped into something pretty important."

   "From the look of your reaction, I suspect we could use some conversation around this one."

   People will probably laugh nervously after you make your observation.

2. Next, ask people to talk to you about why the room went silent. Tell them that this is exactly the kind of discussion that needs to take place before you can collectively move forward to reduce the amount of fear in the work environment.

3. Then be quiet and listen to what people have to say.

Suggestions such as these are informal methods that can be woven into day-to-day interactions. They get people thinking and let them know where you are coming from. Along the way you get a chance to practice the vocabulary of fear—words such as *scared, anxious, hesitant,* and *afraid*—in a confident, supportive tone that assures others that you are not implying criticism. Broaching the subject of fear informally also gives you a chance to monitor the responses you get in return. If people jump into the discussion freely, you are already miles ahead. If not, it could be simply that they have not thought about fear as a workplace issue. Keep up the informal comments and storytelling. Eventually, others will begin to add stories of their own.

Enlist the Support of Other Managers Who Report to You

Midlevel managers and first-line supervisors often voice concerns about being caught in the middle. When the folks at the top get a new idea, these midlevel people are sometimes involved in the initial thinking and decision making. Frequently, they are not. Yet they are the individuals who are usually charged with implementing countless new programs and initiatives, many of which languish after a flurry of executive attention and the spending of much money. These requests come, of course, while they are also expected to maintain smooth daily operations. This double demand causes middle managers to become understandably skeptical about "another new management program."

If you supervise people who manage others, it is very important for you to actively engage them in the process of reducing fear and building trust. If you do not do this, hesitancy, skepticism, or a lack of cooperation on their part may limit the eventual effectiveness of your effort.

Share your reasons for wanting to reduce fear and build trust. When you sincerely and enthusiastically tell people why you want to make changes in the work culture, they will be more open to joining you in that effort. To build this support:

1. Individually or in a group, lay out the reasons behind your interest in creating a more trusting, collaborative work environment.

2. Describe the process you have gone through to come to this decision.

3. Share data that they may find convincing related to customer requirements, production rates, the cost of waste, and the results of employee opinion surveys.

4. Ask for their perspective on these issues and ask for their help. Get their assessment of how fear affects the whole organization.

5. Share with them your preliminary thinking about approaches to take and ask for their feedback on these ideas. Together, build a plan of action.

Explore their concerns about your action plan. Those who report to you need a chance to raise concerns about the changes you want to make. Some of these issues may be undiscussable. For example:

- How will operations continue at a full pace if managers are asked to pay special attention to initiatives in organizational culture?
- Where will the time come from to manage these initiatives?
- What new expectations will be placed on managers?
- Are these new expectations the latest "management fad," or will they be consistently supported and reinforced?
- What kind of support will managers be given to learn new ways of doing things?

It is important to create as much psychological safety as possible so that people will be honest with you about what they really think of your plans to reduce fear. Until their underlying concerns are on the table and you have had a chance to address them, you should expect people to have a divided response. If you have more than one level of managers and supervisors reporting to you:

1. Give those at the higher levels a chance to think through these issues for themselves before their direct reports are involved.

2. In any such discussions, remember that these managers and supervisors may simply try to tell you what they think you want to hear. After all, you are the boss. If you believe that this is the case, use an easy, low-key approach.

Use a checklist of the possible symptoms and costs of fear. A checklist can be a helpful way for many people to begin understanding how fear affects the workplace. The following list of possible "symptoms" of fear provides a good way to build awareness, particularly if you have encountered some elements of denial. Three fundamental questions should be asked for each item:

1. Is it happening here?

2. What might it have to do with fear, particularly the fear of speaking up?

3. What costs—tangible or intangible—are associated with each item for employees, managers, the organization, or the customers?

The possible symptoms include

- Lawsuits against the company
- Labor unrest, formation of unions, and hard bargaining; strikes
- A lack of suggestions for improvements and innovations
- The loss of customers who complain about poor service or products
- Turf battles over resources, assignments, and roles
- Us-versus-them talk
- Complaints after a meeting is over
- Unwillingness to take responsibility for mistakes; cover-ups
- An overly large number of personnel policies; an enforcement approach to rules; continuous arguments about the rules
- Many layers of approval for simple decisions
- Many sequences of checking for simple transactions
- "CYA" ("cover your ass") activities
- People behaving politically
- Negative feelings about the company; lack of pride or commitment
- An "I could care less" approach to the work
- Stressful work conditions or relationships
- Cynicism
- Bad decisions or indecision
- Grievances and employee complaints
- Resistance to performance appraisals
- A feeling by people that they get no feedback
- Expensive training programs aimed to "fix" employee or management performance
- Meetings where no one asks questions or no problems are solved
- Recurrent problems with absenteeism and tardiness
- Missed schedules
- Instances of unethical behavior
- Financial or budgetary problems

- Continual equal employment opportunity issues and harassment charges

- Resignation of high-quality performers and creative thinkers

- Eleventh-hour reports admitting that a project will not work or cannot be delivered on time

- A commitment to projects that people know are a waste of time and money

- A very active rumor mill

- Widespread dissatisfaction with promotions, assignments, and terminations

- Threatening behavior by supervisors, managers, or employees

Not every item on the list necessarily represents a sign that fear is alive and well in your workplace. Yet the list gives individuals something concrete against which to test their own experience. Discussing it can lead people to observe how easy it is to take fear and its costs for granted. As people share their perspectives, they may begin to see behavioral patterns in a new light, understanding the sometimes subtle way fear and mistrust influence daily activities.

You may find, especially at this early stage, that it is important to reassure people that you are not just looking for problems and things that are wrong. For example, it may be helpful to offer a list of what is going well along with the symptoms of fear so people know that their positive contributions are appreciated and are not being ignored.

Overcome Denial

Denial is an instinctive retreat from something that is potentially threatening. It is a very natural response to a topic like fear in the workplace. Denial can often be detected by the different types of objections people raise when you tell them of your plans to do things differently. Grid 8.2 captures some of the patterns you may observe.

These variations of denial boil down to the feeling, "That's not us," or "That's not me." Usually objections like these are warning signals that the topic has been communicated in a threatening way that implies criticism, blame, or a negative intent. We learned this lesson the hard way, as the following story reveals.

When People	You May Hear
Don't see fear as part of their work environment or as applying to their organization and relationships	"I just don't see how this fear issue applies around here. It might be true for other people or someplace else, but I don't see how it fits the operations division."
Do see fear, but as a human relations issue unrelated to the "real" work of the organization	"I don't see why we should spend more time talking about this stuff. I just want to do my job."
Are personally very confident and consider fear a sign of immaturity, inexperience, or personal weakness	"It's not my problem if other people don't speak up. If people are too mealymouthed or insecure to talk about what's bothering them, then maybe they haven't got a point."
Think of fear as an inevitable part of organizations	"Sure there's fear around here, and you're never going to get rid of it, either."
Don't see fear as having much of an impact on quality or productivity or may think it increases them	"Frankly, a little fear isn't such a bad thing to keep people on their toes."
Are concerned that they will have to make personal changes if this topic is "taken too far"	"This training is all well and good, but it doesn't apply to the real world."

Grid 8.2. Expressions of Denial.

 *Presentation to the Management Team*

During part of our research effort, we made a presentation to the management team of one of the participating companies. The team was made up of about 175 executives, managers, and supervisors and included the chairman of the board, the vice chairman, and the CEO. Earlier in the day, we had been quite successful in reporting to a small group of top officers a summary of responses from a sample of previously interviewed company employees. We reported how the sample group's answers to the questions about undiscussables, reasons for not speaking up, and the impact of fear compared with results from our research effort as a whole.

At the evening presentation for the larger group of managers, we followed a nearly identical format. We included an opportunity for the managers, working in small groups, to briefly identify what they believed were the company's undiscussables. In a gratifying way, the undiscussables surfaced by these small groups seemed to match the data we were about to report from the interviewed employees. Once those sample data had been presented by us and compared to the broader research findings, we turned to the whole group and asked the leading question: "Does this mirror your experience with this company? Do these data points ring true?" Loud shouts of "No way!" echoed across the room. We were shocked and a bit confused. "How come?" we asked the managers. Suddenly, we found ourselves answering lots of questions about how the sample of employees had been chosen, whether it reflected a vertical slice of the organization (it did), and whether it included enough people. We had a classic "That's not us" response on our hands. We forged ahead with the presentation, feeling as if we had endured a sufficient gash in our credibility for one day.

Ultimately the evening was saved by two events. First, the HR director pointed out before our talk finished that we had omitted one vital piece of information used at the earlier presentation to the officers. We had reported to the officers, but not the managers, that many of the employees interviewed had commented on how much they liked working at the company. The second event was the commentary made by the CEO at the end of the presentation. He reminded his team that the glass at their company was more than half full. He then told them of his own experiences in getting personal feedback and the need to listen to the news, good or bad, about management conduct and performance.

This was a sharp lesson for us about flooding people with data that could be heard as critical of their organization or their own performance. The HR director's reminder and the CEO's "more than half full" line go right to the core of the issue of denial. No matter how bad things might be, people want to feel good about themselves and their circumstances.

To avoid being on the receiving end of defensive reactions like those we experienced, focus on creating an understanding of the need for change. Here are two very effective methods.

Place the topic of fear in context. In most organizations, fear is part of the background, not the foreground. To help people feel more comfortable exploring some of this neglected terrain:

1. Remind people of the many things that are already going right and celebrate these things.

2. Encourage people, however, to look for the "silent" organization, the opportunities that are lost because people hesitate to offer their ideas.

3. Informally weave these concepts, ideas, and questions into your interactions with most of the people you encounter.

4. More formally, at large or small staff meetings, ask structured discussion questions such as these, using a brainstorming technique:

"What strengths do you see in our current operations?"

"What barriers keep you from being as successful as you would like to be?"

"Which of those barriers involve undiscussable issues? Fear of repercussions? A sense that things won't change?"

"If this were an organization where all people offered their ideas without hesitation, how would things be different? What kinds of things would we be doing? How would our customers be served differently?"

Apply the cycle of mistrust to better understand the patterns of fear. As a catalyst to conversation, go over the cycle of mistrust in Chapter Two. This can help everyone to better understand how fear begins and is perpetuated in your organization. In one-on-one situations or small groups:

1. Apply the cycle of mistrust to a recent situation that people would easily characterize as negative or mistrustful. Walk through the model, identifying the negative assumptions supervisors make about employees and vice versa. If your situation did not involve mistrust between supervisors and employees, adapt the model as needed—for example, between two departments, between two individuals, between a customer and a supplier. Pose questions like the following ones:

"What negative assumptions do you see going on in this situation?"

"What kinds of self-protective behavior do the negative assumptions inspire on both sides?"

"Generally speaking, what's the gap between our intended behavior and how it is perceived by others?"

"What can we do to turn a cycle like this around?"

2. Save your perspectives until others have had a chance to share their point of view. Describe how you feel about things. Let people know that you get frustrated and are sometimes tense or anxious.

3. Make sure the tone in your voice is open and interested, rather than interrogative. Your questions and manner should convey genuine interest and a desire for a mutual exchange of ideas.

Stay positively focused and respectful of others if the denial continues. These steps will not address all types of denial. Some individuals may want "proof" of fear's negative impact and may voice that desire in an aggressive way. Others may be convinced that fear is too big or too entrenched in organizations to be turned around. Their cynicism may be discouraging and can seem to be an unreasonable barrier to your desires to create a different kind of work environment. In these cases:

1. Accept the denial and doubts of others as interesting and legitimate counterpoints to your own thinking.

2. Ask people to keep those questions handy and to watch for evidence that answers their concerns.

3. Work past your sense of disappointment about the denial as you implement other strategies that will help to illuminate the presence of fear and its negative impact in the workplace.

Acknowledging the presence of fear requires a willingness to be open and stay open as you initiate all sorts of discussions with others. In the give-and-take of the conversations that unfold, you will encounter a challenging mix of opinions, experiences, data, and emotions. Some of these conversations may be very frustrating, particularly when denial is in full bloom. Over time, however, more and more people will appreciate and respond to your consistent interest in understanding and surfacing the patterns of fear in the work environment.

To illustrate this point, we would like to return to the story we told earlier about our poorly received presentation. During the evening, we saw the corporation's second-highest officer do a simple thing. He turned to the person next to him at the dinner table, a customer relations supervisor many layers lower in the organization, and asked the question, "What do you think? Is there fear in this organization?" His tone was very natural and sincere. He was not at all defensive. He just wanted to know. The customer relations supervisor turned to him and said with equal naturalness and candor, "Of course." "Really?" he asked. "Oh sure," she replied. "It's all over the place. I see it every day." "You do?" he asked. "I'd really be interested in hearing about what you are seeing."

They spent the next few minutes in an engaged, illuminating conversation. He had demonstrated perfectly, perhaps without really knowing it, a powerful step someone in his position might take to acknowledge fear's presence.

New Lessons and Reflections

Thoughts on Organizational Culture

If people suggest that driving out fear and building trust is "not the real work of the organization," you might want to create some focused time to explore the questions: What is the real work of this organization? What is the real work of our work group? The view that tending an organization's culture is not real work can be the easy way out for people who are uncomfortable with emotions, relationships, and ambiguity in the work environment. In most cases it is an unintentional, yet unfortunate, put-down of some of the most difficult and important work faced by leaders today. It is important to address this opinion, because if this notion spreads to others, you will have a much harder time reducing fear and increasing trust.

Prior to these discussions, you might want to reread Chapter Seven, which references studies about companies that consistently demonstrate success over long periods of time. Additionally, think about the future directions of organizations and work (see Chapter Sixteen). In particular, you might want to read Arie de Geus's *The Living Company* (1997b) and Thomas Stewart's *Intellectual Capital* (1997). Each of these presents a very provocative view about real work, especially as we move into the next century.

In your discussions, it is important to ask the following questions: Once the real work is defined, how do we best accomplish that work? To what degree do fear-based habits (see Chapter Four) and assumptions (think about the cycle of mistrust) block our ability to do this work? Isn't the removal of these barriers part of the real work that needs to be done?

Thoughts on Personal Leadership

Perhaps one of the most sensitive aspects of acknowledging fear's presence has to do with accepting that *all* of us have the potential to create fear and mistrust. While it may not feel good to know that you have not spoken up or have experienced fear yourself, often far more threatening is the idea that you may be exhibiting personal behaviors that erode trust.

The deputy manager of a complex, multimillion-dollar engineering project was frustrated because others did not always share their opinions candidly in his presence. However, after thinking over the matter, he decided that an old pattern of personal criticism and blame might be showing through in his behavior toward others. His ability to share this piece of self-knowledge with the professional managers with whom he worked signaled to them his willingness to learn and change. As he came to understand these reactions and their true impact on others, alternative behaviors, including a greater tolerance for listening to others' explanations without interruption, began to reveal themselves. While he still works on this problem "every day," he is respected for his personal insight into behaviors that many of his colleagues thought were unchangeable.

A common misconception among leaders is that personal disclosure is a weakness. As one executive commented, "They ultimately depend on me. It's better not to tell them about my flaws." But nondisclosure looks false, creates further tension and undiscussables, and ultimately fools no one.

9

Pay Attention to Interpersonal Conduct

Once fear's presence and negative impact are acknowledged, leaders can begin to think about steps to isolate and reduce it. A solid first step is to help supervisors, managers, and executives avoid abrasive or abusive conduct. This is an excellent starting point for several reasons:

- Abrasive and abusive behaviors create immediate and direct repercussions for others and contribute to a longer-term perception of a fear-based work environment.

- Most of those who hold leadership responsibilities already agree that these behaviors are unsatisfactory.

- In order to prevent problems, it is always helpful to know what to do and what *not* to do.

- When people in management roles demonstrate trust-inspiring rather than fear-producing behaviors, others in the organization will be more likely to follow suit.

Strategy	What This Will Accomplish
Establish positive group norms	A shared vision of the way in which people will work together
	A shared sense of ownership for supporting a positive work environment
Provide feedback to managers who report to you	Information and insight to individuals about how they come across to others
	Reinforces a sense of responsibility for maintaining a positive work environment
Coach managers who report to you	Increases the likelihood that managers will be successful in demonstrating the group norms
Work with unmet expectations	Directly eliminates the fear-causing behavior of managers

Grid 9.1. How to Pay Attention to Interpersonal Conduct.

For these reasons, this chapter emphasizes things that leaders can do to positively influence their direct reports, who also manage or supervise others. The goal is to eliminate as many of the abrasive and abusive behaviors as possible among those in recognized leadership roles. These strategies are summarized in Grid 9.1.

Establish Positive Group Norms

Group norms are the commonly accepted ways people go about doing things when they are members of a particular group. As habits, they become ingrained and almost disappear from people's consciousness—until someone does not follow the norm. Think about how you would react if you were in an elevator with a group of strangers and someone had an angry, obscene argument on a cell phone. You would probably be surprised and irritated, and no doubt you'd be glad to get off the elevator. Norms shape our behavior in powerful, unseen ways, because they represent an accepted standard, a set of assumed expectations for behavior. Loud arguments and vulgar comments are not accepted practice for people who ride elevators.

In some organizations, it is still an acceptable norm for people to behave in dictatorial, competitive, and threatening ways. The behaviors called out on the abrasive-abusive scale in Figure 4.1 were easily identified by those involved in our field study as common practice in certain organizations or within particular work groups. In workplaces where those behaviors—even the subtle ones—are accepted as normal, people feel threatened and are less likely to speak up.

When leaders consciously shape work environments around a set of trust-based, collaborative norms, they are well on their way to reversing the negative impact of fear. This work is highly visible at first and says loud and clear: "We expect people to work together in collaborative, respectful, and creative ways in this organization." Once the positive norms have been established, they too become invisible and will be noticed primarily when someone breaks them, for example, by withholding information or spreading a rumor that discredits a coworker.

The following story illustrates the great potential benefits of norm-setting work.

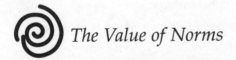 *The Value of Norms*

In one organization where top leadership has made a serious commitment to build trust and reduce fear, the strategy of setting positive group norms has been very useful. Here are three examples.

Early in trust-building work, the executive team carefully developed the following set of behaviorally defined organizational values:

> As people serving others, we respect each other and commit ourselves to these values:
>
> ■ Integrity: We will say what we will do and do what we say.
> ■ Trust: We will tell the truth.
> ■ Unity: We will get the job done together.
> ■ Improvement: We will work to get better at what we do.

The executive team knew that others in the organization would not adopt these values unless they saw that the behavior and decisions of those in leadership reflected the same values. Therefore, the executives created a meeting norm: the values would be posted in their meeting room, and when they made decisions they would do a quick check to make sure that the decision would reflect these values. More than once, this norm has caused them to back off from a plan that would send mixed messages to employees and undercut other efforts being made to reduce fear and build trust.

A second example of the value of norms comes from one of the operating divisions. There a management group of forty members agreed to a new set of norms to guide their meetings and approach to leadership. Within the first year of implementing these guidelines, the sudden termination of one manager created a storm of rumors and worries about "what might happen to the rest of us." Recognizing that the cycle of mistrust had reared its ugly head, the group voiced their need for a specific norm to use when unexpected and potentially upsetting personnel changes took place within their group. The agreement was as follows:

■ Whoever was in charge of the decision for the personnel change—whether it was a promotion, a shift in role, or a termination—would call a special meeting to take place that day.

■ All who could attend would make every effort to do so.

■ At the meeting, the information would be shared and people would have a chance to discuss their reactions and ask questions.

■ If certain things could not be said by the decision maker because of confidentiality, members would respect that position.

■ Members who were not able to attend would be informed as quickly as possible by the decision maker.

■ No further discussion of the ins and outs of the changes would take place.

This agreement has been used reliably and successfully for over three years to minimize gossip, rumors, and fear-producing innuendo, even in difficult and controversial situations, such as terminations.

A third example has to do with a restructuring effort by the organization that aimed to unify two key, historically separate divisions. The two groups of professionals, traditionally suspicious of each other, now reported to the same vice president. Having previously worked with both divisions, we were asked to facilitate an off-site, two-day meeting to begin building bridges among a group of ninety managers. Our previous work in the two divisions had included norm setting and training in consensus decision making, so people were already familiar with the importance of norms and had been working to apply them. By 10:00 A.M., in the midst of discussions that would lead to a new, unifying vision statement, we were approached separately by three individuals. Each delivered the same message: the vision work would lead nowhere until some important background undiscussables were publicly identified and addressed. After a break, we shared this feedback and asked for a response from the group. The group agreed to change the agenda and spend the rest of the day dealing with its "hot topics."

When the meeting adjourned the next afternoon, it was clear that the shift in the agenda was a crucial step in trust building because the group had chosen to deal with its threatening issues together, with all the parties present. Had this not occurred, there was every chance that the meeting time would have been wasted because the real issues had been avoided. The previous norm-setting work had given the groups a solid platform for moving forward—in this case, a norm of discussing undiscussables. As months passed, the off-site meeting came to be regarded as a significant moment in creating a new and positive collective identity.

As this story indicates, the outcome of norm-setting work can be a firm foundation for trust. This work provides explicit guidance for people as they respond to the challenges of everyday situations as well as less routine challenges. The following guidelines help in the creation of norms.

Develop agreement about ways people should work together. Begin this process by bringing together the managers and supervisors who report to you. If this is a large group or if there is a fair amount of mistrust, you may want to have an outside facilitator present. Your goal is to develop a common picture of the positive relationships you collectively want to maintain with employees. This picture of desirable relationships, when it is jointly created, inspires people to work hard to achieve it. To secure that commitment, strive for consensus about the norms. You might want to refer to Chapter Thirteen for guidance on decision making. The basic steps are as follows:

1. Brainstorm possibilities by posing the question:

   "How would people work together if we were known for the quality of our work, the loyalty of our customers, and the high level of job satisfaction of our employees?"

2. Discuss the items listed, getting clear about the meaning of key phrases.

3. Select the vital few items that are most important to creating your desired work environment, making sure that each one is written in a way that will be understood by those who have not been involved in your discussions.

4. Let the list rest in draft form for at least a week.

5. Return to the list, asking:

   "Does this list still make sense? Are there changes we want to make? Why?"

6. Make changes as necessary, again using consensus.

Decide how you will reinforce the norms. The commitment that members of the group make to help one another act according to these norms is a very important part of the process, requiring follow-up once the norms have been agreed to. In fact, if you do not take this step, all the time and effort that went into developing your norms will later be regarded as a waste, and as another example of inconsistent leadership (yours). To prevent this from happening:

1. Distribute the list of norms to all members of the group, allowing a few days for people to reflect on each item.

2. As soon as possible, meet again to explore the ways in which these norms can become a kind of self- and group measurement tool, enabling people to reinforce positive behavior and take action if it strays from the agreement.

3. Facilitate discussions around the following questions:

   "What are our agreements about giving one another feedback on behaviors that support or contradict the norms?"

   "How will we measure progress toward meeting these norms as a part of day-to-day interactions?"

   "What barriers do we foresee in meeting them and how will we overcome them?"

   "How will we hold ourselves accountable for living up to those expectations, yet give ourselves permission to be human and make mistakes from time to time?"

   "When will we meet next to assess our successes and potential areas for improvement?"

4. Make sure your group answers the last question and follows through on this commitment. We recommend reviewing progress on newly established norms every three to four months for the first year.

Share the norms with all employees. The next step in this effort is to share the norms and the reasoning behind them with employees in your portion of the organization. Some leadership teams delay this rollout until they see some obvious progress in their own ability to live according to the norms. When your team is ready, here are some steps to take:

1. Prior to sharing this information, have your group answer the question:

   "Do we expect employees to live by the same norms or do we encourage each work group to develop its own norms designed to support what we have started?"

2. If you decide that you want your norms adopted by every-one, arrange for a variety of meetings that will allow employees to learn about

   The concept of norms and why it is important to con-sciously establish ones that are positive

   The norms and the way they will be used to guide behavior

   Why these norms, in particular, were selected

   What process was used to arrive at this list

   How that experience has affected those who were involved

   What kind of support will be given to employees so that they can be successful in behaving according to the norms

3. If your group wants to allow each work group to have its own norm-building experience, take steps to repeat the process that you have just experienced. Realize that certain modifications may need to be made given the dynamics of each work unit.

4. Remember to think carefully about whether or not outside facilitation will be necessary for success in any of these steps.

Provide Feedback to Managers Who Report to You

In order for a new set of norms to have a positive impact, they must be reinforced. As the initiator of this effort, you need to offer obser-vations to those who report to you about how they are demonstrat-ing the new norms.

Notice and comment when people support the norms. The more you acknowledge the positive ways managers work with others, the more you are likely to see a repetition of those behaviors. Use statements like these:

> *"Ben, I really appreciated the way you encouraged Santos to take the lead in last week's public meeting. He represented this company very well and your trust in him showed. I know that was a good learning experience for him."*

> *"Joan, I know you went out of your way to get others involved in this project, even though it took extra time on your part. I could tell that it meant a lot to them by the way they have followed through on all the details. That's a great way to show that we are walking the talk with our norms!"*

Intervene when you see people violating the norms. A more challenging situation occurs when you see people exhibiting behaviors that contradict the spirit conveyed in your norms. These are the behaviors that may threaten others and cause them to hesitate to speak up. In such cases:

1. Assume that the other person wants to support the new norms.

2. Remember that feedback is most effective when it is offered as a gift, something designed to help the other person grow and succeed.

3. Use neutral, rather than judgmental, words to describe the behavior you have observed and its impact.

4. Let the person receiving your feedback choose whether or not to make any changes in response to what you are saying.

The following are examples of feedback given about a newly established set of norms:

> *"Jerry, I have some thoughts on how yesterday's meeting might have gone a bit more smoothly. If you are interested, I'd be glad to share them with you."*

> *"I'm concerned, Mike, about your pattern of interrupting people before they finish what they are saying. I notice that you tend to do this most often when you are rushed."*

"Alice, you seem really on edge these days. There's an impatient tone in your voice that subtly conveys disapproval. I wonder if you are entirely aware of how you are coming across."

Coach Managers Who Report to You

When one of the managers who reports to you shows a tendency to rely on old-style, directive approaches, you will want to add a coaching element to strengthen your feedback. The extra effort on your part is necessary because the other person may not even see the problem behavior, let alone view it as something that needs to change. He or she may never have received feedback on personal conduct before. In situations like this, you may end up dealing with the individual's image of who he or she is at work. These concepts are usually well formed and not easy to change.

Help people to understand the impact of their behavior by asking questions and giving examples. Most people know beforehand when a problem at work is caused by their behavior. Typically, they do not change because they do not see the impact of the problem. The leader's role is to help people recognize vividly how certain behavior negatively affects others, the work, and the organization. Stowell and Starcevich (1987) point out that this is usually best done by asking good questions and providing good examples. Here are some possibilities; notice how the questions build on the concept of feedback and push the conversation to a different and more pointed level.

> *"Nguyen, if that same comment had been made about you, how would you respond?"*
>
> *"Ted, I've heard from some of your employees that you can be really sarcastic at times: having an edge in your voice, using double meanings to make your point. These things always make someone feel uncomfortable. I know your job can be very frustrating, but I wonder if you have really evaluated the effects of this behavior. How do you think this type of thing is interpreted by your employees? What kind of impact do you think it has on the work?"*
>
> *"Marcia, I've heard it said that you intimidate people with your communication style. It's in the look of impatience you give people*

sometimes and the abrupt tone in your voice. I know these may seem like small behaviors, but they are having a significant impact. I believe you are leaving the impression that your employees aren't any good at their jobs and should be scared of you. Is that what you mean to convey?"

"Javier, when you break a pencil to make a point about how upset you are, people focus on how they are being treated, not the message you are trying to send. What would you think if someone did that to you?"

"Susan, I could hear you shouting on the other side of the office. For about the next hour, all people did was talk and wonder who was getting it this time. My bet is that they will remember this incident for a long time. What do you think about all this?"

When you need to provide this type of direct feedback and coaching:

1. Focus on describing concrete behaviors: what the person specifically has done or said and the problems that resulted.

2. Listen to the employee's explanations carefully for clues as to why these behaviors are occurring.

3. Watch the tone in your voice when doing this; stay open, reflecting a desire to learn and to support positive change. If you adopt a judgmental or interrogative tone, you will threaten the person you are trying to coach, and your efforts will fail.

Work in a collaborative way to understand the reasons behind the troublesome behavior. In situations where you shift to a coaching strategy, there is usually a pattern of behavior that you believe needs to be changed. Working in a supportive way with your direct report:

1. Explore why this pattern—which runs counter to the norms this person helped to create—takes place. By doing so you give the person a chance to share the problem rather than face it alone. Ask:

   "What assumptions do you make about people who work for you or with you? Do you believe these individuals are cynical or suspicious?"

   "Do certain events or characteristics of others trigger the unwanted pattern?"

*"Do strong emotions or judgments take over and result in unin-
tended threats or punishment for employees?"*

2. Be prepared to hear strong emotion from the other person,
   who may be frustrated in her or his attempts to manage others. For example, a person might feel put on the spot by
   employees she sees as "a bunch of ungrateful whiners."
   Perhaps she's feeling, "I shouldn't have to deal with this!
   People just need to do their work!"

3. If strong emotions persist and seem beyond a predictable
   range, you might want to consult an employee assistance
   counselor for advice or collaborate with a higher-level manager about what to do.

Work together to develop a plan for change. Once you and the manager who reports to you have identified the causes or triggering
events for the unwanted behavior, you are in a better position to figure out how to reinforce the positive norms and reduce the unpro-
ductive pattern. Encourage your employee by asking:

*"Have you ever faced situations like this in the past? If so, what
helped you to break the old habit and establish a new one?"*

*"What new skills or ideas might help you to stay on track with
our norms? Is there education or training you might want to
sign up for? Are there certain people already in the organization
you might want to learn from?"*

*"Could we agree to shift some aspects of your job structure or
responsibilities as a way to support the new behaviors? What
might that shift be?"*

*"What kind of support do you need from me? From others in our
group?"*

In the course of such discussions, you can make some very
specific contributions:

1. Be very clear that you want to see the behavior changed and
   why that is important to you; express confidence that the
   manager has the same intention.

2. During the conversation, offer concrete suggestions that sup-
   plement what your employee-leader is saying.

3. As appropriate, share some of your own past experiences,

gaffes, and blunders as a way to help build trust and reduce the sense of aloneness that your employee might feel.

4. Along with your constructive comments, point out the others person's special skills, talents, and accomplishments.

5. Do what you say you will do once your plan is in place.

6. Afterward, continue this supportive approach but be persistent in your requirement for change. Forgive mistakes, but find time to talk about them and understand their causes. Do not let opportunities for learning go to waste. You must follow through.

Be open to hearing feedback about your own leadership. These discussions may lead to feedback from your employee about your own leadership style. Discovering how she or he sees you can provide a rich opportunity to explore the nuances of your own interpersonal relations and to tear down a fence or two along the way.

1. Take advantage of the opportunities that come up by saying such things as these:

   "You mentioned a few minutes ago that something I said was confusing to you. I'd like to understand more about that. Would you tell me more?"

   "I've been giving you a lot of information, but I'd like to know how I'm doing. What feedback do you have for me?"

   "How are these sessions going from your point of view? Is this being helpful to you or not? Is my role as your boss getting in the way?"

   "Are there changes I need to be making so you can be more successful?"

2. When your employee shares his or her thoughts with you, use your best listening skills. Ask good clarifying questions if you don't understand something that is said.

3. Accept what is offered as information to consider. Remember that becoming defensive or conveying a curt or judgmental tone will risk shutting down the openness you have worked very hard to establish.

Work with Unmet Expectations

When individuals are working to achieve behavioral norms, there is usually positive evidence of this, such as

- Observable changes in behavior at meetings and in one-on-one conversations

- Discussion and use of the norms when making decisions

- Spontaneous reports by group members about how the norms have been used to help address conflicts or improve communications

- Improvements reported by third parties unfamiliar with the work ("Wow, Jean is different! What happened?")

However, sometimes group norms do not influence individual behaviors. If someone's behavior consistently violates the spirit of the norms, it is tempting to immediately jump to requiring changes in behavior. This is a slippery point because the power of the norms comes from their development by the group. They are essentially a promise about behavior from one colleague to another.

Nevertheless, there may be a moment when it becomes necessary to deliberately convert the norms into performance expectations. This happens after you have engaged in one-on-one discussions to clarify the norms, provided feedback and coaching, and perhaps made referrals to other resources to help a person improve. This chapter would not be complete if we did not offer some suggestions about what to do when you decide that an employee or manager is truly unwilling or unable to live up to the norms that have been established. To begin with, five points are worth mentioning:

1. If you want to create a trust-based, high-performance organization, be aware that certain fear-producing behaviors must stop.

2. Deal with obvious breaches of the norms in the managers who report to you if you want to maintain credibility as a leader.

3. Do your homework by gathering as much accurate information as you can before meeting with your direct reports.

4. Develop a thorough understanding of your organization's HR procedures related to feedback, disciplinary action, and termination. This will enable you to move ahead in these situations with greater clarity and confidence. In particular, learn how to conduct a fair investigation of incidents so that you do not rush to action without all the facts.

5. Don't hesitate to ask for help from an HR specialist or consultant if you feel you need it.

The situations highlighted in the next sections represent times when a manager has been overly harsh, for example, inappropriately disciplining an employee, bullying someone, or harassing a person about a mistake. These are the circumstances when a direct report has taken action toward an employee that appears to be or is retaliatory, a payback for speaking up, or punishment for taking a risk while in pursuit of the organization's mission. For each of these circumstances, it makes sense to do the following as an initial part of your conversation.

Stipulate, or remind the manager, that you are using the norms as the basis for a personal performance expectation. Since the norms originally were set collaboratively in a group setting, it is essential to make sure that the person knows that you are now establishing a performance standard for him or her (or have already done so) as part of your leadership role. Clearly state that the reason for this shift is your personal observation of the individual's apparent unwillingness or inability to achieve the behaviors associated with the norm. Be prepared to discuss what you have observed in detail.

When Actions Seem Retaliatory but Motives Are Not

With individuals whose actions look intimidating but who deny any retaliatory motive, be clear what the expectations are and hold the individuals increasingly accountable for their actions. Employ the suggestions made earlier about coaching.

Begin with a warning about what the situation looks like to you and to others. Reassure the manager of your commitment to a fair and complete exploration of events. Then jointly analyze the situation in question, and perhaps other past incidents, to show why the behavior seems retaliatory. Replay the events, identifying different ways the manager or employee could have handled the situation, without being intimidating yourself. At times like these, you might say:

> *"Elizabeth, as you know, I take our leadership commitment to our norms very seriously and believe it is a solid basis for performance expectations. Unless you can help me see it another way, the incident involving you and Peter contradicts those expectations in a big way. Walk me through what happened, so I can see the events from your point of view."*

Continuing on, you might use phrases like the following:

> *"I can see that you would be very disappointed in how the presentation turned out. How else might you have handled things?"*
>
> *"Is there any connection between this situation and the tension that came up last summer between you and Eddie? I know you worked hard on that one and did a great job of resolving your differences successfully."*
>
> *"Tell me what you intend to do next with Peter."*

Work with the manager to develop a performance improvement plan. Effective performance improvement plans begin with clearly stated and well-understood goals for changed behavior. They call out specific steps that will be taken and identify times for check-in points and reviews of progress. They also note the resources that will be provided to help the person be successful. In this process, your attention to and support for your report cannot be understated. If you do your part to help this person succeed, the chance of his or her behavior changing will be significantly heightened.

Consider using the services of a third-party consultant or a coach from somewhere else in the organization to support the individual. The nature of your relationship with the person and your skills may indicate the need to bring someone else in to support the performance improvement effort. Use this procedure:

1. Ask the individual to identify someone else in the organization who possesses the skills and characteristics he or she wants to develop. It may be possible to set up periodic meetings between the two for coaching or other useful discussions.

2. If no one is available within the organization, locate an external consultant to serve as an objective sounding board and coach. Investing in an outside resource and continuing your own personal involvement would be a clear demonstration of your commitment to help the person succeed.

Design ways to get objective feedback for the manager. Many of the people who exhibit abrasive or abusive behavior at work never know it. Getting feedback for a manager from his or her employees and coworkers therefore may be vital. Anyone who is trying hard to improve needs to have some trusted source of feedback about how it is going, what is working well, and what needs extra effort. The "360-degree" approach offered by several external vendors of evaluation instruments can be effective. In this case, the manager who wants feedback would select several people—employees, peers, and supervisors—to comment on her or his leadership performance and characteristics. Standardized questions, analyzed anonymously, with a follow-up report and coaching built in, make this a useful package for some.

For less extensive efforts, you might engage an outside consultant to interview a set of people who are in a position to comment on the manager's behavior. Again, the important notion here is feedback gathered in a thoughtful, thorough way, analyzed and presented by someone who is both skillful at this type of work and disconnected from the organization.

If change does not occur as a result of these steps, try to restructure the employee's position to a nonsupervisory role. This is sometimes possible, depending on the skills and knowledge of the manager and the needs of the organization. Some people can be far more successful as individual contributors than they are in a supervisory capacity. The point of this restructuring is to remove the manager from any position where he or she might be inclined to use an ingrained abrasive or abusive style of leadership with others. Restructuring can be very sensitive. It should be done in a way that enables the person to genuinely learn from the experience without undermining her or his self-esteem. Human resources professionals are often an important support for leaders facing such situations. If you do not believe that the manager has enough to offer the organization, if you do not have an organizational flexibility or need that would justify such an action, or if you do not care enough, then you may simply decide to ask for the manager's resignation.

When Someone Intentionally Threatens an Employee

If a manager who reports to you takes action that, upon investigation, is found to be intentionally retaliatory, intervene quickly, being direct and to the point.

Ask the manager to reevaluate his or her personal behavior in depth. Without demeaning the other person, say that it is time to compare his or her motives, interests, and style to the needs and expectations of the organization. For example:

> "Francis, it is time to carefully think about whether or not you are a good fit with this organization. I want to know why you have behaved in ways that directly contradict the norms we've all agreed to."

> "Cherie, this recent incident is a serious violation of what all of us in leadership roles have agreed to. I want to know, in detail, what you think is behind this and what you intend to do in the future."

Depending on the severity of an incident or pattern, ask for a decision: to participate constructively or to resign. Sometimes, it takes a focused discussion about the possibility of requesting a resignation to make the point that you are serious about wanting to see behavior change. In such cases you might say:

> "Marco, I would like to see you stay in this organization, because you have many fine qualities. However, this abrasive and abusive behavior must stop. Either you immediately start acting according to the expectations I've outlined for you, or I will ask for your resignation. Do you understand what I am saying?"

> "Pauline, the incident that took place last week so violates the work environment we are trying to build that I must ask for your resignation."

If an individual acknowledges an abrasive or abusive style and is unwilling to change, remove all leadership responsibilities or proceed with a termination action. If you believe that there is a way this person can be a valuable contributor to the organization, offer that possibility, making it clear that no formal leadership or supervisory responsibilities will be included in the new job. If that is not doable or appropriate, announce your decision to terminate the manager. In this situation, you might use the following words:

> *"Eric, I had hoped to avoid this situation. I must ask you to leave this organization. Your unwillingness to alter your approach and your continued violation of the expectations we have for those in leadership positions leaves me no choice."*

> *"Henrietta, this is not going to work. You obviously understand that your behavior toward employees is overbearing and intimidating, yet you are unwilling to change the way you respond. Your employment here is now terminated."*

When Someone Wants to Change, but Cannot

Give attention and support to the person who cannot change an abrasive or abusive style but who is sincerely trying to do so.

Provide a referral to a helping agency or employee assistance program. Your HR department or a local mental health center should be able to assist you with this type of referral. Before making the referral:

1. Get the basic facts about the type and amount of the service provided, the program's track record in dealing with individuals like your direct report, and any financial issues.

2. Find out how you can support this counseling effort from behind the scenes at work.

3. Share this information with your employee, emphasizing that your motivation is to help him or her be successful at making the desired changes.

Help to arrange a mentoring relationship with another experienced manager. See the preceding suggestions.

Consider restructuring the position to one that does not involve supervision. See the preceding suggestions.

If problems persist, face up to them and help your direct report to do the same. Sometimes all your best efforts and those of the other person will not produce the desired changes in behavior. If your direct report cannot behave in ways that are acceptable, it may be time for this person to leave the organization. In such moments:

1. Be truthful and supportive, acknowledging what has worked, what has not, and why you are asking this individual to leave.

2. Engage the services of a competent outplacement counseling service or career development firm to help the individual become successfully reestablished in new employment.

When a Termination Occurs

If a termination occurs, remember that others may be scared. People close to the individual who has left the organization will probably have feelings about the situation. Suspicion, worst-case thinking, and the cycle of mistrust will be swirling. People will have two primary questions:

1. Was the individual who left treated fairly by the organization?
2. Will what happened to this person happen to them?

This most delicate of workplace circumstances must be handled with clarity and caring in a straightforward way. If you avoid dealing with this situation, you will fan the flames of mistrust, confusion, and fear. Take the following steps:

1. With your manager and any key human resources professionals who have been involved, agree on what can and cannot be said publicly about the individual's departure.

2. Without violating the dictates of conscience, company policy, or advice of legal counsel, talk to your other employees about this event. Do this as soon as possible.

3. Give them a chance to express their feelings and concerns and ask questions. Paraphrase to demonstrate that you understand the points of view that are expressed.

4. Describe, if only in general terms, the efforts that were made to correct the problem before the termination occurred.

5. Reinforce your commitment to support people in their development efforts. Make statements like these:

"There are things about Perry's departure that I cannot talk about because I want to protect the confidentiality that he, and any other employee in this organization, is entitled to."

"I will answer your questions as best I can. I hope you will respect the fact that there are some things I am not at liberty to share."

"If, after this meeting, any of you have concerns about your position in this organization, please come to see me. I would be happy to talk about how I see your contributions and career potential."

In the long haul, we believe that paying direct attention to interpersonal conduct is a vitally important way to build trust, respect, and integrity in the organization. This can happen even in the toughest of cases. People become proud of their ability to improve communication with one another and become increasingly interested in the skills required to do so. Establishing and adhering to positive norms, educating people about behaviors to avoid, and providing day-to-day feedback give direction and energy to working relationships. These steps overturn negative practices and feelings and directly address the behaviors that are most likely to cause fear. They also chart a positive course for ways to behave that support increasing levels of trust and cooperation.

New Lessons and Reflections

Thoughts on Organizational Culture

Once group norms are created, they must be attended to. The points made in this chapter about periodic review of the norms and giving feedback to people who do—or do not—live up to them cannot be overemphasized. If these steps are not taken seriously, it would be better not to set group norms at all. Letting a group drift away from its commitments only builds cynicism and fear. Chapter Twelve offers help on these issues as does *The Courageous Messenger* (Ryan, Oestreich, and Orr, 1996).

Thoughts on Personal Leadership

While it may be unavoidable in some cases to talk about group norms without calling them "standards" or "expectations," the less frequently you must do this, the better. The norms people set for themselves should be discussed as a matter of personal and group choice. They should be regarded as a form of "liftoff" for the team in obtaining a higher level of trust and communication, not a set of laws by which people police one another. Chapter Three expresses the feeling of hope and optimism that should come from the norm-setting process and the norms themselves.

When a team realizes that it is *choosing* its norms—not just following a human relations process of some kind—a strong sense of identity and pride can quickly follow. You can lead a team toward this moment by highlighting the freedom of the group to decide for itself its own path toward high trust. Use the team's language, not your own.

10

Value Criticism: Reward the Messenger

The phrase "shoot the messenger" is a cultural and historical symbol for what can happen to people who speak up. In three words, the implication is clear: "If I say what is really on my mind, I will suffer for it." In this chapter, we describe why messengers are shot and provide recommendations to overcome this pattern. These are summarized in Grid 10.1.

First, a Word About Language

Messengers usually point out problems with people or systems; typically, they are messy situations that seldom have a simple answer or a quick fix. Unfortunately, this information is commonly termed "bad news." Historically, those who bring it forward have been seen as "bearers of bad tidings." Language like this, along with phrases such as "shoot the messenger," perpetuate the difficulty experienced by those who have something to say and

Strategy	What This Should Accomplish
Hear the message	Gain information and insight about opportunities for improvements and innovation

Increased understanding of the experience of employees

Increased positive relationships with messengers |
| Seek the message | Gain information and insight about opportunities for improvements and innovation

Gain feedback about the impact of your performance and leadership style

Increase in your reputation as a leader who sincerely wants to build trust and reduce fear |
| Reward messengers | Current messengers will continue to speak up

Increased numbers of those who are willing to speak up

Increased understanding of employees about what people in leadership roles are doing to respond to their suggestions

Increased belief among employees that their suggestions and concerns are important |

Grid 10.1. How to Value Criticism.

those who are listening. The negativity connected to this type of exchange conveys trouble for the messenger, who will suffer some type of repercussion, and trouble for the receiver of the message, who will have to do something once the difficult message has been delivered. In our work we have decided to recast this negative tone with a set of related points:

- Messengers bring forward information and perspective.
- As such, the message is neither good nor bad, although it frequently sounds and feels like criticism.

- Messages may focus on complex, sensitive, or difficult issues.
- Those who make the effort to share and hear such messages do their organization a great service and demonstrate strong leadership.
- If the news does not get through, the information cannot be utilized to solve problems or make improvements.

Why and How the Messenger Gets Shot

Those who hear what messengers have to say as "bad news" and shut off discussion may do so because they do not, in fact, know how to solve the problem. They worry, along with the messenger, that if the problem comes to light, "I'll get in trouble" or "People will think I can't handle it." As one middle manager for a public agency commented, the "shoot the messenger" syndrome "comes from managers' fear of looking bad in front of their bosses. They all want to look like they are doing a good job." The presence of many messages suggests that the plans, pet projects, and assumed understandings have flaws, gaps, and glitches. Slowing down, listening to, and then responding to these messages is not easy and certainly not fun, especially when one is under the stress of a fast-paced, constantly changing work environment. Messengers become the unfair targets for repercussions when the receiver's pride, convenience, or political success is more important than building an open, collaborative workplace where problems are identified and quickly solved.

Messengers also get shot because their listeners make negative assumptions about their motives. Some imagine that the messenger is doing something other than simply bringing news. A retired manager we spoke with asked us, "Don't you think these fellows who show up on your doorstep usually have a grudge of their own they are trying to work out?" Discounting the messenger in this way is self-protective. It is a sign of a negative assumption about the messenger's goodwill. When people "show up on the doorstep," the self-protective manager first wants to know what ax the messenger has to grind. The message gets lost as the cycle of mistrust invades with an evaluation of motives.

To change the perception that messengers ultimately cause harm requires commitment to the larger picture of organizational improvement. It also requires a willingness to take the risk of hearing a sensitive or complex message that may mean more work for the listener. What is necessary is the attitude, personally and throughout the organization, that problems are prized possessions—learning opportunities that are essential to continued improvement and innovation. It takes a recognition that the messengers do not create the problems; they simply help to identify them. If, as a manager, you have a reputation for genuinely wanting to hear criticisms and handling them in a responsible, nondefensive way, people will talk to you. They will do so even if they do not know you personally or if they report to you directly.

Hear the Message

We have often heard from clients that messengers' viewpoints may be hard to accept because of the way they are brought forward. To illustrate, let's play out an uncomfortable—and not uncommon—scenario where the messenger's manner is openly aggressive.

> A vocal member of the union executive committee comes to you with a complaint from a coworker. He is blunt, accusatory, frustrated, and argumentative. He carries a raft of negative assumptions about your behavior and motives that feel like an attack on your integrity. His history is not easy; the two of you have disagreed openly before and his own job performance leaves a lot to be desired. Now, suddenly, he is in your office complaining about how a coworker has been mistreated by her supervisor. Neither he nor his coworker has talked to the supervisor directly and the complaint seems altogether minor. You find yourself wanting to snarl: "It's none of your damn business. Get back to work!"

Stop. Take a breath. Think for a moment. Do not expect messages to come to you in a palatable way. What you have in front of you is the concern of an employee whose values and approaches, for whatever reason, may reflect the cycle of mistrust. Recognize that there may be more to the situation than what is initially verbalized and that this is an opportunity for you to exercise an important aspect of leadership.

Maintain an open attitude. Keep in mind that the issue is not *how* the message first arrives, but *what* the message is. When messengers, like the one in our scenario, come on strong, it is easy to become defensive and self-protective. Resist the temptation to slide into the cycle of mistrust or take things too personally. Stay open-minded by doing some of these things:

1. Recognize that the messenger's bravado may be a mask for her or his own nervousness or fear about the subject of the message or about talking with you.

2. Without seeming to be interrogating the messenger, ask questions that get at the core issue of concern.

3. Consider that the messenger's aggressive tone might reflect other problems that are surfacing with other employees.

4. Paraphrase to make sure you understand the key points.

5. Ask your messenger what he or she wants you to do and why.

6. If you disagree or hesitate to comply, say so and give your reasons for your response.

7. Ask the messenger to tell you her or his understanding of what you've said.

8. Acknowledge any points of common ground and build upon them.

9. Say what you will do and give your reasons, making sure that they are commitments you will fulfill.

10. Keep your tone of voice respectful.

11. If you have a hard time staying open, pay attention to what that might say about your relationship with the messenger (or others) and steps you might want to take to improve it.

If you are overly sensitive to the manner in which a message is delivered, you make it more difficult for individuals who may already be fearful that coming to you will cause them to be seen as troublemakers. Requiring that people always be 100 percent polite and constructive and that they have solutions, not just a problem, will narrow the number of individuals who will ever come to you. Such expectations will almost guarantee that when somebody does show up, that person will be angry, frustrated, and outspoken—or vague and indirect. Either of these options only makes your job of hearing the news that much harder.

Hear out the messenger's full message. The value of effective listening skills in situations like this cannot be overemphasized. To listen effectively:

1. Ask clear, open-ended questions and paraphrase what you hear to make sure you've understood things correctly.

2. Remember the big picture as you put on the hat of the investigative reporter: seek as much perspective as you can in the moment, and worry about putting it all together later on.

3. Ask questions such as:

   "Who else, besides yourself, is concerned about this issue?"

   "How does this situation negatively affect things—relationships, the work to be done, feelings about the organization?"

   "What do you believe is behind it all?"

   "Have any efforts been made so far to try to improve things? Did they work? If not, why not?"

   "Tell me how I'm connected to this problem. What can I do to help things improve?"

   "Are there other things I should know about?"

   "What would you like me to do once we've finished talking? Why is this important?"

No matter how unpleasant the manner of the messenger may be, his or her willingness to share a personal perspective is an opportunity. If it is, in fact, the tip of the iceberg, you will want to use this conversation as a means of learning as much as you can about what is going on with others in the organization. Once everything is on the table, you may find that there is quite a bit of work for you to do. That's okay. Now you have a basis for further investigation and contact with other people. By listening carefully to this "troublemaker," you have gained insight about a problem between an employee and a supervisor and about your organization as a whole.

Create a comfort zone. One of the reasons a messenger's style may be offensive is that he or she might be tense about approaching you, the subject of the conversation, or both. When people are uptight they do not express themselves as well as they might. In addition to having a nervous tone of voice, they may stumble over their words and ideas. They may be unclear, exaggerate, express anger, present inappropriately rosy or negative opinions, overly simplify things, or make them too complex. You can help this situation by bringing down the tension level so that the messenger is more likely to say what he or she really means. This is more complicated than offering a comfortable chair and a cup of coffee, although those things sometimes help. It is more a matter of tone, openness, and a willingness to slow down and listen. Even if the other person seems hostile, say things like these:

> *"Okay, this sounds like it's pretty sensitive and important. Let's start at the beginning."*

> *"I'd like to get a sense of the full situation and how you and others are feeling about it."*

> *"I'm here to listen. I appreciate your views on this problem and I'd like to know why you personally think we've got it."*

> *"I know that coming here to talk to me is not the easiest thing to do. Before we go any further, I want you to know that I appreciate your willingness to do so."*

Phrases like these defuse the tension by saying that you are open and accessible, and that you care about the other person's feelings and perspective. They are a mark of personal strength and the capacity to show respect in the face of a tough situation. They are, in the terms of conflict experts Roger Fisher and Scott Brown (1988, p. 37), an "unconditionally constructive" approach to others. They may also have the effect of bringing down your own tension level by reminding you that your focus is to listen, gain information, and operate from a position of integrity. Keep in mind the phrase: "Better to hear it now than later."

With the messenger, identify the systems issues. The messenger may define the problem as "that manager" or "that customer." The behavior of those parties may well be involved. The bigger picture is that the problems brought by the messenger may also have to do with work systems, roles, policies, organizational structures, ambiguities of all kinds, or other problems that have little to do with individual behavior. By identifying the needed improvements in the systems behind the presenting concerns, you depersonalize the problem. The conversation can then be directed toward a collaborative analysis of the business issues that need to be addressed. Consider the examples in Grid 10.2.

To get to the possible underlying systems issues, ask questions like these:

> *"What do you think might be the cause of the behavior that is so troubling to you?"*

"Is [name of person] really to blame? What else might be going on that could be behind his or her behavior?"

"Are there ways our work is organized that contribute to this problem?"

This is more than just a technique to get people to talk. Our interviews suggest that individuals' first concerns are personal, self-protective, and more oriented to management practice issues than to suggestions for improving work. By helping to move the conversation toward those larger issues, you encourage people to evaluate how their initial complaint relates to the systems by which the work gets done. This defuses tension and asks the messenger to become an active participant in the problem-solving process.

Seek the News

Responding to the problems that come to you is a critical skill, but it is still a reactive one. To really open up communication, more forthright action is required. Go out and find the problems and the new ideas. The phrase "If it ain't broke, don't fix it" leads to a certain degree of armchair confidence. It is as if you are saying, "If nobody is bringing me problems, I guess there aren't any." A different approach is to find out what condition the organization is really in by being more visible, participative, and openly receptive to information. This requires time and effort and a willingness to push yourself out of your daily routine to understand the routines of others.

The suggestions we emphasize ask you to communicate in person with those who work for you. Organizational assessments done by outside consultants, employee satisfaction surveys, employee task forces and standing committees, and electronic hot lines are other methods many organizations use very effectively. However, because reducing fear and building trust require improvements in the manager-employee relationship, we call your attention to approaches that are targeted specifically toward enhancing those vital interpersonal interactions.

Ask open-ended questions about the work. In this process, you ask people directly for thoughts on possible problems or ideas that might represent new approaches. Direct these questions toward work groups or individuals. You might say:

Presenting Concerns	Possible Systems Issues
"Jane has completely unrealistic expectations about what I can do in the time available. I've tried to tell her that but she doesn't get it."	Confusion about roles Poor project or work-flow planning Inadequate resources
"We've been working on this project for two years. Every time the design team recommends action, the executives back away from it. They obviously don't want anything to really change."	Confusion about direction Conflict over resources Politics at higher levels in the organization
"When I told Charlie where the equipment should be stored, he started hollering at me, telling me that I was not his boss. I don't deserve to be treated that way!"	Unclear expectations about workplace norms of behavior Lack of employee orientation or training on interpersonal skills Possible role confusion

Grid 10.2. Possible Systems Issues.

> *"How are things going?"*
>
> *"What kinds of problems are you running into?"*
>
> *"If you were going to do this again, how would you improve it?"*
>
> *"What barriers do you anticipate in the next phase of the work?"*
>
> *"What are our customers saying about us these days—both complaints and compliments?"*
>
> *"What is working well from your point of view?"*
> *"Can you suggest any different ways of doing things?"*

Use the following guidelines in asking for more information:

1. If people are slow to respond, make an observation or share a related experience of your own to let them know that you sincerely want to find out what is going on.

2. Say clearly that you are interested in being of help and want to support their efforts.

3. Listen carefully to their responses, then paraphrase what they tell you to make sure that you got their message.

Take on an actual front-line role for a day. One health care administrator we know uses this technique on a regular basis. Once every two months, she makes sure that she is scheduled into one of the six outpatient clinics she oversees. There she assumes the role of the receptionist, working a full shift. She sees patients, their families, physicians, nurses, and technicians. And, perhaps more importantly, they see her working the front line, trying to understand their experience and the issues from their vantage point. This sends an important message about her respect for the work, the ideas, and the feelings of her employees. If you use this strategy:

1. Watch, learn, and ask questions about the processes people use to produce a product or service.

2. Get to know people, their names, what they do, and what they care about.

3. Pay attention to your own experience during the day—what you enjoy, what frustrates you, what helps you to do quality work for the customer.

4. Follow up with discussions with both front-line and supervisory staff to identify problems and possible improvements.

Talk about how your mistakes have been learning opportunities. When you tell people about what you've learned from a mistake you've made, you demonstrate that you are willing to examine your behavior, gain insight, and move on. In fact, telling a few selected stories about yourself—how you goofed, what you learned from it, how you did things differently the next time, how you accepted responsibility for what went wrong—does three things. First, it sends the message that it is okay to make mistakes as long as lessons are learned that will result in improvement in the future. Second, it makes you seem "more human" to people who might have a tendency to put you on a pedestal or in a box and makes it easier for them to approach you about their mistakes. Third, it models your willingness to take responsibility for your own actions. This gives you a chance to make the point that mistakes can have negative consequences for the individual or the organization, but that a negative consequence does not mean the end of one's job or career. Here are some useful phrases to begin such acknowledgments:

> *"Let me tell you about a time I had a similar experience. Here's what happened . . . Here's what I learned . . ."*

"I was able to use what I learned from that experience in the following ways . . ."

"The decision I made created a lot of difficulty. When it was all over, I realized . . ."

"Now, of course, I wish I had handled that situation differently. But through that experience, I learned the invaluable lesson that . . ."

In *The Abilene Paradox*, Jerry Harvey writes, "When we make it difficult for organization members to acknowledge their mistakes and have them forgiven, we have designed organizations that reduce risk-taking, encourage lying, foment distrust, and, as a consequence, decrease productivity" (1988, p. 59). Harvey observes that a manager's ability to tell the simple truth and accept responsibility for a mistake is amazing to people who expect excuses or implications that others are really to blame. When managers tell the truth about themselves and their experiences, it comes as a breath of fresh air to those who expect anyone in a supervisory capacity to be distant or defensive. Such an act of self-disclosure "provides the basis for human connection. It relieves our alienation from one another" (p. 66). As a result, it makes it much easier for others to do the same.

Ask directly for feedback. Strong leadership is demonstrated when you ask for feedback and respond to it in an open, appreciative way. Asking for feedback gives you a better picture of the effects of your behavior on others and the overall results of your work. It also reassures people of your positive intentions and desire to improve. Statements like the ones that follow can be used with your customers, employees, coworkers, or supervisor:

"Like most people, I am trying to make a conscious effort to improve my performance and my communication skills. I am interested in thoughts, positive and negative, about how you see me operating in my role."

"I'd love to know what you thought about how I handled myself at the meeting on Friday afternoon. I felt a bit awkward afterward and wasn't sure if I had helped things or not. Please tell me what you think."

"One of my goals is to make sure you get the support you need. Would you be willing to think about the work we've done in the last six months and tell me what I should do more of, less of, or continue? I sure would appreciate that feedback."

"Honestly, I want the good news and the bad. I want to hear the truth, and I am not interested in this just for the sake of some type of personal validation. I need the facts in order to improve."

Requests for such feedback can be made one-on-one or in group settings, although we find that individual meetings are typically the best settings to hear the perceptions of others. To prepare for these meetings:

1. Remember that some people may want to know in advance the specific areas you'd like to discuss; giving them a few days to think about your request often leads to a more meaningful discussion.

2. Take a warm, natural approach to these meetings and do whatever you can to keep them private and uninterrupted.

3. Be sure to ask about the impact of the behaviors they identify, on themselves and the organization.

4. If you sense that people's fear and cynicism may get in the way of their being honest with you, bring in an outside consultant to confidentially interview them, whether they are your employees, coworkers, or supervisors. Using a standard set of questions, this person can summarize the trends for you without revealing who said what.

Share the feedback and your plans for change. Once the feedback has been collected by you or a third-party consultant, build a composite picture of how others view your leadership. Look for patterns that have emerged, including both strengths and areas needing improvement. Invite to one meeting all those who gave their input. At this meeting:

1. Report back what you heard and allow for some discussion and verification of your perceptions.

2. Tell how you reacted to hearing the feedback—what was gratifying, what was upsetting, what was confusing.

3. Communicate your plan of action, while asking for reactions or additional thoughts.

4. Close the meeting by publicly thanking people for their input.

5. If you do not feel comfortable leading this meeting yourself or believe others would be suspicious of your intent, ask a neutral person (your consultant, if you used one) to facilitate.

Asking for feedback does two things at once. First, you are getting information about yourself and your skills that can be vital to making personal improvements. Second, you are leading others to do the same thing. By example, you are encouraging them to seek information on their own performance and style.

Reward Messengers

To fully turn around the "shoot the messenger" syndrome, leaders need to make a conscious effort to reward people who speak up. The rewards we highlight are not tangible ones. They emphasize appreciation for the openness and risk taking of the messenger, demonstrate respect for the messenger's suggestions and observations through attentive follow-up action, and focus on building a constructive and ongoing relationship between you and the messenger. This will ensure your continued access to the information and insight of others.

Personally thank people for bringing forward their concerns and ideas. Most messengers come forward because they want to contribute to positive change in their work environment. Specifically thanking them for their contribution will encourage them to continue to bring things up. While you are doing this:

1. Acknowledge that speaking up is not always the easiest thing to do, particularly when it includes potential criticism or feedback on a person's style.

2. Say what you will do, when you will do it, and when and how you will report about your progress.

3. If possible, describe the way their message will have a positive impact on the organization.

4. Express your personal appreciation for the efforts that have been made.

Tell natural messengers how much you value them. Some people naturally speak up, no matter what the organizational environment is. These are individuals who have not bought into the cycle of mistrust and who are naturally open with their feedback by virtue of temperament or experience. They are willing to raise issues and challenge conventional thinking. With such characteristics, these people are invaluable in your efforts to build an environment where others who are less confident and straightforward will speak up. To reinforce their contributions:

1. Ask them to help you out by keeping you informed about issues and concerns.
2. Thank them when they bring you the news, whether it is easy or tough to hear.
3. Consider their advice carefully, and act on their suggestions whenever it is feasible.

Make changes based upon what messenger tell you. Messengers bring their news because they want things to change. If, over time, they see few results of their efforts, their willingness to bring forward tough issues will diminish, no matter how much thanks and verbal acknowledgment you give. The implication of your action is very clear: if you want to encourage people to speak up, you must—now and then—take visible action based upon their messages. A story helps to illustrate this point.

> One executive we know relies on a director of research to bring him information about the organization and feedback on his management style. On more than one occasion, he has sincerely expressed his appreciation for her straightforward candor and commitment to communicating the bad news. Frequently, the research director has provided tactful, direct feedback regarding practical changes in the executive's interpersonal style that would make communication go more smoothly in the operational units. While acknowledging the importance of these ideas, the executive's actual behavior has remained essentially the same. This apparent reluctance to respond to the research director's messages has unfortunately given a frustrating double message to this loyal messenger and seriously eroded her trust in the executive. She has begun to wonder if it is worth the effort to keep bringing him feedback when she sees so little change.

Here's an example of how another leader took a different approach.

> A front-line employee in a public agency talked to us about layoffs that had happened some years previously. The executive was criticized heavily by employees for the abrupt way in which these layoffs occurred. The employee we spoke with shared these concerns but also commended him for the way he handled the criticism: "He asked us [the employee association] to

meet with him. He didn't bury our memo criticizing the way he had handled the layoffs. He took action, setting up an employee task force to make recommendations for change. Then he acted on those recommendations. He went up in front of employees at the height of their anger. He took it all. I'll always respect him for that."

The executive did more. He continued to investigate the problems and brought in an outside consultant to assist him. This work led to several additional steps: organization-wide training in communication skills, the beginnings of a supervisory training program, revisions to policies that inhibited communication flow within the organization, and team development for people at senior levels.

Provide concrete examples of how criticism has led to improvements, savings, or innovations. Improvement efforts in an organization are often a rich source of stories that reinforce the value of tough news while praising the messengers. In one company, a staff department discovered that about 30 percent of its time was spent checking or correcting the work of others. The good news is that by evaluating several overly complex procedures, the department was able to reduce the amount of checking time significantly, along with reducing errors. The team saved about one-quarter of a staff analyst's time per year. Sharing information such as this is a way to promote the belief that tough news can be the catalyst for success. To do this:

1. Use hard data when possible, telling of production time cut, dollars saved, market share increased, customer complaints down, and compliments up.

2. Describe the personal reactions to the message, letting people know that while complex issues are not necessarily easy to hear, you have a strong desire to hear and work with the situation so that improvements can take place.

3. Celebrate and publicize this information, emphasizing learnings.

Ensure some type of response to every employee suggestion. When suggestions are made by employees, follow up on them. In Chapter Four we described a variety of behaviors that trigger fear. Failing to follow up on good-faith suggestions made by employees creates ambiguity and stimulates, for many, anxious and fearful reactions. Some people will begin to wonder if you really thought their ideas were valuable after all. From this perspective, it is an easy slide into guessing that they might have offended you or others in the hierarchy and that they are on the verge of being in big trouble. Others will interpret the situation as indicating that you don't really care about their concerns, and that your commitments were simply convenient lies to get them out of your office. To prevent such an unfortunate emergence of the cycle of mistrust, make sure you do what you say you will do:

1. Get back to people to let them know what is going to happen as a result of their suggestions. Typically, you have three options: you decide that follow-up is not necessary or possible at this time, you intend to get personally involved, or you delegate the follow-up to someone else.

2. Thank the messenger for his or her efforts, describe what you are inclined to do, and give your reasoning.

3. If the messenger does not agree or understand your point of view, be willing to discuss it; be open to reconsidering your plan if new information surfaces during this exchange.

4. If you delegate the response, describe what you will do to monitor the work someone else will do.

5. When appropriate, create some type of involvement for the messenger, for example, offer membership on a problem-solving task force or plan to meet again in a month to discuss progress.

6. If, when you delegate a response, the follow-up does not occur as planned, investigate the situation, looking for clues about communication and problem-solving barriers in your organization that need to be addressed.

Establish response to employee ideas as a priority for the managers who report to you. As with many of our suggestions for ways to build trust and reduce fear in your organization, it is important to make sure that the managers who report to you share your commitment to responding to employee suggestions. To do so:

1. Talk about these issues and strategies at your staff meetings, emphasizing the negative impact when follow-up does not occur.

2. Encourage your direct reports to reflect on and share their

own experiences of offering suggestions and getting no visible response.

3. Ensure that ways to respond to employee suggestions make up a routine part of supervisor and management training.

4. Remind people that when action has been taken, it is important to be sure that the messenger is informed about what happened and why.

Put together, these strategies create a strong statement of support for existing messengers and encouragement for new ones. In fact, the goal of the effort ought to be to make every person a messenger for the organization. A story about a manager who asks for feedback illustrates this point.

 *The Marketing Director*

A marketing department director we worked with is an enthusiastic advocate of self-managing work teams. She passionately believes in pushing decision making down in the organization and has spent a lot of time and money on pilot projects and training to help managers and employees to be effective in this new way of approaching work. Unfortunately, her personal style has been one that has confused people and caused them to hesitate to bring their concerns forward. When we first were asked to assist this person, both those who reported directly to her and employees further down in the organization told us that they could not speak freely about the concept of self-managing work teams. They did not know what it really meant for them and their roles, but they felt that speaking up would be negatively interpreted as resistance by our client.

The department director was perceived to give mixed messages about involvement and openness. A noticeable proportion of her department said that "no matter what she says, she doesn't walk the talk. So how can we trust her?" When things were not moving fast enough, she would get a sarcastic edge in her voice, rather than acknowledging, up front, her frustration and impatience. She was famous for her "look," which conveyed strong disapproval. When she would ask for input and no one spoke up, she would make the decision herself.

The director knew that things were not right but did not know what was going wrong. Fortunately, a few people within her department took the risk of talking about low morale and confusion about what "self-managing work teams really mean." With some help from us, the director sought feedback on the pilot projects as well as on her own personal style. When, at a recent staff meeting, her direct subordinates teased her, saying, "This will be remembered as the year Celia gave up 'the look,'" trust was obviously on the rise.

Being open to the messages about her personal communication style had other payoffs. Members of the group could express their confusion about the self-managing teams. Up to that point, there had been much suspicion and cynicism about "all the money that has been wasted on the self-managing work-team pilots." These comments came primarily from people who had not been directly involved in the pilots, but who had heard stories about the "amount of time spent in meetings and away from the real work."

Opening up the discussion to consider this bad news led to a more systematic survey of how people who had been directly involved felt about the pilot projects. In fact, only one out of the fifty people involved said that he would not want to be part of a pilot project if he could do it again. This surprising result caused many to rethink their assumptions about the teams. If the bad news had not surfaced, the good news would never have been believed.

The door this leader opened was one to herself. She made a concerted attempt to model the willingness to seek feedback. In fact, she asked us, as consultants, to give her feedback on her management and communication style in front of her direct subordinates. We gave her that feedback honestly, and she used it as a catalyst for further input from those who reported to her. Near the close of the discussion, the director made clear her intention to change some of her unconscious yet intimidating behaviors. She said that she hoped, and expected, that her managers would give her ongoing feedback in the areas she was trying to improve, especially in getting rid of "the look." One manager asked the important, but often unspoken, question, "And how would you like us to give you that feedback?"

This meeting represented significant progress for both the marketing director and her group of managers. The director boldly demonstrated her commitment to getting the news—positive or negative—about herself and her organization. She made it clear that she needed and wanted the support of those who work for her. And when she answered the question about how she wanted to receive the additional feedback, she paved the way for her managers to give her the support she needed to be successful.

In fact, that is exactly what occurred. In that same meeting, the group as a whole talked about their decision-making methods and the ways their habits contributed to the impression of top-down decision making in a department where there was a push toward self-managing teams. The group agreed that some of their collective patterns were a problem and made a commitment to use different methods in the future. This change fulfilled a basic objective behind our client's introduction of the pilot teams.

In this case, the marketing director stopped short of saying that she expected her managers to seek feedback on their own management and communication styles. She also did not reaffirm the need to raise and solve problems collectively in order to improve. Her actions, however, demonstrated her belief in this approach. Her willingness to publicly receive personal feedback and discuss it with her direct reports set the stage for rewarding messengers throughout the department.

New Lessons and Reflections

Thoughts on Organizational Culture

Be careful about suggestion systems that are overly complicated and time-consuming and that cannot easily be maintained. In traditional programs, employees invest many personal hours and great energy in writing up and presenting their ideas. When ideas are not responded to in a timely way or "get lost in the black hole" of a bureaucratic system, the spirit of suggestion-giving and idea-sharing is polluted. Cynicism and self-motivated competition can quickly take over. That is largely why we encourage approaches that use less formal, more personal, more spontaneous ways to ask for, respond to, and acknowledge the ideas brought forward.

Thoughts on Personal Leadership

Many organizations have spent a great deal of money training leaders to give feedback to others (for example, through performance appraisals), but few have provided training in directly asking for feedback. For this reason, many managers feel awkward and tense about the process of gathering information from others about their leadership style or other sensitive topics.

A helpful exercise is to create a script that relates to asking for feedback. Write down what your exact words would be in opening the conversation with a specific employee, colleague, or manager. Then write down how you think the other person would actually respond. Next, write down your reply or another statement and then your receiver's response. Continue the process for as long as you like. The exercise can help you prepare for tense moments you may be expecting, such as when the receiver is silent, is defensive, or provides uncomfortable information. Having visualized the conversation in this way, you are likely to feel more prepared for the real thing. You may also discover that some of your preconceptions about this type of conversation are close to worst-case thinking.

11

Reduce
Ambiguous
Behavior

In Chapter Four, we identified the ambiguous behavior of supervisors and managers as a major source of mistrust and cynicism in the workplace. In this chapter, we offer three information-oriented strategies to help reduce ambiguous behavior, shown in Grid 11.1:

■ Invite people in and help them feel welcome.

■ Give people as much clear information as possible.

■ Do not put people into double binds.

These strategies respond to the need of employees to know in clear terms what is meant by a particular communication, what is happening, or what is likely to happen.

Two other principles are important in reducing ambiguity:

■ Listen to and respond to suggestions for action.

■ Involve people in decisions.

Strategy	What This Should Accomplish
Invite people in and help them feel welcome	Help people feel valued and more comfortable with you as a person
Give as much clear information as possible	Work gets done more efficiently because people have the information they need Increased sense of ownership because people are included in the information flow
Do not put people in double binds	Reduction in the number of undiscussables Minimize the cycle of mistrust People act with integrity at work

Grid 11.1. How to Reduce Ambiguous Behaviors.

The first was addressed in Chapter Ten, and the second is examined in Chapter Thirteen.

How Ambiguous Behaviors Create Fear

The behaviors that come across as vague, confusing, and fear-producing to others at work include

- Secretive decision making
- Uninviting behaviors
- Lack of, or indirect, communication
- Lack of responsiveness to suggestions
- Inconsistency and mixed messages
- Unethical conduct

These patterns provoke fear, mistrust, and cynicism because they do not provide needed, reliable information. The facts, issues, or intentions are absent, unclear, or contradictory. This lack of information triggers a chain of events that eventually leads to fear. Consider this pattern:

- An employee sees his manager behaving in a confusing, ambiguous way.
- The employee tries to interpret this unclear or insufficient information and, in doing so, questions the manager's intentions or wonders about the extent to which he is valued, trusted, or viewed as competent.
- In the absence of additional information, the cycle of mistrust provides negative explanations for the ambiguous behavior.
- The employee becomes anxious about what the ambiguous behaviors might mean, what is really expected by the manager, or what kind of trouble might result if he asks for clarification.

In cases such as this, people frequently do not know what to do. They grope in darkness and worry about what will befall them. All they know is that they do not know. This leads to speculation, concern, and worst-case thinking. Unfortunately, when reliable information is unavailable, many people rely on the cycle of mistrust. The cycle is a ready reservoir of explanations for a mixed message, lack of feedback, or indirect communication. It encourages people to decipher in a negative way the unclarified who, what, why, and how. Lack of information combined with negative assumptions and mistrust cause people to be afraid.

Ambiguity is in the eye of the beholder. What one person sees as a practical, situational response, another views as suspicious inconsistency. One person might be confused about the accuracy of information, while another does not understand why the information was presented in the first place. While "no news is good news" for one work unit, for another it indicates that information is being hidden. Given the complexity of this response, is it possible for managers to overcome this problem of perceptions? Our answer is, in fact, a mixed message. Yes, a lot can be done to create a clear flow of information throughout an organization. No, there will probably never be a time when things are not misinterpreted to some degree. Hence, the title of this chapter asks readers to reduce ambiguous behavior, rather than eliminate it.

Invite People In and Help Them Feel Welcome

The words and actions of leaders can help people feel important and valued. Just as when you welcome a new neighbor or invite someone to your home for the first time, there is a more personal sharing of information. It is communication that says, "I want to get to know you and I want you to get to know me." This getting-acquainted process is an essential base for ongoing relationships.

In the current business environment, this is not necessarily an easy thing to do. Organizational environments are usually geared more to the head than the heart. People become oriented to using their time efficiently, taking action, and using their brains to solve problems. Talking about feelings is often regarded as a nonessential activity. In climbing the traditional corporate success ladder, some people may have learned to play their cards close to their chest. They have learned that opening up can be interpreted as a sign of naïveté or vulnerability—something that might eventually damage their credibility and influence. And of course, as a matter of culture and temperament, some people are simply less outgoing than others, less likely to disclose information about themselves or their feelings about issues at hand.

And yet employees want to know who their managers are. Their desire to get acquainted pertains to work-related competencies, personal values that guide decision making at work, the genuine feelings experienced by their managers, and other areas. They long for their managers to behave like "real-life human beings" and are delighted when it happens. When you as a manager do not come across in a full, open sense, others do not know what to expect. If you and your values and feelings remain hidden, your employees will be left to speculate and interpret both your intentions and your behavior. They will then give you what they believe you want, which may not be what you are interested in at all.

Getting close enough to people so that they have a keener, more immediate grasp of who you are as a person does not mean being friends with everyone, continually going out to lunch, or meeting each other's families. It does mean talking now and then about your feelings, values, and perceptions and encouraging others to talk about theirs. This can sometimes seem slow and unimportant but, in fact, it is a wise investment in personal credibility.

Let people know how you feel. Most people do not talk a lot about their emotions at work. Here are some things you can do to appropriately open up this aspect of the work environment:

1. Watch others who are able to share some of their emotions; notice how they do this successfully and what kind of impact they have on others.

2. As you describe your reactions to events, use "feeling" terms, such as *elated, frustrated, disappointed, grateful, angry,* and *relieved.* These are words that describe your emotional experience and give others insight into your more personal reactions to events at work.

Make time. Absence, in the business world, generally does not make the heart grow fonder. Just the opposite—it can cause people to feel unwelcome. A professional-level employee spoke with us about her manager, with whom she consulted for only one hour per month. She felt that it negatively influenced her performance to have so little contact. She wanted to be clearer about performance expectations and her role. She noticed that a coworker seemed to have almost daily contact with their supervisor and that their discussions seemed more social. Her interpretation was that favoritism was at work and that she was disadvantaged because of it.

Situations like this one bring to mind one of the difficulties supervisors must manage: the balance between too much and too little intrusion into the work of employees. As this example illustrates, this can be a problem of both amount and equity. There are individual differences in how much time a person would like with a manager and how much he or she is concerned about the closeness or distance of others. Here are some steps to take:

1. Ask people whether they are getting enough or too much of your time. Keep track of who wants more contact, who may prefer less, and their reasons.

2. Once people's individual needs are understood, do your best to accommodate them.

3. Resolve the overall question of equity by creating a routine of interactions. For example, you might decide to meet with each individual once a month for two hours and have a Monday-morning staff meeting where everyone is present.

4. Follow through on this schedule.

5. If an issue like favoritism is hot in your group, bring it out into the open and discuss it collectively. Chapter Twelve offers advice that may help you to proceed.

Use a process check. One technique that is common to group process training and that helps people feel valued in group settings is called a "process check." This is just a stopping point, during or at the close of a meeting, that gives people a chance to talk about what they like, dislike, or have questions about. If strong concerns are voiced, decisions can be made about how to improve interaction, in the remaining part of the meeting or at some designated future time. The process check gives people a chance to talk about issues that are confusing or vague. The following lead-ins are helpful in getting people to volunteer their observations about the meeting:

> *"How is this going so far? Are we getting at the things that are most important to you?"*
>
> *"Before we move on, is there anything that needs to be clarified?"*
>
> *"How is the pace? Are we going too fast? Too slow?"*
>
> *"What would make this a better use of your time?"*
>
> *"Are there any undiscussables that we've avoided here?"*
>
> *"If we were to play this conversation over again, what might we do to improve it?"*

The process check can be used in one-on-one situations as well as with groups. It can be applied in person or over the telephone. It essentially consists of slowing down the interaction to see if people's needs are being met and if course corrections need to be made.

Use common courtesy. Keep in mind the importance of basic good manners. Graciousness in interpersonal dealings invites others to feel comfortable and valued. Good manners are signs of respect that are often neglected in the pace of a busy day. Following are some of the little things that make a big difference:

- Say "please" and "thank you," and say "hello" when you see people in the hallway. If possible, call people by name.

- Do your fair share of loading paper in the copy machine or making or pouring coffee; do not act as though you are above such ordinary tasks.

- Make genuine inquiries about people's weekends, vacations, health, and family members.

- Acknowledge success or discouragement with honest enthusiasm or empathy.

When they are done sincerely, such actions are remembered as indicators of both personality and values. They imply sensitivity, concern, and respect for others. They tell people that you do not take yourself too seriously and that you do value the roles others play. To be effective, of course, these small but powerful interactions must be genuine.

Give As Much Clear Information As Possible

Managers would be wise to consider these two questions related to information flow:

- What information should be shared and with whom?

- What methods are best to ensure a fast and consistent flow of information throughout the organization?

These two concerns have a direct link to the amount of fear or trust that is present in the work environment. Access to accurate and timely information is a primary factor in making people feel included, valued, and trusted. Lack of access, or information that is wrong or late, creates the opposite effect.

Having worked with employee communication issues for years, we are always surprised at the various ways in which information is communicated to different parts of the organization. In one department a memo from the executive arrives on the front lines within an hour of its distribution to department heads. In other cases, it does not make it at all. Those who inherit their news from the grapevine rather than from their leader usually wonder what this pattern means. Being left out of the official information loop sets people up to feel excluded, as symbolized by the popular definition of "mushroom management": a philosophy of "keeping people in the dark and heaping manure on them."

The problem may be one of efficiencies rather than negative intentions. The supervisor's office may be so clogged with technical tasks and requirements that it takes a week's turnaround to get mail to the next layer of the organization. That is not how the situation will be read, however. People are most likely to perceive this as a more intentional put-down of those on the front lines who "do not need to know." That negative assumption, which properly belongs to the cycle of mistrust, may be mirrored by the past behavior of managers who honestly felt that people on the front lines should have very limited access to information.

Managers caught in the cycle of mistrust want loyalty and commitment without having to provide information. They literally ask for "blind" obedience. Instead we see people giving their best work and long-term loyalty to organizations that trust employees. Bringing people quickly into the information loop about critical issues is a symbolic and practical way to do this. Such sharing of information contributes to a sense of community and teamwork.

Clarify what information cannot be broadly shared. Given that rumor mills in most organizations are fast and fairly reliable, sooner or later most employees hear most things. In fact, very little information cannot be shared with employees throughout an organization. Some issues, however, must remain confidential. To get clear on what information needs to be tightly guarded and what can and should be quickly shared, consider questions such as the following:

- What issues need to remain confidential—by law, regulation, or business ethics?

- What other reasons would cause us to hold this information confidential or delay sharing it?

- Which of these reasons should be reconsidered because they come from negative assumptions about our employees' intentions?

- Are these reasons strong enough to outweigh the benefits that would come from being open with our employees about the issues?

- What can be said about the confidential issues without revealing information that is privileged?

Once you are clear on these issues, make sure that there is agreement among those who are involved in confidential matters as to what will and will not be said. Sometimes developing a script of words to say is a way to prevent rumors from spreading or to avoid mixed messages.

Share accurate information in a timely manner. With all other information, especially information related to changes that affect individuals and how they do their work, it is wise to figure out ways to exchange and discuss it as soon as possible. To do this:

1. Assume the positive about your employees; believe that they are interested in what is going on and will put any information you give them to good use.

2. Ask people what type of information and how much of it they need to do quality work and to feel good about the organization.

3. Once this assessment is complete, do your best to provide people with what they want and need.

4. Use e-mail and voice-mail systems to get information to people quickly and in a consistent manner.

5. Remember that information flow does not equal understanding; therefore, follow up on important and complex messages in person so that discussion can take place.

Here is an example of how one organization improved its communication system:

> In one research project funded through yearly grants of federal money, funding updates were included on the agenda of every staff meeting, even though there was frequently no news to report. Given the volatile nature of the project's funding source, staff members appreciated knowing that there was no change. Simply knowing that funding issues were a standing item on the agenda of each staff meeting helped them to feel more confident that they would be kept informed of any changes. The project director also agreed that as a standard practice, whenever she received any type of news regarding future funding she would pass it along to staff members in the form of a handwritten note that would be duplicated and distributed on the spot.

Decode confusing systems. Pay systems, performance appraisals, job placement, terminations, and budgeting are just a few of the systems that can be problematic because of their complexity and the actual or presumed need for confidentiality. Mysterious systems, combined with ambiguous behavior, can create a fearful combination for people who must operate within them. Here is an example of how complicated—and full of fear—a situation can become, even when all involved have a positive intent and basic agreement about what ought to be done.

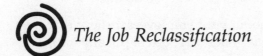 *The Job Reclassification*

A manager we know was faced with a difficult job reclassification issue. Her employee, a skilled administrative assistant in a highly visible office, had asked that her job be upgraded. When the position was evaluated by staff in the HR department, the employee's job was discovered to be three levels too low. While a promotion was clearly in order, advancing her to the level of her current work would have caused internal political problems. In working with the HR department, the manager decided that the job should be reclassified to a level one step lower than the one the assistant had expected. The manager then announced the new classification at a staff meeting, without consulting with the employee first. Because of the many projects assigned to her and other unfortunate time constraints, the manager was unable to talk to the employee about the decision in detail for several weeks. The assistant did not understand why the job had been reclassified this way and simply had to wait for the explanation.

The employee reported that she got much less work done during this time period, experienced considerable self-doubts, and had many questions about the meaning of the manager's behavior. She wanted very much to talk with her manager to find out why the reclassification was lower than she believed it ought to be. However, she was afraid that the manager might think she was challenging her, and so out of fear for her reputation she did not confront her. She also did not want to impair any future reclassification efforts. Instead, she talked to others in her office and consulted with HR staff. While nothing malicious or negative was intended on the manager's part, the ambiguity of her conduct and her lack of information about the decision created tension and a loss of credibility. It surely triggered fear, anger, and frustration for the administrative assistant.

In this case, the manager made a significant error in not immediately talking to the administrative assistant about the politics involved in her situation. Ideally, she would have talked with the employee first, before announcing the reclassification to the rest of the staff. She would have helped the assistant to understand the office dynamics, talked about her feelings, and discussed whether or not future efforts at reclassification were feasible. The manager certainly should not have delayed the discussion until several weeks after the announcement. To avoid situations like this, consider the following actions:

1. In situations where you are not inhibited by legal or procedural restraints, act quickly to let people know what is happening and why; be sensitive to the ways in which your silence can be misconstrued.

2. When it is impossible to communicate openly about a specific issue, say so to the people most affected by the situation.

3. Ask that they understand the sensitive circumstances and support you as you work with the issue in an appropriate and confidential manner.

4. Let people know why you are withholding information—for example, to protect someone's privacy or the company's competitive advantage, or perhaps on the advice of corporate attorneys.

5. Ask to be informed about rumors as soon as they surface; correct misinformation immediately and, as you do, engage people in an exploration of related undiscussable issues.

Answer people's questions. Especially in times of change, people need to have their questions answered. The trick, of course, is knowing which issues to address if they are not voicing their concerns. Thus, two skills become very helpful: anticipating questions someone might have and sensing when questions remain unanswered even after discussion. Several techniques can help you in this process:

1. In your communication, cover the basic who, what, why, and when questions.

2. Talk about the long-term and short-term benefits of the change, as well as the problems you anticipate.

3. Give background information and take extra time to allow people to understand the circumstances or reasoning behind a particular approach or decision.

4. Make sure time is set aside for discussion so that communication is two-way; during this time, ask if others have unanswered questions or confusion about points you've shared.

5. Watch for nonverbal cues from others that suggest whether or not your points are being understood and believed; if you sense they are not, ask questions to test this perception.

6. Overall, use your experience when you are in the employee role to anticipate the type of questions those who report to you might have.

Unfortunately, effective communication and efficient communication are not necessarily represented by the same conversation. While content—the what, why, and who—is essential, many people need a more deliberate discussion of the implications, feelings, and future directions associated with any particular issue. This is particularly true if emotions are high and fear is present. Be prepared to slow down and shift from content to process issues based upon what you hear from others. Asking good process questions is an effective means of finding out what else needs to be talked about. Sometimes these questions are similar to those in the process check described earlier in this chapter, but other, broader questions about how work is going can be included. Some examples are:

"Now, where are we?"

"Can you give me your understanding of my position on this issue?"

"What is it we have agreed upon?"

"What still needs to be resolved?"

"What will happen as a result of this meeting? When? Who will do it?"

"When do we check in again on this project?"

"How should we communicate what we have agreed upon to others?"

"What else do we need to talk about?"

"Have we left anything out?"

These and other similar process questions will help you to effectively answer others' questions and thus reduce the levels of fear or cynicism that may be present. They are all based on the principles of open feedback and convey the thought: "We are all in this together."

Let people know where they stand. Because people care about being well regarded at work, they want to know where they stand with their supervisors. They want to know how they are doing in terms of the quality of their work, their productivity, and their relationships with others in their work environment. And they want supportive, not threatening, ideas on how to improve in all these areas. When people do not know what is expected and do not get feedback regularly about how they are doing, they have a hard time improving their performance and often become anxious. Without performance feedback, by definition, people are working in an ambiguous work environment.

Much information about how to give ongoing performance feedback and conduct formal appraisals is available from your HR department and through libraries, bookstores, or short training sessions. Consider the following reminders as being particularly useful in reducing the ambiguity and threat frequently associated with performance feedback or appraisal:

1. Remember that performance feedback is more than an appraisal; it is an ongoing part of the supervisor-employee relationship and should be present on a daily basis.

2. Be clear about what you want from your employees and develop the ability to express those wishes so that others understand what you want and why it is important.

3. Sharpen your skills at describing behavior in neutral terms.

4. Make feedback a two-way street; ask others to share their perceptions of your performance with you.

5. With an official performance appraisal, remember that the key phrase is "no surprises within formal appraisals."

6. Conduct formal appraisals on time; late appraisals are a classic example of ambiguous behavior.

Do Not Put People into Double Binds

Double binds not only create tension; they also immobilize people, making them less capable of exhibiting the initiative and judgment that organizations need. A double bind asks people to do something that compromises their values and sets them up for confusion, disappointment, or failure. Double binds demand that a person act in a certain way while simultaneously creating barriers to behaving in that way. Managers create double binds for their employees in two ways: by sending mixed messages and by asking others to operate unethically.

Recognize and acknowledge the mixed messages you send. Given the complexity of organizational life, even the best-skilled and best-intentioned managers are likely to put out mixed messages from time to time. These are some classic examples:

- Telling people to use their discretion but warning them not to make any mistakes
- Encouraging the consideration of new approaches but cautioning people not to contradict certain established policies
- Emphasizing the need to get the job done fast—within the existing budget

Mixed messages feel like riddles handed off to others with the command, "You figure it out." They cause anyone who hears them to instinctively say, "Wait a minute. What do you really mean?" While they are far easier to recognize from the listener's perspective, it is also important for managers, as senders, to recognize and acknowledge their own mixed messages. This enables them to cut down on the number of confusing, ambiguous messages they send and to minimize the impact of those they do send. To avoid mixed messages:

1. Listen for the conditions you impose when you make an assignment or request to see if you are asking someone to do two incompatible things at once.

2. Acknowledge it when you realize that you have sent a mixed message because of your own confusion or a values conflict.

3. Engage your employees in strategy discussions about the political, operational, and human realities that have created this situation and ask how you can manage the dilemma together.

4. Consider using the following useful phrases:

   "Wait a minute. As I think about what I just asked you to do, I may have given a mixed message. Let me clarify what is most important in this situation."

"I can tell by the expression on your face that I must not have been very clear. I have to admit this is a confusing situation for me. Let me try again."

"Frankly, I feel a bit caught between two ends. I'd love to know what you think about all this and if you've got thoughts about what our best next steps should be."

Ask people to highlight mixed messages. No matter how hard you try, it is not likely that you will be able to catch all the mixed messages you send. Asking others to identify the mixed messages they hear can yield enormous clues about what people see as inconsistencies. For example, you may learn that people see a major discrepancy between the abrasive behavior of managers to employees and a demand for warm, friendly customer relations. Or they may think that current belt-tightening measures and staff reductions are related to the recent refurbishing of executives' offices.

The dilemmas that are highlighted can provide exceptional feedback to managers about the measures and explanations needed to build support from employees. In other cases, the dilemmas may not be entirely resolvable. But as the systems and business issues behind them are explored, people may come to understand and appreciate the complicated circumstances you and the organization face. And, in the long run, this effort may lead to some truly innovative solutions.

Here are some actions you might want to take with the group of people who report to you:

1. Explain the pressures and political realities that sometimes cause you to ask people to do two opposing things at once. Help people to see that what appears to be a mixed message on the surface may be, in fact, the presence of two opposing forces.

2. Ask for others' perspectives on the presence of mixed messages. Is it a big problem? What kind of confusion, frustration, anxiety, or fear does it cause for them? What patterns do they see in your behavior?

3. Tell people that you would like help in identifying mixed messages and you need their assistance.

4. If you sense that your employees might be reluctant to give such direct feedback to you, suggest the following formula.

When people hear you give a mixed message, they can say, "I hear you saying _____ but I see you doing _____," or "I hear you asking me to _____ but at the same time you want me to _____."

5. When people give you feedback, use paraphrases and clarifying questions to make sure you understood the point that was made. When appropriate, engage others who are present in a discussion that focuses on understanding the contradictory dynamics or developing action steps to minimize the confusion.

When work groups adopt specific agreements for handling mixed messages, including a method for conveying feedback, they take a giant step toward operating in a more trusting, collaborative way. Discussions and agreements like the ones we have suggested here can make it easier for members to give tough feedback, to work successfully within a changing and confusing environment, and to be forgiving and supportive of others. Be aware that these actions can open some threatening doors for people. If your situation is extreme and you know that a large amount of fear and mistrust exists in the work group, do not hesitate to bring in an outside facilitator to assist you.

Do not ask people to act unethically. Our interviews and experience tell us that only rarely do managers ask employees to do something ethically wrong. What is more likely is that a request will create a conflict in values for the employee and will thus be perceived to be unethical. In such situations, the individual is caught between the manager's demands, the organization's code of conduct, and the person's own sense of integrity. Here is an example:

> In one public agency, employees felt they had been instructed to advise citizens that a certain service was not available, but they were not to indicate that this was the result of lack of money. In fact, no other explanation seemed reasonable, so employees did not know what else to say. The directive was heard by employees as asking them to lie to the agency's customers about its services. This situation created ambiguity and tremendous frustration for employees. They could not carry out management's request without feeling compromised in some way.

Although people certainly vary in terms of their adherence to basic values, common situations to avoid include asking employees to knowingly do things that cause them to

- Lie or hide the truth
- Manipulate resources or people
- Take or use things that do not belong to them
- Hurt others
- Break or bend the law or established policies
- Say one thing and do another

Situations such as this can become extraordinarily complex to manage, even though they can crop up very quickly, sometimes when you do not anticipate a problem. Keeping communication as honest and open as possible will help to reduce the confusion, minimize fear, and—now and then—result in a reasonable solution. For example, in a hospital, an employee had to wheel abortion patients to the operating room, violating his personal values. Over time, his supervisor observed that his performance and attitude were suffering. She asked what was wrong and he was willing to explain his dilemma. Through some creative staffing efforts, she was able to arrange for him to work with other cases.

As with mixed messages, if you find that you must ask employees to do things that might put them in a compromising situation, consider taking these steps:

1. Let them know that you are aware of the dilemma you are creating.

2. Explore the situation with them so they understand the competing circumstances you face.

3. If possible, allow them to choose their level of participation.

4. If there is no choice—if you must have their involvement— let them know how much you appreciate their support.

5. If they choose to leave your work group or the organization rather than go along with what you need them to do, help them to make this transition with their integrity intact.

Given the complexity of any workday, managers have continual opportunities to behave in ambiguous and confusing ways. Because of its slippery nature, this aspect of managerial performance is difficult to evaluate and hard to target. The suggestions we have provided are offered as a place to begin. The goal is to reduce the number of inaccurate, confusing, or incomplete communications that can cause people to get caught in the cycle of mistrust.

New Lessons and Reflections

Thoughts on Organizational Culture

One of the obvious challenges of the information age is how to efficiently handle the mountain of information that technology now makes available to people. Most of us operate in a world where a touch can send information to a whole host of people, some of whom may not need or be interested in the subject. It is not uncommon for busy managers and executives to spend up to two hours a day simply answering their e-mail. The result is that many people feel overwhelmed with the flood of information. They can miss important items because they have difficulty sorting out what's important and what's not. That sense of losing track of things and not being able to keep up gets added to the pressures of a constantly changing work environment.

Even though it is part of the problem, technology can be part of the answer to this dilemma. Many types of information and knowledge can be put into on-line "pull" systems, in which the monthly report, the data summary, the list of lessons learned from a particular project, and the person to call for a certain service can be made available when people request it, rather than simply showing up on a screen or on paper, as in a "push" approach. Two key questions should be asked:

> *"What kind of information or knowledge do we need in order to be effective?"*
>
> *"How can the system make it easily available to us when we need it, and not before?"*

Thoughts on Personal Leadership

Leaders can easily become caught in the trap of not wanting to *impose* on their employees. As a result, they may not publicly share personal viewpoints that some have heard them express in private. A classic example is the leader who has a vision for the future of an enterprise but does not freely articulate it because others might assume that it is cast in concrete. People often respond to the ambiguity this lack of open communication creates by suggesting that the leader has a hidden agenda—an allegation that usually results in some loss of credibility.

If you identify with this or similar dilemmas, talk about it with your team. This can lead to a rich discussion of their background expectations of you as a leader and can begin to free everyone from making inappropriate assumptions about your role. This effort can also begin to bring to the surface key questions the team needs to ask itself:

"How much latitude do we have to set our own course—as individuals and as a team?"

"Why do we meet? What is the real aim and charter of our group?"

"How willing are we to disagree with one another and with the leader?"

As a group grapples with these questions, the level of ambiguity that is taken for granted recedes. Openness to questioning the background assumptions fosters team learning and enhances everyone's leadership.

12

Discuss the Undiscussables

One of the best and most powerful ways to begin overcoming fear's influence is to discuss the undiscussables. It is a rich technique for accessing the hidden issues and problems covered up in relationships, work groups, and the organization as a whole. As with all the strategies we present, discussing the undiscussables is not a one-time event. It can be an excellent approach for a team-building retreat or special problem-solving meeting. It is also a principle of disclosure that should become a part of everyday communication. Of all the ideas and suggestions included in the first edition of this book, we have relied on discussing undiscussables—along with the cycle of mistrust—most of all.

This chapter offers a variety of ideas that you can use to reduce the number of undiscussables in your work environment, captured in Grid 12.1. Even though we most frequently refer to group situations, the techniques we suggest are also applicable to individual settings.

Strategy	What This Should Accomplish
Introduce the concept	Others will understand the dynamics of issues that are hard to bring up A common terminology will make it easier to discuss complex issues
Describe the process and set the ground rules	People will feel safe in moving ahead with the discussion Clear agreements will help guide behavior if discussion becomes difficult People see a model that they can use in other situations
Identify the undiscussables	People will know what others have a hard time talking about People will learn what issues have priority for discussion
Talk about the undiscussable issues	Shared clarity and understanding about troubling issues Resolution of some issues Increased trust of and insight about group members
Follow through	Ensure action on issues that need to be and can be addressed
Work with core undiscussables	People leave the discussion with an understanding of the emotions at the heart of their reluctance to speak up Open acknowledgment of the patterns of fear and powerlessness experienced in the organization

Grid 12.1. How to Discuss the Undiscussables.

Some Reminders About Undiscussables

As you put our suggestions to work, remember that undiscussables should be treated with respect and handled with care. Uncovering what people are not talking about and why they are not talking requires sensitivity. Such discussions frequently involve self-esteem, private work anxieties, and strong feelings such as anger or frustration. People take their undiscussables personally. Yet given the right environment and the right leadership, individuals can become remarkably open about issues that may have been hidden for a long time.

Definition

As we emphasized in Chapter Five, the focus is on issues that people hesitate to talk about in legitimate problem-solving forums. Sometimes they are brought up and discussed, but doing this requires thought and courage. The subjects feel risky. Those who do bring them up worry that they may suffer some type of repercussion for doing so. Mostly people talk about undiscussables in settings where no action can take place to resolve their concerns. These conversations feed the rumor mill and take on the tone of gossip, unresolved complaints, and other sources of cynicism.

Descriptions and Metaphors

When setting the stage for talking about undiscussable issues, it is sometimes useful to have well-tested phrases that explain the process you will follow and the issues themselves. Here are some that we have found useful:

> *"Undiscussables are secrets everyone knows. The process we'll be using is a safe one that is respectful of each person involved. We'll all agree on how to have this conversation before we move ahead."*

> *"Before we get into our discussion of the issues, we will help people feel ready to explore the concerns that have been identified. One way to think about this is as a series of pools and waterfalls, where we fill up the first pool with understanding and clarity before the water spills out, naturally moving us on to the next pool."*

"Undiscussable issues are often like onions or rings on a cross section of a tree trunk. Some are on the external surface and are easier to see or get to. Other issues, at the core, take a bit more work and care."

Guidelines for Use

The irony in all this is that people very much want to talk about what they have a hard time talking about. The key to liberating this willingness has everything to do with your leadership. To get the best from discussing undiscussables, you will want to do the following things.

Create a safe, blame-free environment. People will talk easily about undiscussables when they are asked in a sincere, natural way. Ensure confidentiality and sufficient time for a thorough discussion.

Accept the undiscussables, whatever they are. Take a nonjudgmental approach. Explore what each issue means to people and how they feel about it. Clarify the issues; share relevant facts, feelings, or perceptions; and identify any necessary changes in behavior, systems, or practices.

Don't try to deal with every undiscussable in a group setting. How a member's family situation or drinking problem affects the work can be better handled through one-on-one coaching plus referral to an employee assistance program or an appropriate agency. If such an issue comes up, tell the group that they have raised a legitimate issue, but one that cannot be resolved by them. Encourage respect for the employee's privacy and feelings. Reassure the others that appropriate action will be taken to help the employee, and make sure that it is. If the employee is present when the issue arises in the group, follow up later to discuss with the person his or her feelings about the meeting.

Remember that a personal circumstance that has no impact on work is not germane. As part of its definition, an undiscussable is an issue that—because it is not discussed—has a negative impact on quality, productivity, or job satisfaction.

Be sure to set ground rules. When you are using a special problem-solving meeting or retreat to discuss undiscussables, remember that the goal is to discuss work-related issues in a constructive, mutually supportive way. Discussing the undiscussables is not like being in a therapy group. Remind people that the purpose of discussion is to identify work-oriented problems in order to move forward together, not to place blame.

Do not use the concept of undiscussables to deal with issues you should manage personally. If you know that one of your employees is having significant performance problems, coach and supervise. Do not set up a "discuss the undiscussables" event that unnecessarily highlights the person's performance failings or uses peer feedback as blackmail.

Introduce the Concept

The first thing to do is to decide how you would like to introduce others to the concept of undiscussable issues. We present two methods that show different levels of involvement. The approach you choose needs to match the current trust levels among members of your team. Your approach should push a little on people's comfort zones without overwhelming them.

Use an informal introduction. One low-key method is to simply raise the idea of discussing undiscussables and see what happens. You will be modeling what it is like to bring up a sensitive topic. One way to do this is by talking about one of your own undiscussables. In the course of operational problem solving with your team, you might informally use the concept to get at a hidden point. A discussion might take the following form.

You say, "Let's go back and talk about scheduling for a minute. I get the feeling that some of these project costs have become undiscussable for us."

"What do you mean, 'undiscussable'?" questions one of the group.

"Undiscussables are things people are feeling hesitant to talk about in this room, with those who can help to resolve the issue," you reply, pausing.

"Well," says somebody else, "those costs might be a little outrageous."

Sprinkling the idea of undiscussables into your day-to-day dealings will encourage others to apply the term on their own. Notice that you have not introduced the concept of fear—why things are undiscussable—at all. This quick and easy approach works because people instinctively know what undiscussables are. They generally dislike them and welcome opportunities to get them out in the open. To begin this approach:

1. Identify an issue that you or others might be worried about discussing because of some type of possible repercussion.

2. Use the term *undiscussable* as a way to naturally describe the point you are raising.

3. Watch for clues from others that will let you know whether or not they understood your point; if not, slow down and explain what you meant, as we illustrated in the scenario.

4. Periodically in your interactions with others, simply use the words *undiscussable* or *undiscussability*.

By raising issues in this way, you reassure others that it is acceptable to talk about sensitive issues. You communicate that openness is valued and, in doing so, encourage others to join you in an honest effort to resolve issues that have been avoided in the past. And all this is done without making a big deal out of the situation.

Brief your group on undiscussable issues. To use the concept of undiscussables in a more direct fashion, follow these steps:

1. Explain to the group that you want to create a more open environment where people talk freely about work-related problems.

2. Tell them that you are intrigued by some new ideas to help teams develop and are interested in getting their reactions.

3. Use the figures in Chapters Five, Six, and Seven to summarize our findings about typical undiscussables, why people don't speak up, and the associated costs.

4. Then ask the group two questions:

"In what ways do these findings mirror or differ from your own experience of organizations in general?"

"To what degree do these findings reflect our own organization, division, or work group?"

5. Accept whatever is said, using it to gauge the readiness of the group to move forward; if you hear denials of any type of problem related to speaking up, say:

   "I'm glad you feel so positive. I want to make sure that feeling always stays with us. I wonder, though, what we—or I—can do to improve things."

   "I wonder if everyone here feels the same way. Does anyone here besides me feel uncomfortable bringing issues up from time to time?"

   "I'd really like to pursue this with our group more fully. How could we go about getting to the heart of some of the issues we know we've avoided?"

6. Don't push hard; let the conversation develop naturally. Be patient and don't overtalk. Suggest that people consider using the concept of undiscussables in future interactions with you and with each other.

7. Within one to three weeks, find a time when the group is together again to ask if people have thought about the concept of undiscussables. Then you might say:

   "I wanted to follow up on our conversations about undiscussables. Has anyone found the idea useful?"

   "How has it come up for you?"

   "There are ways to more deliberately look at the undiscussables in our group. Is there interest in moving ahead with that?"

Describe the Process and Set the Ground Rules

When interest in talking about undiscussable issues is expressed, it is important to quickly let people know that there are safe ways to proceed. Describing the process and setting the ground rules for discussing undiscussables is an important first step. If your group already has established norms for effective meetings, you may be able to simply remind people that your normal agreements apply to this particular discussion. If these norms do not exist, you may want to create some special guidelines for moving ahead. To begin:

1. Identify the steps in the process as (a) agreeing to the ground rules, (b) listing the undiscussables, (c) talking about the issues, and (d) following through with needed actions to resolve the remaining concerns.

2. Consider bringing in an outside facilitator if your group experiences a lot of mistrust and cynicism or if you want to participate fully as a group member and not worry about leading the discussion. You might want to consult the group on this issue to see if there is a strong preference.

3. To clarify the ground rules, ask questions like these:

   "What agreements can we make about how we want to approach the discussion of these tough issues?"

   "Do we want to add any special guidelines to the way we already go about our meetings?"

   "How will we handle something if people show strong emotion or if there is significant disagreement?"

4. Use a brainstorming technique, listing all the suggestions before the group shifts to discussion. In certain cases, each item suggested is valuable and can stay on the list; at other times there needs to be some discussion and elimination or rewording of items. Use consensus as a way to make these decisions (see Chapter Fifteen).

5. Once the list has been agreed to, make sure that it is in plain sight during the next steps in the process. If people seem nervous about moving ahead, you may want to write up the list and distribute a copy to each person in the group.

There is no one right set of ground rules for discussing undiscussables. As you can tell from the questions we have suggested, it is important to have agreement about how people will behave if strong emotions and conflict surface. It is not uncommon for groups to identify agreements such as these:

Speak for yourself, from your own experience.

Describe the issue and be ready to say how it gets in your way.

Be honest about your feelings and what you'd like to see.

Don't blame.

Use neutral, rather than judgmental, words to describe things.

Separate the systems issues from interpersonal concerns.

Paraphrase when you don't understand or when you disagree.

Remember that we are all in this together and that we all want things to improve.

Be willing to give and receive feedback.

Identify the Undiscussables

There are three basic ways to identify undiscussable issues. People can identify them on the spot, in the meeting where you plan to discuss them. Members of the group can bring a list of them to the meeting. Or, if you are using an outside consultant, this person can meet individually with people to confidentially record the issues, then report them back to the whole group at the discussion meeting, without using names. Whatever method you use, the primary question to ask is this:

"What issues do you [or we] have a hard time talking about with the people needed to resolve the concerns?"

If the question is phrased as "What issues do *you* have a hard time talking about?" it is more personal, more powerful, and more threatening than if the question is "What issues do *we* have a hard time talking about?" Either approach will surface important concerns. Some groups like the bolder, more personally focused approach, sensing that it creates greater ownership for what is about to be discussed. In other situations, the more gentle and general method creates greater comfort for moving ahead. Typically, undiscussables fall into one or more of the following categories:

- Unfavorable situations or events
- Complex issues, programs, or initiatives
- System inadequacies
- Another person's behavior, style, competence, or motives, especially those characteristics in leaders
- Personal doubts, questions, or fears
- Cycles of mistrust

Before moving ahead with any discussion, make sure that people understand the definition of undiscussables and the problems they can cause, agree to the ground rules for the conversation, and know the general process for conducting the discussion. Allow at least two hours for this type of meeting if your group consists of twelve or fewer people; if it is larger, allow at least three to four hours. When the issues are complex and the group is large, an entire day can be spent in fruitful exploration of undiscussable issues.

Identify the issues at the discussion meeting. This approach works well for groups that are ready to take greater risks, or where people agree that the issues need to be explored *right now*. To identify the issues:

1. When the discussion begins, remind people of the ground rules for discussing undiscussables.

2. Ask those present to form small groups of three to five people. With someone in each group recording the issues, give the groups time to each build a list. After twenty to thirty minutes, ask one person to report on the issues that have been discussed. Then build a list for the whole group, using flip-chart pages or a white board, where all concerns are recorded.

3. If the group size is under twelve, another, more direct, way to build the list is simply to ask the question and record the answers that people offer, using the flip chart or white board.

4. Once the list has been built, ask the whole group to look for overlaps and commonalities in the undiscussables that were identified. Eliminate duplicate items. Give people a chance to ask for clarification of the meaning of items they do not understand.

5. Once the items have been clarified, prioritize the list. This can be done by rank-ordering the issues for discussion. Here are two options for the questions that you might ask to narrow the group's focus. Use either method 1 or method 2. The two-question approach creates a safe way to get to the most valuable undiscussables to address.

Method 1:

"Which of these issues can we do something about?"

feedback requesting uninterrupted staff meetings and seek agreement on this one issue.

This process usually convinces people that they have more power than they had imagined. People recognize that they can have an influence when they commit to a plan of action, and cynicism, powerlessness, and fear have less room to grow.

Use powerlessness as a bridge to explore fear of repercussions. When the issue of powerlessness surfaces, the stage is often set to more fully examine the patterns involved in the fear of repercussions. The following questions may prompt high-risk, yet highly important, discussions:

> *"Which of the barriers to our influence or control relate to systems in the organization? To personnel systems in particular? Which relate to the general way we go about doing things around here?"*
>
> *"When people talk about powerlessness, how much of that reflects a cynicism about management in general? About top management? About me?"*
>
> *"How many of the undiscussable items reflect a fear of repercussions? What kind of repercussions? What is our evidence for believing that this is the case? What influence do we have on eliminating these repercussions?"*

Such questions can lead the group to a new level of communication and may result in another round of discussions about undiscussables. As people search for the sources of their thoughts and feelings, they may uncover past events: an experience at the negotiating table, a derogatory comment from an upper-level manager, a negative experience with a coworker, or something else that still operates behind their feelings. Individuals have a chance to test their own perceptions against the general assessment of the group and determine for themselves whether their private anxieties are justified. As with all undiscussables, bringing the core issues into the bright light of group discussion reduces their mysterious power and usually proves them to be normal-sized concerns quite capable of being resolved.

By being willing to directly discuss the perception of powerlessness and the fear of repercussions, you and your team will be addressing the most central fears of people at work. As a manager, you will be demonstrating in a very genuine way that you

- Do not discount people's fears
- Are willing to remove the labels, judgments, and loss of credibility that traditionally go with speaking up about repercussions
- Are willing to consider information collaboratively and hunt with others for the facts of particular situations

On the surface, this may not seem like anything radical. But in organizations where people have avoided undiscussables for years, such an action can represent a significant new trend. Talking about these core issues is a vital point in the effort to reduce fear, because it deals with the reasons why people do not speak up. It addresses these fears directly, bringing a new openness to communication within your immediate work environment.

What to Do If Things Begin to Go Wrong

In most cases, discussions of undiscussable issues go very well, provided that the process is clear and the mutually agreed-upon ground rules are observed and supported. However, given the powerful emotions that are often at the source of people's experience with undiscussability, it is wise to be prepared for whatever may come along. If things begin to feel out of hand:

1. Slow down. Take a deep breath and pause to observe what is happening inside yourself and with members of the group.

2. Ask others for observations about how things are going. Make statements like these:

   "All of a sudden it feels as though the tension has shot straight up. Can we pause for a few minutes to talk about what's happening and how people are feeling?"

   "The issues that have surfaced have obviously triggered some strong emotions. I'm wondering how people are feeling about what's just been said."

3. Review the ground rules and reinforce the value of abiding by them. You might want to say:

   "Our ground rules remind us to paraphrase each other's comments at moments like this. Can we do that for what's just been said?"

"I think it's important that we remember to speak for ourselves and not cast blame on others. Joe, is there another way you can express what you've just said?"

4. Ask how people are feeling and why. This is particularly useful when someone has behaved in a way that breaks the ground rules or has shared information that others find upsetting. It is important, when people share their feelings, to allow time in between statements so that they do not feel rushed.

5. Talk about the process problems with the group. Summarize how you see the issues and ask others for their viewpoints. Say:

"Some people seem ready to go on to action steps, yet others have said we need to take more time to talk about what caused the problem in the first place. Are there any thoughts about how we can handle the remaining time we have today?"

"It seems as though we've reached an impasse here, where we cannot come to agreement about what to do next. What suggestions do you have for how we might move ahead?"

"Frankly, I feel stuck at this moment and need some ideas about how to clarify these points, which seem so confusing. Can someone help out?"

6. Call a break and evaluate the situation privately or with key members. This tried-and-true technique gives people a chance to stretch, get a breath of fresh air, and come back to a meeting room where the tension has been at least slightly relieved. During the break, check with people who represent different perspectives about what has happened in order to gather input on how to move ahead. Quickly evaluate how you are feeling and the possible actions the group might take.

7. Decide whether or not to proceed. If you believe that tensions are so high and good judgment is so limited that people will not be able to honestly abide by the ground rules, bring the discussion to a close. If you do this, say what you want to do, give your reasons, ask for support of your decision, and say what you will do next to continue the work on resolving the issues that have surfaced. Be prepared for the possibility that others might want to keep going. If you truly believe that the conversation cannot get back to a constructive and respectful track, reassert your decision to end the meeting.

8. Close down the discussion, and soon after the meeting seek advice and make a decision about what to do next. Let people know as soon as possible how you'd like to move ahead. Reopen the discussions with a plan to resolve the problem.

9. After the meeting, talk to people individually to resolve concerns and reinforce your positive intention of moving forward with positive results and positive relationships.

The Power of Discussing Undiscussables

It is not uncommon for a group that has identified fifteen or twenty undiscussable issues to see no need to continue with the rest of the list after they have discussed the first five. The magic of this strategy is that it powerfully demonstrates trust, open communication, and collaboration—so much so that sometimes certain issues disappear because of what is happening in the group.

Discussing undiscussables is a powerful technique. In our experience, it has always been worth the time and effort put into the preparation, discussion, and follow-up. In some cases, the discussions turn out to be much less scary than people think they will be. But this approach should never be taken lightly, because some very serious matters can be put on the table for discussion. For example, in one organization, a small team of middle managers and their leader used a discussion of undiscussables to initiate a long-term team development process.

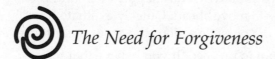 *The Need for Forgiveness*

The team of eight looked back over the almost forty undiscussable issues on several pages of flip charts and began to think about the most important and sensitive of the topics. Decisions of all kinds had become stalled in the team, and a facilitator had been hired to help members find out what the problem was. Now, rating their undiscussables carefully, it became apparent that one, "Racial tension in the group," was at the top of the list. Just seeing this outcome for the four white and four African American middle managers raised the anxiety level in the room. This wasn't a new problem for the team, but they had never talked about it openly.

To help the conversation get started, their facilitator began to ask some open-ended questions: "What has caused this issue to come to the top now? To what extent do you agree that this is what needs to be addressed?" The group remained silent.

To break the tension, the facilitator asked the group to get up out of their chairs and move to more comfortable seats in another part of the room. The move helped to get a large conference table out of the way and enabled people to sit in a more informal setting. "Let's try it again," the facilitator suggested. "Could someone start our discussion by sharing personal feelings about this issue?"

"Well," began one of the team, with a slight tremor in her voice, "if we are going to really talk about this, there will need to be some real forgiveness in this room. I'm going to have to tell some of you how I think you've helped create this tension and I expect you'll want to tell me how I've helped it along, too. We'll need to be honest." She sat back in her chair. Others acknowledged that what she had said was true, that honesty and forgiveness needed to be the norms for the group as they worked together.

Slowly, other members of the group began to communicate. One said, "I think you all have a certain opinion of me—that I'm a very territorial manager. I'd like to tell my story so you understand why I've acted the way I have."

"You knew we thought that about you?" said another member, a little shocked. "Sure," came the reply. "Let me explain why I didn't say anything." When he finished, the team members recognized how quick and inaccurate their judgment of their colleague had been. Soon other perceptions that had been locked behind a wall of undiscussability began to surface.

From this awkward—and heartfelt—starting point, the group's conversation began to gather steam. The team spent the entire afternoon exploring one issue after the next that had never been aired directly and openly. By the time the session ended, it was apparent that many issues had become entangled with perceptions of racial tension in the group. By honestly acknowledging that tension, they were able to move constructively into the host of negative assumptions about one another that had accumulated over the years. They set up a schedule to meet regularly over the next few months to clear the air, deal with their differences, and do some healing. The meeting to discuss undiscussables became a powerful starting point for this work.

As this story reveals, discussing undiscussables can be hard work that taps into people's deepest values, beliefs, and emotions. But it can also be just the breakthrough called for to begin moving toward the trust end of the continuum.

Carrying out the steps we've suggested in this chapter is likely to institutionalize the concept of undiscussables. The concept will surface from time to time in conversation as an introduction to a sensitive topic, a red flag on an issue that needs attention. This ongoing search for undiscussables becomes a means to ensure that trust is continually being built. It helps to guarantee that new, better ways of doing things are not quashed under the weight of some possible repercussion or the conclusion that speaking up will do no good. You and your team will find yourselves talking about concerns as they come up, long before they become sensitive and frightening topics. In such cases you will no doubt observe the delightful irony that the more you are able to talk about undiscussables, the fewer there will be to discuss.

New Lessons and Reflections

Thoughts on Organizational Culture

When people are asked to identify undiscussables, they will often take advantage of the opportunity to raise concerns about systems or policies. Once the beliefs about these issues, their impact, and emotional reactions relating to them have been explored, a decision needs to be made: should any action be taken to help resolve these concerns? If the answer is yes, focus the group on what they can do to help move the issues to the next step. Good questions to ask include these:

"Is this an issue that we control or that we can influence?"

"If we can only influence the outcomes, who are the key decision makers we need to influence?"

"What do we know about them? What types of information or arguments might sway their thinking?"

"Are there any timelines that need to be taken into consideration?"

"Do we have all the information and understanding we need in order to resolve this issue or make a solid recommendation to someone else?"

"If not, what else do we need to learn?"

"Where might we find this information?"

"Who might help to improve our understanding of the issues?"

At the close of such discussions, it is possible to quickly create an informal action plan. This will aid people in following through on their commitments and help the group to keep track of its strategy for resolving concerns or influencing those who can. So that everyone involved can see, create a three-column grid, with the words "What," "Who," and "By When" at the top of the columns. Then list the actions the group has decided to take, filling in who will do them and the completion date. Make sure to include the date when the group will meet again to review its progress. Put today's date on the notes, duplicate them, and distribute them to all members immediately.

Do whatever is necessary to keep the group moving forward on its action plans. If you do, confidence and trust will increase as people see that their concerns are being taken seriously and that things can change as a result of their collective effort. Throughout all this, your role may include playing the facilitator, the strategist, the information giver, and the advocate.

Thoughts on Personal Leadership

When frustrations have been repressed for a long time, it is easy to worry that discussing undiscussables will cause negative emotions and feelings to come to the surface in an uncontrolled way. If you are concerned about this, it is a good idea to talk about your responsibilities as leader before the discussion begins. People may expect you to intervene, to protect them, or to take sides as they express their perspectives. Make it clear that you *share* the responsibility for keeping things constructive, but that you cannot—and should not—try to fully control the discussion. Such statements can feel threatening to teams where little emotion has been expressed in the past, so, if necessary, go back to establishing ground rules and stay with that part of the discussion until people are comfortable moving forward.

One simple question that can help as people open the door to tough or sensitive issues is "What are we learning?" This question can be used to help people summarize new understandings about the topic under consideration or it can be used to help them evaluate *how* they are talking about this topic.

In an executive team meeting where frustrations and pressures were running high, several people expressed deep personal discouragement about being able to make progress with undiscussable issues. Some angry personal criticisms slipped into the conversation along with several indirect, ambiguous statements that caused confusion and mistrust. Within moments, the tension level escalated dramatically. Luckily a facilitator was present and asked what the group was learning from this uncomfortable exchange.

The next hour was spent carefully reviewing what had happened at each step in the conversation and exploring the way that misunderstandings had quickly turned to accusations. What at the outset had seemed like an awkward and painful meeting became a source of new information about the people who were present, their styles, their assumptions, and their legitimate grievances. Members learned that to go forward they would need to avoid general or indirect disagreements, a hostile tone of voice, and all forms of "sniping." They saw how failing to look into one another's eyes as they spoke and forgetting to use one another's names led to misunderstandings and reinforcement of negative assumptions about motives. While these were tough lessons, their in-the-moment quality left an indelible impression on the team. The learnings from the meeting quickly generated a powerful new set of norms for the future.

13

Collaborate
on Decisions

D ecision-making processes are at the core of organizational life. Responsibility for particular decisions determines the nature of jobs and roles; the power structure and hierarchy; peer, supervisor, and employee relations; one's influence on others; and, thus, the organization. In this chapter we offer an easy-to-use model for decision making and a variety of suggestions on how to increase collaboration in your work group. These strategies are summarized in Grid 13.1.

The patterns of decision making have an enormous impact on how people think and feel. Concerns about this area appeared throughout our interviews in a variety of ways. For example, of the behaviors that generate fear, secretive decision making was singled out as a critical component of ambiguous behavior (see Chapter Four). When people have been left out of decisions, they often feel powerless and unneeded. They become dependent on others, anxious about their value to the organization, cynical in their dealings, and understandably resistant to well-intentioned

Strategy	What This Should Accomplish
Become aware of current decision-making patterns	Increases insight about present decision-making habits and preferences for the future
Seek input on decisions	Broadens the base of ideas and information to improve decisions and support for those decisions Increases trust and communication
Manage consensus	Effective and efficient group decisions that will be easier and faster to implement Increases trust, communication, and teamwork
Communicate about decisions that have been made	Increases the likelihood that those who are not highly involved in making the decision will support it Increases trust and communication

Grid 13.1. How to Collaborate on Decisions.

efforts to empower people. This leads them to experience the meaning of Peter Block's observation: "I fear those that I feel dependent on" (1987, p. 10).

There is increasing pressure on anyone in a leadership role today to involve people in decisions. Our workforce is now composed of people who expect to participate. Management theory has evolved over the last forty years to encourage participative and delegated decisions. For many leaders it is taken as an article of faith that

- Those who make the product or provide the service have essential information necessary for improving quality and making sound decisions

- People who have some say in decisions that affect them are much more likely to carry out those decisions with enthusiasm and effectiveness

And yet, from our interviews and what we see with our clients, we have come to believe that many managers' good intentions about effective decision making go unfulfilled. This is particularly the case when decisions require collaboration between levels of an organization. Frequently, there is a lack of clarity about the real decision that needs to be made, how it is to be made, and who to involve. It is not uncommon for leaders who see themselves as open and participative to be viewed by those who work for them as top-down managers who are inconsistent in the way they handle decisions. In such cases, unclear or misunderstood decision making causes mistrust, confusion, miscommunication, a sense of powerlessness, and alienation. As the many stories we have told in previous chapters attest, where feelings such as these exist, fear is not far behind.

A Simple Model for Decision Making

Many models have been created that can help individuals and groups to be more effective in their decision making. The model in Figure 13.1 has been used successfully with a variety of clients. It was developed several years ago as part of an effort to help the leadership group of a six-hundred-member city department better understand employee complaints about decision making. The model modifies Tannenbaum and Schmidt's well-known leadership styles continuum (1957, p. 96). We also use a continuum, but we have five points on our scale, rather than seven.

The model asserts that leaders make decisions using five methods. By the term *leader*, we mean the person responsible for making sure that the decision is made.

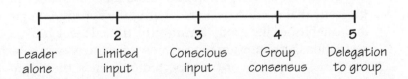

1	2	3	4	5
Leader alone	Limited input	Conscious input	Group consensus	Delegation to group

Figure 13.1. Five-Point Decision-Making Model.

Source: Adapted from Tannenbaum and Schmidt, 1957.

■ *In method 1, the leader makes the decision alone.* No outside input is sought.

■ *In method 2, the leader makes the decision with limited input.* This input is informal and unplanned, from the person the leader has lunch with, carpools with, or meets with late on a Thursday afternoon, or from a next-door neighbor.

■ *In method 3, the leader makes the decision with consciously designed input.* Here the leader assembles a plan that will gather helpful input, considering who will be affected by the decision; various expertise, experience, and values that need to be heard; representation of different levels of the organization; who will be important in implementing this decision; and the data relating to the issue to be decided. We use the term *participative* to describe this type of decision making.

■ *In method 4, the leader and the group make the decision together.* This is what we refer to as *collaborative* decision making. With this method, the leader may initiate the decision-making process but essentially operates as an equal member of the team. Sometimes a facilitator is called in to allow the leader to fully participate as an equal member of the group. The group operates from a consensus model, in which members work together so that the decisions are acceptable to everyone. This does not mean that everyone is in total agreement, but all members do agree that the decisions made will guide their individual actions. We recommend "what we can agree to so we can move forward together" as an operational definition of consensus.

■ *In method 5, the leader delegates the decision to a group.* In this last method, the group collectively makes the decision without the leader's presence. In such situations, the leader turns the issue that needs a decision over to the appropriate group and establishes the group's authority. If the leader has restrictions or minimum requirements for the way in which the decision is made or the expected outcomes, they should be identified and understood up front. After that, the group handles the decision in whatever way it sees fit—usually modeling method 4 by consensus without the leader. The leader becomes reinvolved only if the decision appears to be significantly off track or if it negatively influences issues out-

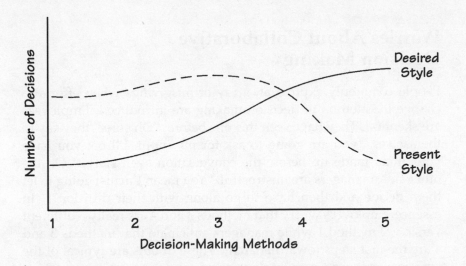

Figure 13.2. Trends Toward Collaboration.

side the group's sphere of knowledge. Otherwise, the group is considered responsible for the decision.

Each of these methods is effective and appropriate depending on the situation. There is no one right way. We have found, however, that many organizations are interested in pushing more decisions toward methods 4 and 5, as illustrated with the graph in Figure 13.2. The point is that not all decisions are made according to methods 4 and 5, but more are being made in that way than have been in the past.

This gradual transition toward more collaborative methods is one that many managers can immediately understand and aim for. The traditional worry that participative methods mean a loss of power or control is mitigated by knowing that not every operational situation or urgent dilemma becomes a group decision. The focus is on finding opportunities to move method 2 decisions toward methods 3 and 4, and method 3 toward methods 4 and 5, when the leader determines that this is appropriate. Generally, this shift occurs slowly as people adjust to new methods and develop their skills. When the use of methods 4 and 5 increases, it is a sure sign that trust is on the rise.

Worries About Collaborative Decision Making

People commonly express an array of misgivings when efforts to change the method of decision making are introduced. Employees are skeptical. They have seen this one before. "Oh sure," they say to themselves, "you are going to ask for my input. I'll bet you have your mind made up before the conversation even starts." On the other side, managers are mistrustful: "You mean I'm just going to let them decide and then have to go along with their decision?!" In essence, employees worry that methods 3 and 4 are really a different version of method 1 while managers anticipate that methods 3 and 4 are the first steps toward anarchy. These doubts are typical of the cynicism and worst-case thinking some employ as the discussion on decision making begins.

In both cases we think that the real source of anxiety is method 4. People are skeptical that it can really work. Because of previous bad experiences, some believe that it is impossible for individuals at different organizational levels to sit down together, thoroughly evaluate a problem, and come to a trustworthy agreement. Both managers and employees imagine that at some time decisions will come down to a matter of rank, and that rank, for better or worse, will prevail.

Collaborative decision making is therefore the most necessary skill to acquire. Of all the decision-making methods, method 4 is the one that most directly results in a reduction of fear. As a group gets better at collaboration, members see that the leader does not have all the right answers, yet does not pull rank. It is possible to work things through to consensus. The leader discovers that the group is rational and committed to a quality decision. It is not necessary to fear that members will force self-interested practices on the organization. The cycle of mistrust is overcome by method 4.

Developing these skills and the trust that goes along with them does not occur quickly. People may have operated for a long time in constricted settings where they believed that only methods 1, 2, or 3 were possible or right. By comparison, method 4 feels very new. They do not know if they can do it, or even if they want to do it. Method 4, after all, implies a level of partnership and

responsibility that can change the whole fabric of their relationships with their peers, customers, and supervisors. It changes the
role of the leader. People's expectations about what they and the
organization can do may be very low, and method 4 can feel like an
incredible stretch. Method 5, for such beginning groups, is usually
unthinkable.

The Role of the Leader

Managers, as leaders of the decision-making process, are responsible for the tasks in the following list. As groups move toward an
increased reliance on methods 4 and 5, some of these tasks may be
de-emphasized or transferred to the group. You will want to become
comfortable with

- Describing the various methods and the roles of people
  within each approach
- Starting the process by deciding which method should be
  used to make the decision and communicating with the
  group about the method
- Initially framing the question to be decided
- Facilitating and/or participating in meetings where methods
  3 and 4 are used
- In methods 1, 2, and 3, clarifying or communicating the decision once it has been made and explaining the reasoning
  behind the decision

One tricky aspect of collaborative decision making is managing your role as the leader throughout the process. You may want
to ask group members to facilitate the decision-making meetings or
to bring in someone from the outside to play that part. This will
enable you to function more as an equal member of the group,
something that is particularly important if you are using method 4.
If that is not possible, you may need to wear two hats at once—the
facilitator of the decision-making process and the person in charge
of the work group. In this case, you will be well served by developing strong skills in group facilitation. To do this, you might want to
seek guidance from your organization's training and development

professionals, local professional associations, or workshops offered by local colleges and universities.

Once you are in the decision-making meetings, regardless of your specific role, follow these guidelines:

1. Hold your comments until several others have spoken. If you jump in right away, you may unnecessarily sway the group.

2. Use your listening skills. Paraphrase what you hear others say, especially before you disagree with them.

3. If you find yourself needing to speak as the leader, announce that you are doing so. For example, you might say:

   "Let me put on my department manager hat for a minute."

   "If you don't mind, I'd let to set aside the facilitator role for a few minutes and share some background information that might prove useful."

4. At the end of a decision-making session, ask the group for feedback. Ask specific questions like these:

   "Did I dominate the conversation at any point? If so, how did that happen? What impact did it have?"

   "Did you have a sense that you were in the decision as an equal?"

   "What could I do next time to increase the sense of collaboration in the group?"

The ultimate goal of this work is to develop an environment where no one is worried about your managerial role and your broader authority. An example of this might be a situation in which people feel free enough to openly ask you to save your ideas until all members of the group have had a chance to express their views. Once such trust has been established, it is possible to imagine a time when you and the team will operate so effectively that no one will worry about when you offer your input.

The end result of performing these tasks is that you will facilitate the development of the group as it moves toward methods 4 and 5, with members building their problem-solving and decision-making skills. Instead of being responsible for tackling all the dilemmas yourself, you share responsibility for them using method 4. This effort is the major tool with which to address the fear caused by secretive decision making.

When people have become skilled at collaborative problem solving, the following traits are typical:

■ The group works from an agenda; it moves quickly from decision to decision as it addresses needed topics within a known but flexible time frame.

■ There are numerous "process" comments, such as "How do the rest of you feel about this?" and "I think we are getting off on a tangent here," that encourage and manage communication; the leader is not the only person making these comments.

■ People feel free to brainstorm informally, to throw new ideas or possibilities on the table rather than making formal pronouncements of opinion.

■ The group has high levels of interaction, usually accompanied by a balance of laughter and moments of serious exchange; everyone participates in a meaningful way.

■ Objections, differing perspectives, and disagreements are welcomed as a way to ensure quality outcomes.

■ There is no sense that any one person's ideas dominate or that someone's private "agenda" has been forced on the group.

■ There is a noncompetitive environment in which people ask for feedback and ideas from one another.

■ People show a willingness to reflect on how the team is operating and how decisions are being made in order to improve group effectiveness.

■ The group has a high sense of accomplishment and achievement.

The suggestions in this chapter can help you and your group approach this goal. Initially they concentrate on examining and cleaning up your current decision-making process. While some of these techniques may seem elementary, they are frequently the very things a group needs to reduce ambiguity and tension. They are techniques that people know they should use but do not take time to include. Without them, groups can easily confuse the decision they are trying to make with the process they are trying to follow.

Become Aware of Current Decision-Making Patterns

If you want to improve your decision making, you need to become aware of your current patterns before you can plan the changes you want and need to make.

Consider your own preferences about decision making. Give consideration to your role as someone who supervises and is supervised. As you respond to the following questions, look for themes that emerge from your answers that tell you something about your biases and preferences.

As a *manager of others,* and as an *employee:*

- Which type of decision making makes you most comfortable?
- Which type do you prefer—intellectually, practically, and emotionally?
- What benefits and detriments are associated with each type?
- When would you be most inclined to use each type?
- What evidence do you find that people regard the decision-making methods of managers and supervisors as secretive or otherwise suspect?

As an *employee:*

- What assumptions do you make about your manager and his or her ability to make sound decisions?
- When do you distrust or feel left out of decisions?
- What impact does this have on your productivity or the quality of your work?
- Does it affect your willingness to speak up?
- Does it affect your willingness to help implement the decision?
- How often do you see your manager making decisions by each of the five methods?

As a *manager:*

- How often do you see yourself making decisions by each of the five methods?
- On what kinds of decisions would you be unwilling to use method 3? method 4? method 5? Why?
- What assumptions do you make about your employees and their ability to make sound decisions?
- How would you describe the decision-making process that is currently employed with your direct subordinates?
- How do you think they would describe it?

■ How effective is your decision making? Where does it work? Where does it break down?

Ask people who work for you about their perceptions of decision making. Insight that you may have gained about your own preferences will prepare you to listen carefully to what others appreciate. Follow these steps:

1. Using some or all of the questions listed above, ask your staff about the decision-making methods they use, their effectiveness, and changes they would recommend.

2. If you sense that there is tension around this issue, bring in an outside person to interview people and prepare a summary statement of the issues that emerge.

3. Share the summary with your staff and discuss its implications.

4. Make agreements about ways to handle decision making more effectively in the future so that everyone involved is more satisfied with the approach.

Ask someone to observe meetings where decisions are made. One of the best ways to become aware of current decision-making patterns is by asking a neutral outsider to observe your group when it is making decisions. At the end of the meeting, or a series of meetings, ask this person to describe for the whole group what has been observed. Include these points:

1. Ask your observer to pay particular attention to the way decisions are approached, discussed, and decided.

2. Listen to his or her feedback and discuss its implications.

3. With your group, make decisions to eliminate current counterproductive practices.
   Here is an example of this process:

   A finance department in a five-thousand-person service organization asked for this type of assistance from us. We observed four senior-level staff meetings and presented a summary of our observations at the fifth. Although the feedback addressed interpersonal communication as well as decision making, it was a catalyst for the group to decide to do a number of specific things to improve its process, including the following three items:

1. When a person brings a decision to the group, the issue will be presented as a question focused on a particular action, for example, "Should we . . . ?" or "What should . . . ?"
2. Each person responsible for bringing a decision to the group will say whether input from the group is desired (method 3) or whether the group is to make the decision together (method 4).
3. At each meeting, someone will be assigned to record decisions. When the meeting concludes, the list of decisions will be read to the group for verification and discussion of appropriate follow-up actions.

These are sound techniques that help groups keep track of what they are deciding and how it is being decided. What makes them seem difficult is that implementing such agreements takes a willingness both to break old habits and, with some discipline, to establish new ones that are more productive.

Seek Input on Decisions

If you do not want to make a decision alone, we suggest that you sidestep method 2 and opt at least for method 3. This requires some thought about who will be affected by the decision and how to gather a representative set of views from them. When interacting with those individuals, you will want to do the following.

Announce the method of decision making that you want to use and your reason for that choice. Many leaders make the mistake of casually saying to a group something like "We need to make some decisions about budget priorities for the coming year. Tell me what you think." While this may represent a friendly way to get a group thinking about a set of concerns, it does not identify the specific issue on which you want their views. Moreover, it suggests a level of involvement and participation that may be higher than the one you truly had in mind. You thought you implied method 3. Your group thought you implied method 4. The miscue on expectations is likely to cause trouble later. Think through the issues, then add comments like these:

> *"For this decision, I'd like to use method 3. I need to know your best thinking and concerns. I'll spend time reflecting on what you tell me and then make the decision."*

"Let's do this with method 4. We all have important points of view and share in the responsibility for making it happen."

"This is a decision that I have made on my own. The time factors and issues of confidentiality were such that it did not feel appropriate to involve others."

Before seeking input from individuals or a group, clarify the key question within the decision. Many miscommunication problems can be prevented by carefully clarifying the wording of the question to be decided. Here are some guidelines.

1. Ask yourself how others will react to the question you have posed:

    ▪ Does it make sense?

    ▪ Will people truly understand the kind of input you want?

    ▪ Are the words or concepts clear?

    ▪ Will people understand the question in the same way you do?

    For example, returning to the budget issue, there are varying levels of clarity:

Unclear	"Tell me what you think about the budget priorities for next year."
Clearer	"We are still undecided on next year's capital improvement budget. What do you think we ought to do with it?"
Better yet	"Give me your yea-or-nay vote on each of the following items that fall into the capital improvement budget: two new cars for the auto pool, PCs for the marketing department, or refurbishing the lobby and customer service counter."

    In refining a question related to decision making, it is not uncommon to rework the phrasing several times.

2. Think about the information you really need to know by playing a future scenario out in your head:

    ▪ What will you do with the information you collect?

    ▪ Given that, what are you looking for:

Data?

Experiences?

Feelings?

Predictions for the future?

Reactions to a past event?

Suggestions for improvements?

Priorities?

3. Make sure that you do not ask people for input that you will not use.

Identify how input will be used, who will make the decision, and how the input will be considered. For example, using method 3, you might say:

> *"If you can get this to me by next Friday, I'll incorporate it into the information I'm getting from Ahmed, Barb, and Josh. I'll get a summary of responses back to all of you at our Tuesday staff meeting so that we can use it as a starting point for a method 3 discussion. I expect to use the ideas that come out of that discussion to make my recommendations to Terry by the end of the month. He's got the final say, but I expect him to go along with what we suggest."*

Let people know what additional information they can expect from you. It is important to inform people about follow-up, especially when they will hear about the final decision. For example, you could say:

> *"Once I get my suggestions off to Terry, I'll send a copy to you. Unfortunately, there's not enough time for me to run this by anybody before I have to meet his deadline. I expect that he'll sign off on this request by a month from now. Once I know, I'll let you know."*

Manage Consensus

The suggestions we have listed so far foster cooperative action and participation. They can help bring groups to the level of collaboration represented in method 4. To move to that next stage of development, you will need to lead the group into an examination of how it is working together to make decisions. This requires that you and the group together

1. Define consensus decision making (what does method 4 really mean to people?)
2. Identify norms for member participation
3. Identify and use methods for handling problems in achieving consensus

At the center of this approach is determining how you and your group will define consensus. In this, you will want to explore such topics as the difference between voting and consensus, the advantages and disadvantages of each, and the level of agreement required of individuals to achieve consensus. All this can lead to a rich discussion of commitment and responsibility and of the complexities of day-to-day work as a member of a team. Members may ask, "Does this mean I can't change my mind?" "When can decisions legitimately be made outside the group?" or "How will this affect us as we work on our separate projects?" Such questions and the dialogue that results help members to know each other better and to gain clarity about values related to teamwork and collaboration.

As mentioned earlier, our own definition of consensus is "what we can agree to so we can move forward together." The focus is on action, on moving forward. This does not necessarily mean that each person is thrilled with, or even fully agrees with, the decision. It does mean that each person buys into the decision and will actively support its implementation. We place emphasis on consensus, rather than on voting (unless consensus cannot be reached after repeated tries), because it is a means of finding the common ground that all members can support in a personal way. With voting, some win and some lose—a pattern that reflects competition more than collaboration. You may find our thoughts about consensus helpful to you as you proceed with the following suggestions.

Clarify your intentions with the group to move toward a consensus-based approach for decisions. This is an opportunity for you to call out some of your hopes for your group, how it works together, and what it accomplishes:

1. Emphasize your faith in the group's competence and skills.
2. Identify your reasons for wanting to move in this direction—

for example, your desire to help the group achieve even higher levels of teamwork or learn to wrestle with and work through business issues that you have been handling alone.

3. Suggest that a first, concrete step is to have the group develop its own operational definition of consensus decision making.

4. Ask for reactions from members of the group and encourage people to share other experiences they have had with collaboration and shared decision making.

Ask the group to develop its own agreements about method 4. Since this exercise is one of consensus building, you immediately ask people to practice a method you hope they will become much more familiar with in the future:

1. Share the five-point model shown at the beginning of this chapter, giving examples, if needed.

2. Ask people about their personal definitions of consensus, taking notes on a flip chart or white board. Say, for example:

   "We've all had different experiences making decisions with others. When you think of consensus, what words come to mind?"

   "Does anyone have an experience with consensus decision making that was really satisfying? If so, what aspects of that experience would you like to see us pay attention to?"

   "As we take a look at these notes, what are the common elements we'd like to include in our own definition of consensus?"

3. Offer our definition of consensus if people seem to have a hard time with these questions. Ask them if this is a definition that they understand and think they could use effectively. Modify it based on their comments.

4. Next, tell the group that it is important to have agreement about how decisions will be made if consensus simply cannot be reached. (There are two common backup methods: first, voting with a two-thirds or three-quarters majority and second, referring the decision to method 3 and having you, as leader, then make it.) Facilitate a discussion that leads to an agreement about a backup method that is acceptable to everyone and an understanding of when it will be used.

5. Recognize that throughout the group's discussions, group norms for decision making will emerge; record and distribute them to all members.

6. At appropriate points in the future, evaluate and change these norms, if necessary.

Stick with your agreements when consensus is difficult. When groups cannot reach consensus they easily become dispirited or immobilized. People may back into finger-pointing, or they may simply push decisions back onto the leader, rather than examining and dealing with the causes of the problem. Moments such as these can be opportunities for the group to learn about its own dynamics and how to work better together. Particularly with groups new to consensus, decisions may seem to take too long and get mired down in windy, nonspecific discussions. At this stage people are learning. You can be helpful by doing the following:

1. Keep the conversation on track and provide reassurance that the group is doing a good job; remind people that consensus is not easy.

2. Reinforce your group norms as a way of minimizing tangential comments, repeated speech-making, or unconscious use of the time available.

3. Throughout the discussion, clarify and paraphrase what people say so that views are both respected and understood.

4. After all members have expressed their opinions and shared the available information about an issue, ask these questions, recording the answers on a flip chart or white board:

   "Where do we have agreement?"

   "Where do we disagree?"

   "On the points where there is disagreement, what are the reasons for the different positions?"

   "Is there any common ground in the reasons why people disagree?"

   "What options do we now see for ways to move ahead together?"

5. When issues seem unresolvable in the whole group, ask people to form trios to discuss any insights gained from listening to the previous large-group discussion.

6. Bring the trios back together for more discussion, asking these questions:

   "Is there any way we can resolve our differences?"

   "Of all that we've talked about, what can we move forward on that represents consensus?"

   "Is it time to use our backup method to resolve the remaining issues?"

7. If people are reluctant to use the backup method, go through one more round of either whole-group or small-group discussions, seeking ways to move forward together. Then ask these three questions again. If unresolved issues remain, use the backup method to move forward.

Communicate About Decisions That Have Been Made

Many well-intentioned, collaborative leaders fail to take this one final and relatively simple step, unknowingly perpetuating the impression that they are autocratic or secretive decision makers. This is especially true when a decision has been made by methods 1, 2, or 3.

Communicate the decision as quickly as possible to those who were involved and those who will be affected by the outcomes. Attending to these follow-up steps does not take a lot of time, yet it strongly demonstrates your respect for those who were not highly involved in the decision:

1. Highlight the options you considered and the reasons you selected your course of action.

2. Review why you chose the method you used, particularly if you are talking to people who will be affected but who have not been involved in the decision-making process. Say who was involved in making the decision.

3. If the input you received is not reflected in the decision, make sure you address that discrepancy. This most important step demonstrates that you truly heard the input and that you considered it. If you do not talk about this, people who offered input that is not reflected in your decision are

likely to assume that you had your mind made up to begin with, to feel cheated because you wasted their time by asking for their input, or to mistrust you in the future when you ask for input.

4. Mention any timelines associated with the implementation of the decision, letting people know what they can expect to see and when. Describe anticipated opportunities for their involvement, being careful not to set unrealistic expectations.

If you and your group have used methods 4 or 5, the group takes on a significant role in communicating its actions. The same guidelines apply, however, and your team should not fail to create a communication plan for informing others whenever it makes decisions. Otherwise, the group will soon be perceived as a "closed club" and will look just as autocratic or secretive as the noncommunicative manager. Management teams that are internally very collaborative can easily fall into this trap.

There is obviously a big difference between making a sound decision and using effective decision-making processes. It is always possible for a fine process to produce an ill-advised decision. However, we believe that under most circumstances, carefully considered decision-making processes will result in better business decisions. The suggestions made in this chapter are well tested. They have made an enormous difference in people's reactions to decisions that were made in work groups. In several situations we know well, building the skills and agreements that support collaborative decision making has represented one very tangible way to turn an environment of mistrust and fear into one of enthusiasm, creativity, and commitment.

New Lessons and Reflections

Thoughts on Organizational Culture

Just as undiscussables are both a cause and a result of fear, so collaboration requires and builds trust. As individuals and groups increase their capacity to reach consensus, they make a significant contribution to the amount of trust in the workplace. In fact, the trust-fear continuum in Figure 1.1 can be used as a reference point to better understand collaboration, as shown in Figure 13.3.

Collaboration	Cooperation	Compliance
Trust ———————————————————————————— Fear		
Full participation		Left out of the process
Commitment to action		Resistance to change

Figure 13.3. From Compliance to Collaboration.

As you consider the connections between consensus, collaboration, and trust, some distinctions may prove useful. With *compliance*, people do what they must, what they are told, without having been included in any aspect of the decision-making process; in this situation, if the fear of repercussions is present, resistance or sabotage is very likely. *Cooperation* is the middle ground, when people do what they are expected to do, meeting basic customer requirements; a moderate level of trust is present and people may have been asked for input on decisions being made. With *collaboration*, people partner with each other, regardless of differences in authority, to solve, create, or discover. High levels of trust are involved, so people can comfortably debate issues, share sensitive information, think outside the normal boundaries, and reach consensus on decisions. High commitment to follow-through is one of the results, because people are invested in seeing their plans and ideas put to use.

Thoughts on Personal Leadership

For many people, collaboration is a highly positive experience. It has a different feel to it than cooperation. It is open-ended, innovative, and energizing. It gives people breathing room and simultaneously builds relationships among them. Yet sometimes it is difficult to initiate, especially in workplaces where people have been taught that they must bargain in order to get what they need. In these situations, people sometimes want to turn efforts to collaborate into negotiation sessions where the general attitude is one of exchange: "I'll do this only if you do that." In extreme forms, this negotiation process causes decision making to come to a halt or slide into an adversarial argument.

You can begin to break through this slide by calling out your observations and asking for a discussion of how negotiation and col-

COLLABORATE ON DECISIONS   **253**

laboration differ. While it is likely that you will find overlap in individuals' understanding of these words, it is common for people to see collaboration as based on finding common ground and building trust rather than solely satisfying self-interests. Your next question can be about how to move the discussion from bargaining toward collaboration. This may lead, for example, to a discussion of the need for a common aim or overarching goal. Stopping to reframe the conversation in this way may result not only in more productive outcomes about a specific issue, but also in a better long-term way of doing business together.

14

Challenge Worst-Case Thinking

Worst-case thinking is "catastrophizing." A direct descendent of the cycle of mistrust, worst-case thinking is a nasty mind trap that darkens people's attitudes and buries their ability to solve problems. It leads them into black-and-white dichotomous thinking that limits their capacity to manage the future.

Frequently obscured by the voices of supposed "realism" or "pragmatism," worst-case thinking snares most people at one time or another. If you listen closely, you can hear it from managers and employees alike. Some statements are more obvious than others:

"I would never dream of telling her that! She'd blow up!"

"We can't just have people making those decisions on their own."

"If we don't have a senior management representative on that task force, who knows where they'll end up?"

Strategy	What This Should Accomplish
Respond initially in a supportive, yet neutral, way	Show your concern for the other person Establish a communication link
Identify the worst case and the most likely case	Greater calm because people see that their worries are taken seriously Insight about fears others experience
Build action plans for each case	Increased confidence that comes when people have agreed to an action plan Decreased isolation
Emphasize strengths, gifts, and opportunities	Increased confidence and sense of being appreciated Focus shifts from protecting the past to exploring the future

Grid 14.1. How to Challenge Worst-Case Thinking.

"This whole program is going down the tubes. I'll probably get fired—and get my boss fired, as well."

"This employee committee is a setup. Do you think anybody is going to seriously consider our suggestions? There's only one person who makes decisions around here, and you know who I'm talking about."

"I wouldn't be surprised if all these delays around the budget mean that there will be another bunch of layoffs."

We devote this chapter to suggestions that encourage people to name their worst fears and, as calmly as possible, figure out ways to deal with them. Once these fears are named and said out loud, their power diminishes significantly. To assist with this reversal, we suggest identifying and planning for both the worst case and the most likely case. Before focusing on the strategies that are outlined in Grid 14.1, we offer some thoughts about the causes of worst-case thinking and clues that will help you to know when those around you are caught in this destructive pattern. Unlike many of the other suggestions made earlier, the actions we recommend here are primarily focused on individual interaction, with you in the role of listener and coach.

Worst-Case Thinking Is Tied to Change

Throughout our research and consulting, we have repeatedly observed how easily people can become trapped by their negative assumptions. The worst case is a way of thinking that builds upon negative assumptions. It happens so naturally and usually so fast that people hardly notice. This is especially true during times of change.

Maggie Moore and Paul Gergen, consultants with a specialty in risk taking and change, have developed a model we find particularly useful (Moore and Gergen, 1985). Their model, shown in Figure 14.1, explains the reasons why more people are likely to be affected by worst-case thinking during times of change. They suggest that when people are bombarded by a change outside their control, the impact is likely to be felt in many different ways. Their model shows how a change such as the introduction of a new production line, a layoff, or a job reclassification can operate like a fast-moving, powerful object descending on a web of interconnected aspects of organizational life.

For example, new safety regulations mandated by the government might influence

- What clothes employees wear to work
- How many people are needed to do a job
- How long it takes to complete a job
- What work methods are used

   In turn, these apparently small adjustments may influence

- Training
- Workloads
- Working relationships and social structure, perhaps including the informal rules of the work group about safety matters

These changes, some obvious and some not, travel through the net shown in Figure 14.1. The bigger the change and the faster it happens, the greater the number of areas that will be affected. All of this begins to have an impact on the emotions of those influenced by the change. As more elements of the net are affected, more people have opportunities for worst-case thinking and for personalizing ways in which the change could negatively affect them. In the scenario we have just created, employees may begin to

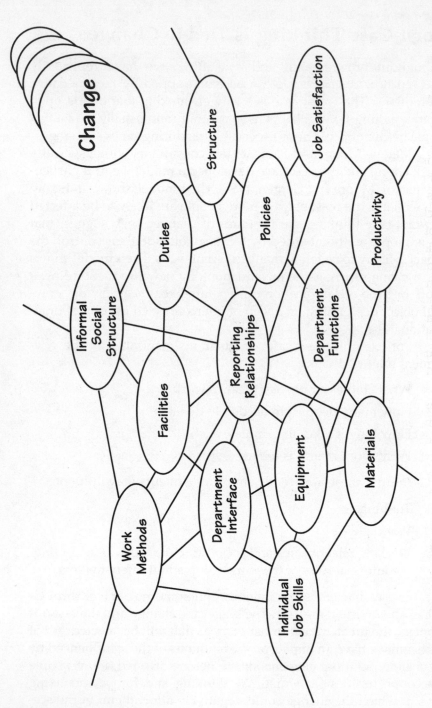

Figure 14.1. The Impact of Change.

Source: Moore and Gergen, 1985. Reprinted by permission.

- See a significant loss of freedom
- Wonder if management will use the new rules to penalize them
- Worry that management will use the cost of implementing the new regulations as a reason to grant smaller pay increases
- Cause some to be concerned about their individual finances and other personal issues

"Nothing's as sure as change" does not offer much solace to the individuals or work groups who are grappling with possibilities that might significantly alter the quality of their work and work life. This is tough enough in organizations where information flows quickly and freely and where managers and employees have a history of planning and working together to solve problems. It is doubly difficult in settings where the cycle of mistrust dominates manager-employee relations and hierarchical traditions limit employee access to information and involvement in decision making.

Any change that is not initiated by the person being affected by it has the potential to threaten his or her sense of credibility, competence, relationships, or security. This is especially so when the individual's relationship with his or her supervisor falls on the fear, rather than the trust, side of the continuum. Externally imposed changes are, of course, common in these times of fast-paced mergers, acquisitions, new-product development, and innovations in technology. Combined, these factors create an environment that is increasingly conducive to worst-case thinking and the accompanying expressions of cynicism, frustration, and anger. This makes it even more important for leaders to concentrate on building trust with employees, as a means of counterbalancing the disrupting impact of change.

The Impact of Worst-Case Thinking

Being stuck in an either-or mentality keeps individuals from thinking rationally and prevents them from successfully collaborating on a plan to manage change. It certainly keeps them from planning what they might do if the worst case actually happened. In such situations, they are also unable to anticipate the events that are most likely to happen. As one technical writer from a manufacturing plant in western New York described it, "It's like crashing and burning." He agreed with the CEO from Atlanta who suggested: "Nine out of ten will assume the worst. When their security is threatened, people don't take risks because of fear of failure, fear of not knowing what to do."

Worst-case thinking causes people to feel threatened by ambiguous behaviors, making the cycle of mistrust particularly hard to reverse. This dynamic explains why some people have such a hard time with change and the ambiguity it inevitably creates. This is true even in a world where change is a constant factor and where it often brings opportunities to enhance one's credibility, competence, relationships, and security. Such people, whether on the front line or in an executive suite, have little interest in or energy for thinking creatively, supporting others, caring about cutting costs, or partnering with others in the pursuit of innovation.

How to Recognize Worst-Case Thinking

Worst-case thinking can happen to anybody, even very positive and rational people. As you read through this material, try to recall the last time you found yourself in this thinking mode. As with most of the dynamics we discuss in this book, the better you understand your own related experience, the more able you will be to assist others.

Worst-case thinking is like unexpectedly breaking through the ice of a frozen pond. In an instant, fear-oriented thinking takes over. People recognize that they are at risk. But instead of figuring out what to do to correct the situation, they frequently become immobilized and panic, unable to think clearly in the frigid water. People who are imagining the worst case lose their ability to see a range of options for future actions. When work problems crop up, some picture a riches-to-rags scenario: successful person with healthy, happy relationships ends up jobless, friendless, and homeless. Others relive the nightmare about missing their college final exam: "At last," they think, "everyone will find out how incompetent and unworthy I really am!"

Strong emotions can be present and are frequently expressed in the form of anxious, panicked requests for assistance. People typically feel unable to turn this downward spiral around and see correcting the situation about as likely as stopping a moving freight train. While others may be helpful and have good ideas, it feels to the person involved as if the only possible remedy is some type of divine intervention, a made-in-Hollywood ending that comes out of nowhere to save the day. When they are caught in this pattern, people obviously are not thinking rationally.

Several observable signs may accompany worst-case thinking. Some are related to statements people make; others are more nonverbal in nature. These are all relative, depending on the normal disposition, communication, and problem-solving style a person usually demonstrates. The actual signs may vary from one person to another. However, each indicates a significant movement toward a bleak and more negative perspective.

Frequently, the first clues are comments that express clear, but not extreme, discouragement, cynicism, frustration, or fear, typically stated with an emphatic tone of voice, such as the following:

"This is not going to work."

"I don't think we've looked at all the risks."

"I'm beginning to wonder where all this is going."

"If we don't pull this off, we're going to be in deep trouble."

"I don't understand what this whole thing is about, anyway."

If you respond to such an opening statement with something as simple as "Oh? What do you mean?" you will most likely hear and see additional signs, such as

- Lessened ability to concentrate
- Absence of positive humor
- Statements predicting impending disaster
- Acknowledgment of only two options, good or bad, with nothing in between
- Strong expressions of cynicism, powerlessness, mistrust, and fear
- Agitation or inability to concentrate on constructive problem solving

Respond Initially in a Supportive, Yet Neutral, Way

When the signs of worst-case thinking are visible, slow down and put yourself into the role of neutral observer, listener, and clarifier. As you interact with the other person, you will be demonstrating your support and interest in helping out. It is important to keep your language calm and neutral in tone so that you do not heighten the anxiety of the other person.

Calmly offer an observation. When you hear or see the clues of worst-case thinking:

1. Notice as much as you can about the circumstances, the behavior, and the tone of the person involved.

2. As soon as possible, perhaps in the moment, offer an observation that will open the door for more conversation. Make statements like these:

   "I noticed at this morning's meeting, Pete, that you seemed quite discouraged about the expansion plans."

   "Henry, you are sounding pretty grim. You must think that this effort is off to a bad start."

   "Alicia, when you answered Jeremy's question, you had a worried tone in your voice."

Ask simple questions and apply your good listening skills. Gentle observations like the ones we have suggested here usually will get some kind of response in which the other person begins to tell you how bad he or she thinks things are. When this happens:

1. Listen carefully, paying attention to nonverbal behavior and the tone of the person's voice.

2. Without rushing, ask open-ended questions or paraphrase what you hear, encouraging the person to tell you more so that you have a better understanding of his or her point of view.

3. Remember that no matter how unlikely someone's worst case seems to you, it is a very serious matter to that person.

Do not escalate the other person's anxiety. Many times, well-meaning listeners raise the worst-case thinker's tension level. If you want to help the other person become calmer:

1. Do not try to fix the problem by offering solutions; stay in the listening mode, paying attention to the emotions that are being reflected.

2. Do not try to diminish the worries of the other person with judgmental phrases such as these:

"Don't be ridiculous. That's never going to happen."

"Oh, that's really easy, all you have to do is . . ."

"Well, you got yourself into this. I guess you'd better get your-self out."

3. Recognize that this type of response will only cause the person you want to help to feel more isolated in his or her worries.

Identify the Worst Case and the Most Likely Case

When they are trapped by worst-case thinking, people frequently cannot even voice what they are worried about. It can be of great assistance to simply help them articulate the fate that might befall them. Exploring imagined worst-case scenarios enables people to let go of a significant amount of emotional tension.

Ask if a person is getting caught up into worst-case thinking. After establishing a connection with the worst-case thinker:

1. Simply ask the person in a caring tone, "Are you getting caught up in worst-case thinking?"

2. When the person responds, typically with "What do you mean?" offer an observation, like the following ones, that includes an explanation for your belief that worst-case think-ing is happening:

   "You just seem to be so convinced that everything will turn out badly. I'm concerned that you are limiting your options and assuming that only the worst will happen."

   "I hear lots of worry in your voice and in your words—and not really anything else. It must be very hard for you to keep mov-ing ahead on this project."

   "I know that you have publicly committed your work group to supporting Jack's new idea, but everything you've said to me pri-vately suggests that you think it is one bad idea after another."

3. Be ready to shift to a listening mode when the other person explains what is going on and why he or she feels scared or stuck.

Ask people what could go wrong. A very practical and acceptable activity with any group or individual grappling with some kind of change is to ask, "What could go wrong?" This question is an easy one for people leaning toward worst-case thinking; it gets them talking so that you can help them to identify the worst-case pattern.

Once the discussion is under way, you may want to ask three additional questions. Do so in a calm, informal way, but stick with the sequence.

> *"What's the worst thing that could happen throughout all this?"*
>
> *"What's the most likely scenario?"*
>
> *"What do you think we need to do in order to make this as successful as possible?"*

This sequence of questions gives those who are uncomfortable talking about their feelings and their fears in a business setting an acceptable way to discuss their opinions, values, and emotions. The last question positions the individual or the group for action. Having a plan of action usually helps people to feel better about the unknown.

Identify hopes, fears, and expectations. Hopes, fears, and expectations can be explored in one-on-one situations as in the previous three suggestions. Posing these same topics for a group, however, can generate an illuminating and energizing discussion. A consulting experience of a colleague illustrates the use of this technique.

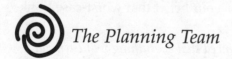 *The Planning Team*

Five months before a major international sporting event, the fifteen senior managers of the sponsoring organization were quite nervous about how the logistics were actually going to come together. In the early part of an all-day retreat, the consultant asked people, in groups of two and three, to talk through their thoughts about the next five months. First, they were asked to describe their hopes about how the event would come together. Next, they were asked to describe their fears regarding the same issue. Those answers were eventually reported to the group as a whole. Fears that were identified included the following concerns:

■ Senior managers would not be able to perform under pressure.

■ Lack of clarity about the budget issues would be a problem and would prevent people from spending the resources that were actually available.

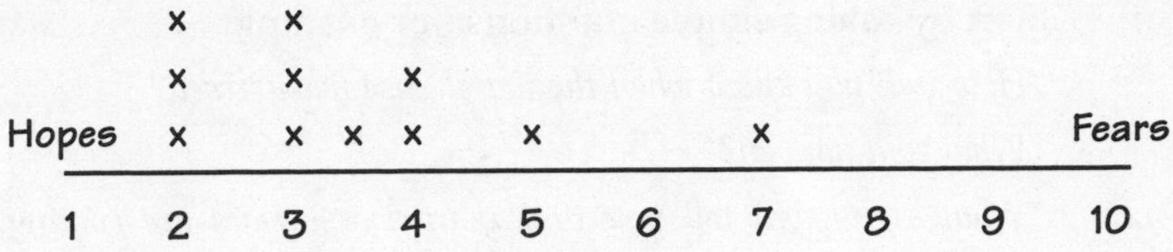

```
         x    x
         x    x    x
Hopes    x    x  x  x     x           x              Fears

         1    2    3    4    5    6    7    8    9    10
```

Figure 14.2. Actual Hopes and Fears.

■ The organization would avoid making difficult or sensitive decisions until it was too late.

Once the hopes and fears had been listed for the group, people engaged in a discussion of their actual expectations. The consultant then drew a continuum with the hopes represented at one end and the fears at the other. He asked people, one by one, to tell their colleagues where on the continuum their own set of expectations fell, with the results shown in Figure 14.2. As a group, their expectations were much closer to their hopes than to their fears. To them, this was a pleasant and surprising revelation.

The consultant applied this exercise on the spot because he saw that many negatives were coming up and he wanted to provide a balanced structure for people to use while they were thinking about their concerns. He also wanted this group of hard-driving, task-oriented senior-level people to think about their feelings and articulate them to their peers. This all took about an hour and a half and enabled people to move through the day with their worst fears openly acknowledged and discussed—and reduced.

Build Action Plans for Each Case

When people manage their worst-case thinking, they recognize it when it happens and move on. They do not get stuck. They have a plan and know when to implement it. This readiness inspires additional confidence that, in turn, reduces the presence of fear.

Develop criteria to identify when the worst case is about to happen. As with all the other suggestions in this chapter, this strategy is designed to get people to slow down and apply some logic to their fears. It also enables them to know what to look for as indicators that the worst case has arrived. Follow these steps:

1. Start by asking simple questions; for example:

   "How will you know when the worst case has arrived?"

   "What will happen?"

   "What signs will tell you that your worst fears are coming true?"

2. Encourage people to be very specific.

3. Verbally reiterate the answers to these questions or take written notes. People might give answers like these:

   "The budget has been reduced another 3 percent."

   "Good people have started leaving of their own accord, and when they do, no one is hired to replace them."

   "Key programs are being cut."

   "I've been asked to change jobs and work for Bart, someone I can't stand."

Lists like this one become yardsticks against which individuals can measure their fears. Until the criteria have been met, people will know that events are still moving at an acceptable level, and when the early warning signs start to appear, they will know when to put their action plans into operation. As a manager or peer, once you know the criteria, you will be in a better position to provide support or guidance if the worst case does come along.

Develop a plan. Although it is certainly possible to work individually with people to help them develop a plan to manage the worst case, we suggest that this happen in a group. Often the fears experienced by one person are shared by others, especially if they concern upcoming changes or an ambiguous organizational future. Follow these steps:

1. Invite those who will be affected by the change to participate. If the fears are truly limited to one person, asking one or two others to serve as consultants can add to the quality of the planning and will let the worst-case thinker know that others are ready to help. Make sure the person you are supporting agrees to this idea.

2. After having identified the worst and most likely cases, pose these planning questions:

   "What can be done to prevent the worst case from happening?"

"What events do we control or have influence over?"

"What events do we need to be ready to accept?"

"What can be done to help people get ready to handle the worst case if and when it comes?"

"If it comes, what can be done to make the situation less troublesome, threatening, confusing, or frustrating?"

"What other options exist for people who cannot manage the worst case?"

3. If a handful of people are involved, facilitate this discussion, refraining from adding your own ideas until you are sure that no one else will contribute them; record the answers to the questions on a flip chart or white board.

4. If a large group is involved, ask one person from each small group to report out the group's answers for more discussion and decision making in the large group.

5. Capture your agreements and any timelines in written notes; copy and distribute them to those involved.

Emphasize Strengths, Gifts, and Opportunities

When you give people the time and support to talk about their worst fears, you make it possible for them to begin to consider their hopes. In doing so, you help them move into the future. In constantly changing environments, people who are on the fear side of the trust-fear continuum will not be willing or able to recognize the positive future possibilities until they feel that their worries have been respected and heard. All of the ideas we've presented in this chapter so far will help that to happen. If you sense that fears have been calmed and that the other person, or the group, is ready to look toward the future with more positive energy, you might want to do the following.

Ask people to describe what is going right. If the organization is coping with major changes in structure, strategy, or culture, encourage people to focus on what is going well with these changes. This encourages them to think about the moments when they and their organization are at their best. This exercise can be expanded to include a discussion of the circumstances that enabled things to go well. In turn, this can lead to action planning to re-create those circumstances more often. This follows an approach recommended by David Cooperrider, as described in Sue Annis Hammond's booklet based on his ideas, *The Thin Book of Appreciative Inquiry* (1996).

For example, suppose that a certain work team seems to be adapting very quickly to a new management information system while other teams are not. Rather than focusing on problems with the new system, shift some attention to the team that is doing well. The circumstances enabling this group to be effective may offer a model for the other teams to use. This appreciative approach has the advantage of feeling like common sense, yet our experience of groups under pressure is that they easily become fixated on solving problems rather than building on successes. As a result, they may ignore existing skills and knowledge that could be useful during a stressful time.

Explore individual and group strengths. Many work environments are considered to be riskier than in the past. People may be asked to take on new roles, new work, and new technologies, increasing tension about keeping up or making mistakes. To counterbalance this tension—and the worst-case thinking that goes with it—encourage people to find and use their unique talents and strengths. Within your work group:

1. Brainstorm each person's unique contributions to the organization.

2. Identify ways for each person to use and build on these talents for the future.

3. Discuss the concepts of individual and team confidence and how they can be increased. Behaviors named by the group, such as using mistakes as learning opportunities, paying attention to the well-being of others, and asking for help, are examples of possible group norms that contribute to a sense of personal esteem and strength.

Some Final Reminders

Challenging worst-case thinking is tough for leaders who are used to solving problems and getting things done in an organized way. Linear thinking and analysis of the facts are not particularly effective when dealing with someone caught in the throes of worst-case thinking. In fact, when you are playing the part of listener and coach, your intuition will serve as an important guide in directing your observations and questions. Here are a few final tips that we have found useful when we've been in this role.

Be ready to attend to strong emotions. Throughout the conversation, be ready to shift your attention to focus on feelings—even though the conversation may have moved on to something logical like action planning. Remain the neutral, clear-headed, and supportive listener who can empathize with the other person's fears or frustrations without adopting those same feelings.

Do something concrete to help out. If you can do something small and tangible to help, offer to do it. Often a small step, like making a phone call or getting a piece of information, will loosen up the other person's ability to act. It is a symbolic gesture, in part, where you figuratively take someone by the arm and, through your offer of help, say, "Come on, let's get started." In doing so, however, be sure that you do not take on responsibility that rightly falls to the other person. If your supportive action ends up as a rescue, it will interfere with the other person's movement toward having more confidence.

Don't try to be a therapist. As with discussions of undiscussables, you may be opening up bigger issues than you imagined when you challenge worst-case thinking. Do not get trapped—or trap yourself—into the role of therapist or personal counselor. The suggestions we have provided can be quite successful with work-related issues and concerns. But we know from experience that self-esteem issues can also surface that may be far beyond the range of a manager's coaching role. If the conversation repeatedly returns to the employee's private view of her or his personal deficits and lasts more than an hour or so, it is time to make a referral to an agency or employee assistance program. You will do the employee a major disservice by getting hooked into the role of amateur psychologist.

Remember that taking constructive action is not always easy. People may find it hard to take action on answering the questions we have posed. If they have become accustomed to a dependent pattern of behavior, taking action to get ready for difficulty or prevent it from happening will represent a major shift. Seeing you or other coworkers acting on collaboratively designed plans will give these individuals extra encouragement to take action of their own.

One of the organizations we visited had recently gone through a restructuring. A senior vice president reflected on the way it was "sprung," in spite of how "we preach partnership and collegiality." He noted, "The change has destroyed the emotional links people had with the organization. People now worry about when the next shoe will drop." Another senior vice president acknowledged that midlevel career employees had to be thinking about what the reorganization meant for their careers and their families.

It is exactly this type of environment where worst-case thinking needs to be managed most carefully. When many people are waiting for the other shoe to drop, they will understandably be inclined toward skeptical, cynical, and fearful thinking. Helping people to name, explore, and plan for their worst-case fears allows them to shape a more positive reality. When people feel attended to, respected, and accepted, they can begin to let go of some of the fear that has felt so overwhelming. The process enables them to take a more realistic view and positions them to be more future-focused, more effective problem solvers, and better contributors in the work environment.

New Lessons and Reflections

Thoughts on Organizational Culture

Two organizational patterns that are frequently tied to leadership decisions make it easier for people to indulge in worst-case thinking. In the first pattern, change upon change is initiated with little respect for how the timing of one change may influence acceptance and support of a previous change. In the second pattern, everything seems to be a top priority. Both of these situations can add a frantic quality to a work environment because people lose track of what they are supposed to do next. Goals become blurry. The tyranny of the urgent takes over. Some people spin into a state of feeling overwhelmed with tasks and performance expectations that seem unreasonable, given everything else they have to do. Worst-case thinking rears its painful head when those who interpret these circumstances declare that "the organization is out of control."

Wise leaders pay attention to the timing of change, so that people are not bombarded with too much, too fast. They consistently remind people of the stability of the organization's vision, mission, and values. They clarify and communicate priorities, focusing attention on key strategies that have impact and meaning.

Thoughts on Personal Leadership

Leaders can fall prey to worst-case thinking, too. If you find yourself in this boat, seek helpful, objective support through a colleague or friend. Talk through your perspectives without looking for commiseration. Notice how your own thinking is colored by images of what *might* happen, not by what *is* happening.

If part of your concern has to do with your own leadership skills or competence, be honest about this. Then refocus on your positive talents and the contributions you make. By bolstering your own confidence level you create a platform for helping others to do the same.

A Future of Trust

15

In the Midst
of Change

Consultant Peter Vaill was right when he suggested that organizations will continue to face the "permanent white water" of constant change (1991). To move confidently into the future, we all need to stop thinking that instability is a temporary condition and deal directly with the effects of turbulent workplaces on our work and personal lives. Much easier to say than to do, this approach is particularly difficult for those unaccustomed to handling ambiguity. For many, change translates directly into fear, quickly followed by cynicism. Among the fears that have been expressed are these:

> "After this merger is over, they won't need people like us anymore."

> "I won't be able to keep up with the technology. It keeps changing so fast and I have so much to do here that I can never get away for training."

"I don't want to travel, so there won't be a place for me here."

"I'll have to work for _____, and she has never liked me. Let's face it, I'm history."

Cynicism is shown in the following statements:

"This reorganization, like all the other things they've tried, will not make a difference. In a couple of years, it will all change back and this current turmoil will be a waste of effort."

"I still don't understand why they want to make these floor changes; why can't they be honest with us?"

"If they want to increase productivity, they should put all the money that is being spent on the new computer system into raises for the hourly workers. That's what would make the real difference, not all this technological window dressing."

"They get started with one change, then somebody else gets a bright idea. Who do they think they're kidding? Nobody has a clue where this organization is headed."

The greater the amount of change and the faster the rate of change, the greater the chance for fear and cynicism to grow. In this type of environment, people are less willing to creatively handle the changes that are so necessary for long-term organizational success. And so a primary responsibility of leadership is to help others move into the future willingly, if not enthusiastically. Again, this is easier said than done. A leadership position does not make a person immune to the fears and cynicism that affect others. And it is very tough to ask people to trust an ambiguous future when the leaders themselves are worried about what that future might bring.

In Chapter Fourteen, we focused on the problems of worst-case thinking as a specific aspect of fear and managing change. In this chapter we broaden the discussion to address the overall challenge of building trust in a work environment where change is a fundamental part of the context. Recalling the trust-fear continuum presented in Figure 1.1, we offer a new model that provides insight about how you may be reacting to change and guidance to help you build trust and motivate those who report to you.

The Old Contract Is Broken

Many changes swirl in and around organizations today: changes in technology, shifts in the customer base, new regulations, mergers with former competitors, fluctuating politics, constant demands for new knowledge and skills. In addition, the shift in the psychological contract between employees and organizations is a core issue with a significant impact on the way people react to many other changes. This contract, frequently unspoken, was assumed by both the prospective employee and the employer: in return for steady effort, compliance, and performance that met basic expectations, workers at all levels would receive ongoing employment in a chosen field, long-term upward mobility, broad fringe benefits, clarity of role and status, and a sense of loyalty between employer and employed.

The staggering rounds of corporate downsizing in the last five years have made it more than evident that the old contract is gone. In its place is something much more ambiguous. With less job security, people must depend more than ever on their own sense of self-direction to get ahead. The corporation is no longer a caretaker, and little if anything can be taken for granted about loyalty. William Bridges (1994) has suggested that even the concept of the job is becoming outmoded, to be replaced by the ability of organization members to define for themselves what work needs to get done and how this should happen.

While for some this is an exciting period, for others the mood is one of deep anxiety, filled with fears about potential loss. People find that the contract has changed with little warning and less training. Permanent white water has become a pressure cooker where support systems seem to have been yanked away, leaving many feeling betrayed, confused, and very worried about the future. Often, people who want to survive and get ahead in this new era believe that they should keep their heads down and privately figure out ways to proceed, one step at a time. They feel that to say, "I need help," could immediately generate the risk of replacement. This fearful, hunkering-down, noncommunicative pattern can be experienced equally by those in leadership and those in front-line positions, regardless of their work history or education.

It is no wonder, given the severity of such shifts, that people react in a personal and emotional way to many of the changes that happen in the workplace. In such settings, the cycle of mistrust is quickly engaged. Leaders themselves can find it a challenge to adjust, let alone to support those who report to them. They can fall prey like anyone else to negative assumptions in their relationships with both their managers and their employees. Here is a story that provides an example of how the fear of change and the fear of speaking up combined in a large manufacturing plant, limiting the ability of those in the first level of leadership to do their jobs effectively.

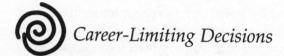 *Career-Limiting Decisions*

At a training session for first-level supervisors, participants talked informally about CLDs, "career-limiting decisions." According to the supervisors, almost anything that involved asking for help from higher management could fall into this category. The group focused their complaints on one particular CLD: whether or not to challenge the number of people they were assigned to directly supervise. A single supervisor might have dozens of immediate employees to train, coach, and encourage on a daily basis, while dealing with the inevitable brush fires and handling the paperwork.

The broad span of employees was the result of a vast reengineering effort to streamline operations within the preceding two years. Although the heavy supervisory load created pressures that made the supervisors' jobs almost undoable, many considered it a considerable risk to bring this up to higher levels of management. The supervisors appreciated the fact that there were not as many of them as there once had been in the company. They worried that speaking up about their concerns might imply that they were not competent and this would lead to some type of repercussion. Talking in an offhand way about CLDs was the grim but humorous way they expressed this fear.

As part of one of the training sessions, a senior vice president talked with participants about the company's plans for the future, discussed other management topics of interest, and invited questions. The workshop leader, having heard the complaints about the large number of employees assigned to supervisors, mentioned that these concerns had been present during the training session.

The senior vice president was surprised to learn how many people some of the workshop participants were asked to supervise directly. He requested details and was able to foster an open discussion of the dilemmas. He intervened immediately and supportively to help, especially with one of the supervisors who was trying to single-handedly manage sixty people. The senior vice president's immediate willingness to understand the problem from the supervisors' perspective was a pleasant surprise and an unexpected benefit of the training sessions.

Hopes and Fears About the Future

We introduced the trust-fear continuum in Figure 1.1 as a way to describe how organizations can be viewed: from trust-based to fear-based to somewhere in between. In this chapter the continuum is presented as a kind of balance that might tip toward the trust or fear end, depending on a variety of factors related to a change and how it is implemented.

To better understand this image, think about your own reactions to a recent workplace change that you were required to make. What was the change? What did it require from you? What were your first reactions when you heard about it? Now notice that in the fulcrum shown in Figure 15.1, trust is linked with hope and looks to the future; fear is accompanied by cynicism and a sense of self-protection related to what has existed in the past.

As externally imposed change enters your work life, you instinctively begin a set of internal measures, trying to assess the

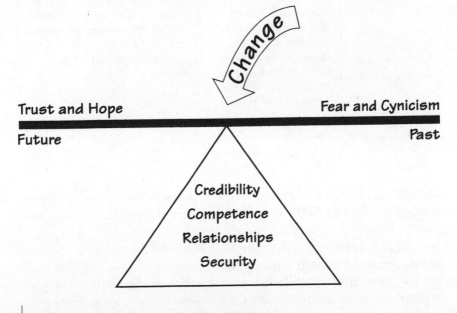

Figure 15.1. Hopes and Fears During Times of Change.

Effect of Change	Definition	What People Say to Themselves
Credibility	Reputation, good name, ability to influence	"I hope people will continue to respect me and I'll continue to be able to influence what happens here. I sure hope nothing happens that will upset this."
Competence	Skills, knowledge, ability to get things done, quality of performance	"I feel competent now and hope this won't change. Sometimes I worry that I might not be able to keep up with all the new things I need to learn."
Relationships	Positive relations with others, being liked and admired, having positive connections that are pleasant and help get things done	"I like the people I'm working with and the kind of relationships I've been able to develop. I wonder about what it would be like if I lost these connections."
Security	Sense of confidence about the future that can include income and earning power, physical safety, a strong sense of personal or professional identity that is sometimes status-related	"I like my job and feel comfortable here. I worry that if there are too many changes, the job itself might be different. In the worst case, I might end up out on the streets."

Grid 15.1. Effects to Consider During a Change.

impact the change will bring. Will the change create loss or opportunity? If it brings both, what will be the balance? In the end, will you be better off than you are right now?

Such questions reflect the four facets of the fulcrum. As you think about the change and its likely impact, if you are like most people, you will probably consider how the change will affect your reputation, your ability to get things done, your connections with others, and your position within the work environment. Although you might not use the actual words *hopes* and *fears*, this is the emotional terrain in which you will find yourself. Frequently unexpressed at work, these hopes and fears are almost always voiced as part of an ongoing internal and highly personal dialogue that takes place as you weigh the pros and cons of change. Understanding this dialogue is a key to helping you and others you work with to move away from the fearful self-protection of the past to the more open, future-oriented other end of the continuum. The four dimensions of the fulcrum are described in Grid 15.1.

People hope that the future—any time beyond the present moment—will bring opportunities to enhance these four elements of their work experience. They also fear that future situations might cause them to *lose* what they currently have in these four areas. The internal conversation circles around the question, "How will this change affect me?"

To illustrate this more fully and to tie change back into issues related to speaking up, let's return to the group of first-level supervisors and their CLDs. Suppose that it was possible to listen in to the inner dialogue that had been going on prior to the session with the senior vice president. In trying to make a decision whether to bring up the issue of too many employees, people might have said certain things to themselves:

About credibility   "I could disappoint those who believed I
                      could do the job. I might be seen as not
                      being very independent or politically savvy,
                      and as not being able to figure things out on
                      my own. This would be humiliating for me."

About competence   "I might be seen by others—and I might see
                      myself—as unable to learn what is necessary
                      to manage in new ways. I might have to face
                      up to some personal limits in my sense of
                      competence and intelligence. I'd feel a lot of
                      regret and personal pain, as if I should have
                      known I wasn't cut out for this job."

About relationships "If I speak up, perhaps my relationship with
                      my manager might be damaged in some
                      way. My manager might spend too much
                      time looking over my shoulder or might
                      withdraw from me. If the situation changes,

I could lose relationships with people I enjoy working with and be left to supervise people who are difficult for me. If my job changes, I might find myself in a whole new part of the plant with an entirely new team, away from the coworkers I really liked. Things could get a whole lot worse."

About security   "Maybe I'd be forced out of my job. *Then* what would I do?"

The supervisors share these fears indirectly through their discussion of CLDs. From the outside, their informal, cynical conversation may seem to define an unresponsive, mean-spirited organization. But listening past their negative assumptions and cynical humor about CLDs, it is possible to gather clues to the inner dialogue in which they reveal their perceived threats to their credibility, competence, relationships, and security. Their sense that "if I ask for help, I'll pay" is a loud signal that feared losses hang undiscussed in the background. The strength of these worries allows little room for the supervisors to find much hope connected to the changes brought by the reengineering efforts. As they look to the future, they worry that theirs is a no-win situation that in the end will lead to some kind of failure.

Luckily, when the senior vice president learned of the supervisors' concerns, he created an environment in which these concerns might start to be explored and resolved. His ability to quickly shift to discussing undiscussables is admirable. And we believe that paying attention to the changes as they occurred would have been an even better approach.

Suppose, in the beginning, back when the reengineering was suddenly causing larger groups of employees to be assigned to a single supervisor, there had been a thorough discussion of the issues involved with the changes, including the losses. At that point, the supervisors could have addressed the challenges they found themselves facing much more easily and openly. One result could have been a collaboration on ways to address this shift, not just among the supervisors, but with upper managers as well.

If that had taken place, trust levels and a sense of connection to corporate strategies would probably have been increased. Performance outcomes might have been enhanced sooner because people felt freer to ask for help. Additionally, this sensitive approach to the supervisors' experience might have influenced the way the supervisors treated their employees, making assistance for everyone more accessible. Unfortunately, the delay and the supervisors' resulting negativity may well have led many people to absorb the notion of CLDs as an organizational fact of life.

In organizations where major changes are taking place, especially at a rapid rate, people can easily feel an increased sense of threat to their current level of credibility, confidence, relationships, and security. When this high level of threat is present, people become understandably self-protective and at least cautious, if not suspicious, about the change effort and those leading it. Cynicism and the cycle of mistrust are easily triggered as people focus on what they may lose. Recalling some of what we learned from our field study, this is especially true when decision making about change is seen as secretive and information about the change has been inconsistent or sporadic.

When changes are externally imposed with implementation plans fully defined, the sense of threat is particularly high. The experience translates like this: "It wasn't my idea, I have to do it, and I can't influence how it will play itself out." Rather than being excited by a potential opportunity, many people feel trapped by the situation. They believe, according to the current psychological contract, that to stay in the organization means that they have no choice but to comply with the change. As Josh Hammond and James Morrison (1996) suggest, this is particularly threatening for those who have grown up in the United States, because the culture encourages people to believe that individuals are in charge of their own destiny. When that sense of choice is removed, fear and anger naturally follow. Is it any wonder that so much current organizational change is met with fear, cynicism, and resistance? Could any of these reasons be behind the resistance you may sometimes feel when asked to lead a change effort on which you have had no influence?

Diminish the Fears of Change by Talking About Them

If you want to help those who report to you overcome their fears of and resistance to change, facilitate meaningful discussions about their worries and fears. This approach reflects points mentioned in

Part Three of this book because it relies on acknowledging the fears of change (see Chapter Eight) and being an open listener to worries that, to you, may seem far-fetched (see Chapter Fourteen). Essentially, the approach helps people to discuss the undiscussables (see Chapter Twelve) because so many worries about change reflect resistance.

When such discussions focus on actual and potential losses, you, like the senior vice president in the CLD story, should demonstrate a level of sensitivity that counteracts the cycle of mistrust lurking behind the scenes in people's worries. To openly initiate and facilitate a discussion of losses says to people, "I respect your experiences and want to understand them" and "If you say you have a problem, then we need to explore your concerns." In these conversations, listen carefully for clues that a person's credibility, competence, relationships, or security are threatened. Remember that these four facets are interrelated, even though one dimension may stand out in a significant way. Ask good clarifying questions and paraphrase what you hear. As with other undiscussables, find out if action needs to be taken or if the opportunity to voice their concern is enough to help people move ahead.

By comparison, if you try to focus on the benefits of a change before people believe that their concerns have received legitimate attention, you will fan the cycle of mistrust. When complaints, questions, and misgivings remain hidden, they will be perceived as undiscussable and politically incorrect. Thus, they will feed the negative assumptions about you as a leader and reinforce resistance to change. Even if misgivings seem irrational, dismissing them by prematurely shifting to a discussion of benefits or implementation schedules will feel like a put-down to the person who sees them as possible. Your response can easily be misinterpreted and can lead to a heightened fear that the losses are coming. Cynthia Scott and Dennis Jaffe's *Managing Organizational Change* (1989) is a useful guide in situations such as these. We particularly appreciate their model called the Transition Grid.

To move people toward trust, hope, and the future during periods of rapid change, leaders must seize the opportunity to bring undiscussed losses into the open. Supporting such discussions is one of the most important ways in which you can communicate a positive, trust-based view of people. In practical terms, this may require, as it did for the senior vice president, responding in the moment to an unexpected complaint before a roomful of tense supervisors. Or it may require thinking through how an overall plan for change should unfold and be communicated. Whatever the context, the goal is to create an environment in which people have a chance to express their concerns without feeling at risk and can therefore develop greater trust and confidence in moving forward.

Helping People to Talk About Loss

Seeing and acting on opportunities to address possible losses connected to change can be highly rewarding. Open discussion can allow people to clear away negative feelings and refocus their energy on the future. People are more likely to see you as a realistic leader who can be trusted and deserves support. As with all the suggestions we've made in this book, this is challenging work. Thus, we would like to offer some reminders that may be helpful as you open up discussions about the losses connected to change. Some of these tips will remind you of other suggestions made in Part Three of this book.

Remember that your job is to listen and understand the levels of concern expressed, not to solve anyone's problem. It is not necessary for you to possess the answers to the many questions employees might ask during these discussions, nor do you need to respond in the moment with solutions that may be better developed at another time and place. More important is your willingness to honor the concerns and questions of those present by helping them to think these issues through. The more ideas, energy, or information you can add to the discussion, the more employees will see you as someone who pays attention, respects others, and is, in return, worthy of trust.

Reframe your worries about gripe sessions. When we suggest that clients slow down to listen to the anticipated losses connected to a change, they often resist; they may say, "I don't want to open up a gripe session." Gripe sessions are usually pictured as conversations in which people endlessly vent about lists of problems and are unwilling to help solve them, yet expect the leaders who are present to quickly resolve their concerns. If you can identify with the worries expressed by some of our clients, here are some points worth remembering:

1. Recognize that your worries about gripe sessions may reflect your negative assumptions about people's intentions: that they want to blame, that they do not want to help solve problems. The words "gripe session" themselves belong to the cycle of mistrust.

2. Replace those thoughts with more positive assumptions, such as believing that employees will not abuse the opportunity to work through the challenges they are facing, having faith that they will honor the realities of the situation, and believing that they will respect the fact that leaders have to make tough decisions about change.

3. Recall times when you've been worried about change and how important it was for you to vent your feelings to someone so that you could "get it out of your system" and move on.

Be prepared to hear strong emotions. During periods of rapid change, people may experience and express strong emotions. The rumor mill may be alive with both accurate and inaccurate views of what is happening. Past work experiences in the same or other organizations may have created enormous baggage. When this baggage is added to the reality that the current change will no doubt bring some type of real loss—of credibility, competence, relationships, or security—feelings about change can be intensely personal. People can be angry or disappointed, cynical, and sarcastic. It is not uncommon today for people to be asked to take on more responsibility, work harder, perform tasks they have not been trained for, and work with new people—all with no increase in pay or benefits, in an environment of potential downsizing and continued restructuring. People will have strong feelings about all this and will need time to express them. Listening patiently is essential, even if what is expressed is uncomfortable to hear or emotional in nature. In those moments, do not try to solve anyone's problem.

Look for small signs that people are beginning to consider future possibilities. At some point, someone may raise the questions, "What's in it for me?" and "Why should I adjust to this change?" As cynical as these questions might sound in the moment, they can also be heard as a heartening sign that people are thinking about the future, rather than focusing on protecting the past. What seems like a negative or undermining question, if honored properly, can lead to a rich discussion of the possible enhancements the change can bring to credibility, competence, relationships, and security.

Involve people in decisions about change. Openly discussing losses associated with change can sometimes result in employees expecting to be more involved in making decisions about the changes. We see this as the good news. In fact, we strongly encourage our clients to use a highly participative approach to planning both the direction and implementation of change. Levels of participation should be clear to all, without false promises or false limitations (see Chapter Thirteen). When a significant cross section of people is so involved, much of the fear-producing perception that change is secretive and top-down disappears.

Use requests for more involvement in decision making as an opportunity to refine agreements about how work gets done. It is possible that complaints about being left out of the decision-making process may surface in discussions about losses connected to change. Take advantage of these comments about organizational power to reexamine the way work gets done. For instance, this might be the perfect time to make new agreements about the following topics:

- How more people can become involved in decision making to implement changes
- The need for greater amounts of information related to changes, including financial data, to be provided at more points and to more people
- Initiation of collaborative work to operationalize the organization's mission, business strategies, and values so that everyone can rely on them for guidance as changes unfold
- A greater commitment to asking for, giving, and receiving performance feedback among peers, managers, and employees
- Higher levels of listening to customers inside and outside the organization

Do not use change as an excuse for returning to a default position of mistrust. Change upon change is a common phenomenon in many organizations. In such settings, the pace seems insane as stress mounts and people get confused about priorities. Out of habit or desperation to feel some kind of control, leaders can be tempted to revert to old dictatorial ways. Announcing, rather than discussing, what needs to be done, by what date, and by whom may seem like an efficient way to proceed. Beware of such moments, for they are leverage points for movement forward or backward on the trust-fear continuum.

Times of great change are some of the best moments to discover the power of trusting relationships. Slowing down to engage people in thoughtful discussions of loss followed by creative group planning sessions will save time down the road. Such attention and participation creates opportunities for people to make choices and influence events. The greater the choice and ability to influence, the greater the likelihood of hope. And the more hope people have, the more energy and heart they invest in helping to create the future.

New Lessons and Reflections

Thoughts on Organizational Culture

Externally imposed change plays very differently than self-initiated change. Leaders who design and plan change are smart to study the differences, becoming sensitive to the way *choice* affects individuals. To better appreciate the dynamics involved, think about your experiences with change in either your work life or personal life. Make a list of times when you have initiated changes, especially ones that were challenging. What were those changes? In the midst of following through, what difference did it make to you that you were the one who decided to make the change? Next, think about changes you felt forced to make. How easy or hard were those changes to implement? To what degree did the imposed nature of the changes influence your experience and your attitude? Was there any room for you to choose certain aspects of the changes or influence the way things happened? What difference did that make?

Choice increases the positive experience with change. The greater the choice, the better the experience, even when the change leads to hours of hard work, the frustration of ambiguity, and the discipline required to develop new skills or knowledge. When choice is not present, people feel trapped; in extreme cases, they feel like victims. Trapped or victimized people are understandably focused on minimizing their own pain and surviving what they see as a bad situation. They cannot be engaged as creative partners in problem solving or innovation. They become the tough-to-supervise, resistant employees who slow down an organization's ability to adapt and succeed. Thus, expanding choice for those involved becomes a primary strategy for effective design and implementation of change.

Thoughts on Personal Leadership

In a world of change, people become numb to possibilities. While much has been predicted about the future, it is often hard for individuals to have a positive vision of what these changes might mean for them personally. In preparing for the future, your role as leader is crucial.

In a recent training session of managers and supervisors, we asked people what they thought the future held for them. We also asked them about the fundamental shift they saw happening around them. The room was quiet and people had a hard time answering, although all agreed that some type of major change was under way. Finally, one supervisor mentioned that "self-responsibility" was likely to be a guiding value in the future. The room was then able to share in a discussion of what this term meant to people and how they and their employees were likely to change as a result of self-responsibility becoming more central as a value.

The lesson is that people may not be talking enough about the broad, underlying shifts, the general destabilization of the workplace. Instead, they focus too rapidly on how to get through "this," meaning a specific change, such as a merger or restructuring. Then, as each change hits, they go through the emotional transitions all over again, including periods of resistance or depression.

As a leader, you can help people to see the larger view of change and envision how to make a better world. For example, the president of a manufacturing company we know spends much of his time helping to create this vision of a "self-organizing" company. His personal investment and contacts with others, his willingness to measure the success of his organization in terms of "whether or not people are learning and growing," is evidence that despite the big shifts, an optimistic view is possible. He is not asking people to cope with a difficult or strenuous present; instead, he helps them to define an exciting future.

16

People Are Ready for a Workplace Without Fear

Those of us who are committed to the work of reducing fear often feel caught between the vision of the high-trust, high-performance organization and the realities around us. To use the phrase of one manager who believes in these ideals, we operate somewhere in the "gray spaces between what ought to be and what can be." The challenge of this work is felt constantly in the tension between our values and the less-than-perfect nature of the organizations in which we operate.

This book has been written for the leaders who constantly probe those uneasy gray spaces, doing their utmost every day to achieve a high-trust organization. These executives, managers, and employees know that fighting the good fight is not easy, yet they believe it is essential. In this last chapter, we would like to acknowledge this hard work and the importance of all those who accept the call to this particular brand of leadership.

Whatever Happened to Paul?

One of the executives we know who best exemplifies trust-based leadership is a man we will refer to here as Paul. In 1990, when we completed the manuscript for the first edition of this book, Paul was forty-one and president and CEO of a service organization owned by a much larger corporation. In the last several years, people who read our first edition would sometimes ask us, "Whatever happened to Paul?" That's a good question, and the answers say a lot about both the importance and the challenges of leadership based on trust. The fact that he requested then—and still does—that we not use his real name is an indication of the realistic trade-offs he makes at work.

When we first interviewed Paul, he had been recruited away from a competitor four years earlier to be the CEO of a company that was $1.5 million in the red. Within eighteen months, his organization broke even. Within two years, its net income was at $2 million and "President" was added to his title. His organization grew from $35 million to $75 million. These numbers described him, in part: intelligent, savvy, and producing results in an incredibly competitive environment.

Those who reported to Paul described his leadership style as "bringing out the best in those who work for him." He saw himself as a facilitator, someone who secures the resources and provides the necessary consultation so that others can do their jobs. When asked about the most satisfying aspects of his work, he referred to times "when a group of us have worked on a problem and come to a solution that we all buy into."

Seven years ago, when he joined the company, success involved more than hard work and long hours for Paul. The corporate environment that surrounded his company was frequently characterized by fear. He spent a large percentage of his time buffering those who reported to him from the bureaucratic, high-control practices of the parent organization. Knowing that he had been hired to turn his company around financially, he chose to do this through decentralized decision making, flexibility, high involvement with customers, and healthy doses of fun.

Sadly, the more successful his organization was, the greater resistance he and his employees experienced from the corporation. On a performance appraisal, he received a mediocre rating. He was told that his consensus style caused him "not to be objective" about those who reported to him. His corporate superiors expressed concern that he was creating too much of a "family" atmosphere.

Within a year, Paul was recruited to a large, multistate competitor. There, over the last six years, he has filled two different executive roles, currently that of vice president for business development. His exposure to line operations and corporate politics and his extensive involvement with customers has refined his sense of leadership. Paul observes that in complex industries like his, where "the economic, information, and customer bases keep changing, people must be free to think holistically and creatively for their organizations to succeed." He also says:

"Listening without bias is the core. Leaders need to be able to listen to the truth without meting out consequences. And then they need to take action. They cannot become paralyzed by having lots of information come at them that may be contradictory to what they believe. You can only discover the solutions to complexity if you don't go in with a bias. You have to have the ability to trust that people have good reasons for doing the things that they do, for saying the things they say. By doing so, you can engage people more creatively in the process and get their participation, rather than their resistance."

Talking About the Future: Knowledge, Learning, and Trust

A new century is an extraordinary concept to ponder. In the last few years and in the next several to come, researchers and pundits and ordinary folks will talk about its implications and wonder about its potential. Peter Senge (1997) has commented:

Almost everyone agrees that the command-and-control corporate model will not carry us into the twenty-first century. In a world of increasing interdependence and rapid change, it is no longer possible to figure it out from the top. Nor, as today's CEOs keep discovering, is it possible to *command* people to make the profound systemic changes needed to transform industrial-age institutions for the next business era. Increasingly, successful organizations

are building competitive advantage through less controlling and more learning—that is, through continually creating and sharing new knowledge [p. 30].

In his recent and provocative book, *Intellectual Capital: The
New Wealth of Organizations* (1997), Thomas Stewart points out that
"knowledge has become the primary raw material and result of economic activity" and that "organizational intelligence—smart people
working in smart ways—has moved from a supporting role to a
starring one" (p. 56). He emphasizes human capital and defines it as
"the capabilities of the individuals required to provide solutions to
customers" (p. 76). Stewart's observations support Kotter and
Heskett (1992), Collins and Porras (1994), and de Geus (1997a,
1997b) and their mutually recognized points about organizational
adaptivity. His perspective is this: "*Human capital* matters because it
is the source of innovation and renewal, whether from brainstorms
in a lab or new leads in a sales rep's little black book" (p. 76).

Stewart glibly makes a point that we believe is central to organizational success in the years ahead:

> For more than a decade business leaders have been taught,
> to the point of being hectored, the virtues of bureaucracy-
> busting, teamwork, coaching, etc. Here's all you really
> have to know about the subject . . . *provide safe places where
> people can share ideas about work without getting shut down by
> bosses and bureaucrats*" [pp. 87–88; emphasis ours].

Senge (1997) also supports this view:

> Top-down directives, even when they are implemented,
> reinforce an environment of fear, distrust, and internal
> competitiveness that reduces collaboration and coopera-
> tion. They foster compliance instead of commitment, yet
> only genuine commitment can bring about the courage,
> imagination, patience, and perseverance necessary in a
> knowledge creating organization [p. 32].

Paul's operational experiences support what both Senge and
Stewart have to say. Paul commented to us: "Many of us have been
trained and facilitated to death. And I mean that positively. We've
learned about the importance of communication, honesty, quality,
and integrity." Indicting those in key positions who "think they're
different than front-line workers," Paul believes that the "hopes,

dreams, and desires of the employee on the front line are the same as those of the people at the top. The problem is leadership, not people. People are ready." What the workplace is ready for, he continues, is leadership that truly supports people: "It feels right, it sounds right, and in their hearts, people know it is right."

Leaders Must Find the Courage to Speak Up

Most of us, like Paul, still work in organizations that are full of conflicting circumstances: environments that are still attached in the background to traditional hierarchies while growing the seeds of new thinking and new energy. To become strong, these tender shoots must be nurtured throughout the organization by people who see themselves as leaders. This means that individuals will need to call out the fear-based practices, systems, and structures that inhibit the open flow of ideas and information. In other words, leaders must find the courage to speak up to their peers and bosses about the negative impact of fear in the workplace. If those in recognized leadership positions do not do this, it is foolish to expect that others will.

This book has focused on what you can do to create a more open, trusting workplace, so that those who report to you will not be afraid to speak up. It is clear, however, that other aspects of leadership are needed to help change the way an entire organization does business. Helping others to speak up ultimately prompts these questions:

"How much am I willing to speak up?"

"How well do I speak up, when I do?"

"What risks am I willing to take in order to have my points be heard?"

These questions underscore what it means to model the courage mentioned by Peter Senge. One manager with whom we have worked told us:

"To begin this work I helped others in my team speak up. Over time this began to raise questions and demand action that I couldn't respond to on my own. Pretty soon, I found I had to do something that would help. I had to drive fear out of myself. I, too, had to be someone who spoke up."

When an open, supportive style of leadership is not reinforced by those to whom you report, it is—without question—discouraging. But this does not have to be a reason to stop. Paul commented to us about his greatest source of impatience: "a whole organization full of bright, well-trained, thoughtful people ready to do extraordinary things" who are blocked by practices and beliefs that are based on negative assumptions of what people can and will do. "The longer I survive," he told us, "the clearer I am about what I need and want to do. I will compromise to preserve my job and my organization. But I cannot go along with some of what I'm asked to do."

When you decide to speak up about fear in the workplace, you demonstrate commitment to the long-term success of the organization. You also show others that you care about them and want to do your part to create a satisfying, humane, and creative work environment. But because of the lingering strength of old-style, hierarchical methods, such actions are not without personal risk. These risks must be balanced with what Paul describes as the need to "hang in there and stay healthy, so you can be a part of leading the change." Acknowledging the tough part of being a trust-based leader in a fear-based organization, he observes, "To stay healthy you have to watch the risk. Your integrity sure gets tested."

If you find yourself in this situation, a companion volume of ours may be useful to you. Coauthored with George Orr, *The Courageous Messenger: How to Successfully Speak Up at Work* (1996) helps people to decide when and how to effectively present sensitive information or points of view to peers, managers, or employees.

The Smart Thing and the Right Thing

In 1991, when the first edition of this book was published, it was much harder to make the business case for building trust in organizations. If people were unimpressed with the findings from our field study or didn't like the theories of those we would quote, our fallback position would highlight the values of participation and openness. We would tell a story or two that emphasized the negative impact of fear, then assert our belief that building trust-based organizations was the right thing to do, especially in societies based on democratic principles.

That is different now. Although there are still few other titles that address the specific issues of fear in the workplace, much research has been done and reported about the essential ingredients needed to build high-performance organizations. Countless organizations have reported on their efforts to increase knowledge, improve quality, build customer loyalty, and reduce costs in a time of dramatic change. Upon examination, whether it is directly stated or not, building trust and reducing the fear of speaking up are consistently part of the core formula.

In addition to the now-available research, we have identified a certain logic that ties successful business outcomes to reducing fear and increasing trust. You might find this useful when you raise concerns about the debilitating effects of fear or when others ask you why building trust is essential to the future success of the enterprise. As one CEO told us, "If I could figure out a way to be the low-cost, high-quality supplier without dealing with all this messy people stuff, I would do it. But there isn't any way."

While this statement may have the feel of begrudging acceptance, we offer it as an example of the pragmatic connection that can be made between the interdependent worlds of feelings and data. Once people begin to see the full extent of the linkages between the business imperatives and human relations, movement toward the high-trust end of the continuum becomes that much easier—and, for some, quite compelling. When leaders start to create a high-trust workplace, things begin to happen:

- People speak up, and in doing so they bring problems and issues to the surface that require attention.

- These previously undiscussed issues may be dilemmas, conflicts, differences, and powerful suggestions for change. They demand new ways of doing business and new ways of relating.

- As new ways to address these dilemmas are discovered, problems are solved and innovations are created.

- People gain a new sense of confidence and energy. If morale has suffered, it improves. If it was already good, loyalty to the organization becomes deeper and help in meeting its challenges increases.

- Accomplishment leads to reflection and learning, and to an increased sense of capacity and a willingness to change as the times demand.

■ This capacity to meet the future with confidence becomes the hallmark of competitiveness and organizational effectiveness.

This chain reaction meets an organization's need to survive and thrive in a world of change. Because it is based as much on the value of people as on business logic, it releases the tremendous energy of a cycle of trust and achievement. The smart thing merges with the right thing: the vision of a high-trust workplace and the core behaviors we described in Chapter Three become a new way of doing business.

Challenges of the Path

W. Edwards Deming was famous for telling those who attended his seminars, "We are here to make another kind of world." We believe that world to be the one described by Paul, Peter Senge, and Thomas Stewart. In Chapter One, a continuum of fear and trust was presented and you were invited to think about where your organization might be placed. Is it characterized more by trust than by fear? If fear is present, how does it manifest itself? How pervasive is it? Our hope is that the awareness you have gained by exploring our various chapters will assist you in creating a work world where trust, creativity, and learning are far more prevalent than fear, cynicism, and resistance to change.

The challenge of building the high-trust, high-performance workplace requires leaders who are willing to do things differently, making both personal and organizational changes. It demands women and men who are willing to admit and learn from their mistakes, to seek feedback and involvement from people throughout their organization, and to work hard in order to eliminate the technical and human barriers that block the practical application of knowledge and creativity. It requires a willingness to stick with the uneasy process of meshing trust-based values with an imperfect, but improving, organizational culture.

We started studying the issues of fear in the workplace in 1988. Since then, there has been an obvious irony associated with writing about and working with fear in the American workplace. We know that each day, in countries far less democratic than ours, people take enormous risks to speak out and face repercussions considerably more serious than being labeled "not a team player." Around the world, people continue to engage in acts of extraordinary personal and political courage, frequently placing their lives on the line for the privileges we take for granted, one of which is self-expression.

Their actions make us feel a little foolish, considering that in "the land of the free and the home of the brave" many still do not feel free to speak up about their concerns at work. From the stories we have heard, we are convinced that each day too many of us—at all levels, in all types of jobs and roles—still perpetuate dependent, bureaucratic, and autocratic work environments, if only in subtle ways. While these actions are largely unconscious, their impact is unacceptable: self-generated and self-imposed patterns of fear and mistrust that restrict collective creativity, energy, and innovation.

Yet increasingly, people continue to see great possibilities as they make their way toward a new century. As for us, we place our faith in our pragmatic national heritage that values choice, freedom of expression, risk taking, and the exploration of unknown territory. We all want to be proud of what we do and the organizations we work for. We want to use our skills constructively, contributing to a product or service valued by others. We want to be listened to, respected, appreciated, and trusted. And increasingly, leaders are ready to facilitate the necessary transformation to the high-trust, high-performance organization in which these experiences are a way of life.

Leaders like Paul are excited about the future and what it will mean for organizations. These leaders are people who possess a vision, have courage, and operate from the belief that successful organizations develop people, not intimidate them. The bright future they see depends on their ability to meet the continuing challenges head-on, working as partners with other leaders, peers, and employees. They understand this basic criterion for success with their brains and their hearts and know that the results are more than long-term financial gains. They feel the pride that flows from enabling good people to do good work. They celebrate the confidence and insight that result from taking risks and trying new approaches. They are willing to work with things the way they are and, in doing so, they derive their satisfaction from making a great difference in a world headed for positive change.

APPENDIX

Field Study Participants

Category	Number of Participants	Percentage of Participants
Level of Position		
CEOs	4	1
Senior managers	16	6
Midlevel managers	62	24
Professional staff (do not supervise)	53	20
First-level supervisors	25	10
Front-line staff		
Technical-paraprofessional	47	18
Clerical	35	14
Blue-collar	18	7
Total	260	100
Number of People by Race and Gender		
White males	98	38
White females	123	47
Men of color	16	6
Women of color	23	9
Total	260	100

Category	Number of Participants	Percentage of Participants
Participating Organizations		
Service	9	41
Government	3	14
Manufacturing	10	45
Total	22	100
Size of Organizations		
Over 10,000 employees	10	46
Between 2,000 and 10,000 employees	6	27
Fewer than 2,000 employees	6	27
Total	22	100

RECOMMENDED RESOURCES

We know very few people who have time to do all the professional development work they would like to do. That is certainly true for us, and we suspect it might be true for you. It seems as though there is always a stack of books and journal articles that go unread, thanks to the more pressing demands of the phone calls to return, the workshop to give, or the report to be written. Often an item from the stack only gets read when someone tells us directly: "You should read this—now!" Always grateful for this encouragement, we would like to do the same for you. Here is a list of some of our favorite resources, all of which connect to themes and issues that are important when leaders make the decision to reduce fear and build trust. Each of these has challenged us and pushed our thinking to a new place.

Argyris, C., Putnam, R., and Smith, D. M. *Action Science: Concepts, Methods, and Skills for Research and Intervention.* San Francisco: Jossey-Bass, 1985. Argyris and his colleagues report that people, when dealing with threatening situations, tend to act in ways that limit valid information and create "self-sealing patterns of escalating error." They see people withholding thoughts and feelings, speaking with high levels of inference, attributing defensiveness and negative motives to others, and placing the responsibility for errors on others or situational factors. Among Argyris's many journal articles, we have found "Skilled Incompetence," in the

September–October 1986 *Harvard Business Review,* to be very useful. He identifies groups of highly skilled communicators who, in their efforts to avoid conflict and upset, did not talk about issues that are critical for organizational problem solving. We are grateful to Argyris for the notion of "undiscussability."

Block, Peter. *The Empowered Manager: Positive Political Skills at Work.* San Francisco: Jossey-Bass, 1987. In this work, Block describes two sides of a self-reinforcing "patriarchal contract." As part of this arrangement, employees submit to authority, deny self-expression, sacrifice for unnamed future rewards, and believe that these three requirements are just. In return, the employees do not have to take responsibility and can blame management, especially when things go wrong. Management must shoulder this load, but in turn it is supported for behaving in controlling and dictatorial ways. This dependent cycle is at the core of bureaucratic behavior. With these dynamics outlined, Block goes on to describe an "entrepreneurial contract" where managers and employees work in interdependent ways, sharing responsibility and pride in mutual efforts that ensure organizational success. Key strategies for establishing this new way of doing business are identified.

Block, Peter. *Stewardship: Choosing Service over Self-Interest.* San Francisco: Berrett-Koehler, 1993. Defining stewardship as "account-ability without control or compliance," Block challenges leaders to rethink the way they inadvertently reinforce patterns of hierarchy and control, even as they believe they are leading in highly partici-pative, trust-based ways. He highlights an important but slippery set of choices: partnership over patriarchy, adventure over safety, and service over self-interest. Exploring roles for both bosses and subordinates, he presents steps that need to be taken in order for the philosophy of stewardship to become real and concrete.

Bridges, William. *JobShift: How to Prosper in a Workplace Without Jobs.* Reading, Mass.: Addison-Wesley, 1994. Continuing his theme of change, Bridges discusses one of the most dramatic, incremental workplace changes: the disappearance of jobs as we have come to know them. He offers explanations of why this "dejobbing" is hap-pening that include researched statistics and case studies. He poses provocative questions to the reader and offers advice on how to suc-cessfully adapt to this new reality. We find this book particularly use-ful for those who recognize that the basic assumptions related to long-term employment have shifted and want to develop a successful strategy to apply to both their careers and their personal life.

Bridges, William. *Managing Transition: Making the Most of Change.* Reading, Mass.: Addison-Wesley, 1991. This is a very practical book for managers who are faced with implementing change. Extending his personal model of endings, the neutral zone, and beginnings (from his book, *Transitions: Making Sense of Life's Changes* [Reading, Mass.: Addison-Wesley, 1980]) to organizations, Bridges outlines a variety of predictable issues that leaders need to address during a change process. He offers concrete advice for what to do during these phases, including how to take care of oneself as the emotion and stress of change play themselves out.

Collins, James C., and Porras, Jerry I. *Built to Last: Successful Habits of Visionary Companies.* New York: HarperCollins, 1994. Reporting on six years of research, Collins and Porras identify and discuss the specific characteristics that account for the extraordinary success of a set of companies. These are organizations—institutions, actually—that have prospered over extended periods of time, surviving many product cycles and several generations of leaders. A lengthy appendix summarizes the details of their research. Collins and Porras present their findings in an easy-to-understand way that enabled us to see how our thoughts about trust and fear connected to their conclusions about long-term success.

Deming, W. Edwards. *Out of the Crisis.* Cambridge, Mass.: MIT Press, 1986. Deming's references to the fears connected to speaking up at work have served as a catalyst for us, and others, who continue to see this dynamic as a most significant barrier to organizational effectiveness and positive human relationships. In his overview of the steps necessary to transform U.S. organizations, he briefly lists the types of fears typically experienced: job loss, poor performance, limited career options, loss of personal credibility, and lack of trust of management. With his directive to "drive out fear," Deming provides a provocative challenge, but he offers limited guidance about how to do it. For the last ten years, filling that gap has been a major focus of our work. His last book, *The New Economics for Industry, Government, Education* (Cambridge, Mass.: Massachusetts Institute of Technology, Center for Advanced Engineering Study, 1994), further refines and develops his seminal ideas into a "system of profound knowledge."

Gibb, Jack. *Trust.* Los Angeles: Guild of Tutors Press, 1978. We are among the many who have been inspired by Jack Gibb. The trust-fear continuum, offered in Chapter One, was inspired by his approach, and much of our early thinking and work on the subject of trust stems from discussions with him in the early 1980s. Among the first to describe the dynamics of trust, Gibb identifies fear as the opposite of trust and suggests that they always go together. He contrasts the behaviors and thinking patterns that are based on defensiveness and fear with those that are based on trust. Other useful readings include "Defensive Communication," in the *Journal of Communication,* 1963, *11*(3), 141–148, and "Fear and Facade: Defensive Management," in R. E. Farson (ed.), *Science and Human Affairs* (Palo Alto, Calif.: Science and Behavior Books, 1965).

Hammond, Josh, and Morrison, James. *The Stuff Americans Are Made Of: The Seven Cultural Forces That Define Americans—A New Framework for Quality, Productivity, and Profitability.* Old Tappan, N.J.: Macmillan, 1996. Hammond and Morrison present a framework that describes how most people born and raised in the United States think about and react to life, action, work, change—and much more. The interconnected forces include insistence on choice, pursuit of impossible dreams, obsession with big and more, impatience with time, acceptance of mistakes, the urge to improvise, and a fixation with what is new. We've been familiar with some of the research behind their book for some time and were glad to see the work published. The seven elements have been very useful to us over time, frequently shaping the way in which we have approached various aspects of our work.

Harvey, Jerry B. *The Abilene Paradox and Other Meditations on Management.* San Francisco: Jossey-Bass, 1988. Still a favorite, this humorous and insightful set of essays raises important and uncomfortable issues worthy of any leader's attention. Of particular relevance to the fear and trust issues are his views on learning to better manage our agreements, rather than our conflicts; why we assume disagreement when it is not present; the importance of forgiveness at work; and the moral courage demanded by many popular strategies for organizational survival.

Kotter, John P., and Heskett, James L. *Corporate Culture and Performance.* New York: Free Press, 1992. This book begins by reminding the reader about some basic aspects of organizational culture. It then proceeds to report on the findings of four different studies that looked at the connection between an organization's culture and its long-term economic performance. An appendix lists the companies involved, describes their methodology, and reports data. Most significant to us was the comparison between organizations that are able to adapt to change in order to continue being successful and those that cannot. The values and behavior of those in management are described for each company.

Quinn, Robert E. *Deep Change: Finding the Leader Within.* San Francisco: Jossey-Bass, 1996. Quinn's book is an insightful examination of the connections between personal change and organizational improvement. His stories as a consultant resonate with the need for leaders to acquire emotional as well as intellectual learning. He encourages careful reflection on how personal behaviors, directions, and assumptions influence relationships and the general life of organizations. His concluding sections on hearing the inner voice of the organization and dealing with undiscussables are elegant testimony to the importance of risk taking and sensitive, nondefensive listening as a leader.

Rachman, S. J. *Fear and Courage.* New York: Freeman, 1978. From the psychological literature, Rachman provides a straightforward definition of fear as "the experience of apprehension" and cites four major causes: exposure to traumatic stimulation; repeated exposures to subtraumatic sensitizing situations; observations, direct or indirect, of people exhibiting fear; and transmission of fear-inducing information. Rachman observes that fears can be acquired by hearing of others' experiences or by direct involvement. He highlights control as a factor and points out that if, in the face of threats, one cannot control the likely outcome, fear will be the most likely experience. Predictability is another factor that can reduce fears.

Schrage, Michael. *No More Teams: Mastering the Dynamics of Creative Collaboration.* New York: Doubleday Currency, 1995. In this revision of *Shared Minds* (New York: Random House, 1990), Schrage argues that teamwork and communication are overused and ambiguous concepts. He believes that collaboration is the essential activity for organizational survival in times of increasing complexity and specialization. With many examples from the arts and sciences, he builds the case for and describes collaboration in business settings. The second half of the book focuses on tools of collaboration, emphasizing ways technology can enhance the creative collaborative process.

Schwarz, Roger M. *The Skilled Facilitator: Practical Wisdom for Developing Effective Groups.* San Francisco: Jossey-Bass, 1994. When managers learn to facilitate effective group work, they begin to free themselves from the traditional habits of directing and controlling. Schwarz's book helps leaders and others to develop the skills that are essential in building trust and reducing fear. The book is loaded with tips and examples of words to say for a wide range of situations that require facilitation or a facilitative style of leadership. Valid information, free and informed choice, and internal commitment to those choices are the values at the core of all the advice offered.

Senge, Peter M. *The Fifth Discipline: The Art and Practice of the Learning Organization.* New York: Doubleday Currency, 1990. Senge's well-known exploration of systems thinking, personal mastery, mental models, shared vision, and team learning represents a comprehensive way to think about the evolution of organizations— and what prevents them from evolving. He draws together a great many threads, including Argyris's concept of undiscussables, to reveal how deeply patterned personal and organizational thinking inhibits learning. The follow-up work, *The Fifth Discipline Fieldbook*, by Senge and others (New York: Doubleday Currency, 1994), is a practical guide to putting his ideas into action. Some exercises, such as those on "the ladder of inference," will especially remind readers of the cycles of mistrust and how they become embedded in relationships through untested assumptions.

Stewart, Thomas A. *Intellectual Capital: The New Wealth of Organizations.* New York: Doubleday Currency, 1997. Stewart makes a strong contribution to the growing literature on knowledge-based work, organizations, and economies. He offers data, case studies, and bits of conversation to help readers see that to be successful in the future, organizations must focus on developing, sharing, and applying knowledge. He explores and links human, structural, and customer capital and offers generalized advice for leaders who want to enhance their organization's ability to identify and manage its intellectual assets. He also provides observations about the information age that are significant for individual careers. An appendix gives an overview of tools to use in measuring intellectual capital.

Suarez, J. Gerald. *Managing Fear; Change, Improvement and Fear;* and *Managing Fear: How to Begin.* Better Management for a Changing World series. Silver Springs, Md.: CC-M Productions. Videotapes. These videotapes show Suarez teaching groups of managers how to recognize and begin to manage fear in the workplace. His approach is thoroughly based in the Deming philosophy. Clear examples and application of quality tools, such as fish-bone diagrams, enable viewers to quickly identify the causes and effects of organizational fear. The tapes show people beginning to talk about fear and the issues fear conceals in their organizations. These tapes are an excellent starting place for understanding how fear undermines quality and productivity and for stimulating broad discussion. Lloyd Dobbins narrates these Clare Crawford-Mason productions.

Wheatley, Margaret J. *Leadership and the New Science: Learning About Organization from an Orderly Universe.* San Francisco: Berrett-Koehler, 1992. Writing in a way that makes hard-science theory accessible to those of us without a science background, Wheatley explores discoveries in quantum physics, chaos theory, and evolutionary biology. She then applies these discoveries to organizations and organizational change. The result is new insight and a compelling theory base to use in understanding, designing, leading, and managing organizations. Along the way, she illuminates the polarities that trouble people in organizations the most: order and change, autonomy and control, structure and flexibility, and planning and innovation.

REFERENCES

Argyris, C. "Skilled Incompetence." *Harvard Business Review,* Sept.–Oct. 1986, pp. 74–79.

Argyris, C., Putnam, R., and Smith, D. M. *Action Science: Concepts, Methods, and Skills for Research and Intervention.* San Francisco: Jossey-Bass, 1985.

Bartolomé, F., and Laurent, A. "The Manager: Master and Servant of Power." *Harvard Business Review,* Nov.–Dec. 1986, pp. 71–81.

Block, P. *The Empowered Manager: Positive Political Skills at Work.* San Francisco: Jossey-Bass, 1987.

Bridges, W. *JobShift: How to Prosper in a Workplace Without Jobs.* Reading, Mass.: Addison-Wesley, 1994.

Collins, J. C., and Porras, J. I. *Built to Last: Successful Habits of Visionary Companies.* New York: HarperCollins, 1994.

De Geus, A. "The Living Company." *Harvard Business Review,* Mar.–Apr. 1997a, pp. 51–59.

De Geus, A. *The Living Company: Habits for Survival in a Turbulent Business Environment.* Boston: Harvard Business School Press, 1997b.

Fisher, R., and Brown, S. *Getting Together.* Boston: Houghton Mifflin, 1988.

Gibb, J. R. *Trust.* Los Angeles: Guild of Tutors Press, 1978.

Gitlow, H. S., and Gitlow, S. J. *The Deming Guide to Quality and Competitive Position.* Englewood Cliffs, N.J.: Prentice Hall, 1987.

Hammond, J., and Morrison, J. *The Stuff Americans Are Made Of.* Old Tappan, N.J.: Macmillan, 1996.

Hammond, S. A. *The Thin Book of Appreciative Inquiry.* Plano, Tex.: By Sue Annis Hammond, 1996.

Handy, C. "The Citizen Corporation." In "Looking Ahead: Implications of the Present." *Harvard Business Review,* Sept.–Oct. 1997, pp. 26–28.

Harvey, J. B. *The Abilene Paradox and Other Meditations on Management.* San Francisco: Jossey-Bass, 1988.

Kotter, J. P., and Heskett, J. L. *Corporate Culture and Performance.* New York: Free Press, 1992.

Moore, M., and Gergen, P. "Risk Taking and Organization Change." *Training and Development Journal,* 1985, *39*(6), 72–76.

Ryan, K. D., Oestreich, D. K., and Orr III, George A. *The Courageous Messenger: How to Successfully Speak Up at Work.* San Francisco: Jossey-Bass, 1996.

Scott, C. D., and Jaffe, D. T. *Managing Organizational Change: A Practical Guide for Managers.* Menlo Park, Calif.: Crisp, 1989.

Senge, P. "Communities of Leaders and Learners." In "Looking Ahead: Implications of the Present." *Harvard Business Review,* Sept.–Oct. 1997, pp. 30–32.

Stewart, T. A. *Intellectual Capital: The New Wealth of Organizations.* New York: Doubleday Currency, 1997.

Stowell, S. J., and Starcevich, M. M. *The Coach: Creating Partnerships for a Competitive Edge.* Salt Lake City, Utah: Center for Management and Organization Effectiveness, 1987.

Tannenbaum, R., and Schmidt, W. "How to Choose a Leadership Pattern." *Harvard Business Review,* 1957, *36,* 95–100.

Vaill, P. B. *Managing as a Performing Art: New Ideas for a World of Chaotic Change.* San Francisco: Jossey-Bass, 1991.

Zand, D. E. "Trust and Administrative Problem Solving." *Administrative Sciences Quarterly,* 1972, *17,* 229–239.

INDEX

A

Abilene Paradox and Other Meditations on Management (Harvey), 44, 179, 306

Abrasive/abusive conduct of managers, 59–66; abruptness as, 62; aggressive, controlling manner as, 64; angry outbursts as, 65; blaming as, 63; causes of, 59–60; coaching for reducing, 155–158; descriptions of, 59; discrediting and discounting as, 63; fear of speaking up about, 97–98; feedback on, 153–155, 162; glaring eye contact as, 61–62; impact of, on employees, 60; insults and put-downs as, 62–63; loss of control as, 65; performance expectations for reducing, 159–166; physical threats as, 65–66; reducing, strategies for, 147–167; retaliatory in appearance, 160–163; retaliatory in intention, 163–164; scope and range of, 60–61; silence as, 61; snubbing as, 62; threats about job security as, 64–65; in top management, 73–74; as trigger of mistrust, 57, 58, 59–66; unintentional versus intentional, 59–60; yelling and shouting as, 65. *See also* Aggressive behavior; Interpersonal conduct; Managers and supervisors

Abrasive-abusive scale, 60–61, 149

Abruptness, 62

Acknowledgment of fear, 129–145; checklist for, 137–139; denial and, 9–10, 139–144; enlisting subordinates' support for, 136–139; informal introduction of, 133–136; initiating discussion for, 130–136; learning about fear in workplace and, 130–133; organizational culture and, 144–145; personal leadership for, 130–144, 145; strategies for, 131. *See also* Assessment of fear

Action planning, 130, 137; for manager behavior change, 157–158, 161; for resolving undiscussables, 210, 222–224, 230–231; sense of powerlessness and, 224–225; for worst-case thinking, 265–267, 270

Action Science: Concepts, Methods, and Skills for Research and Intervention (Argyris, Putnam, Smith), 303–304

Age, as undiscussable, 83–84

Aggressive behavior: in cycles of mistrust, 20–24; as trigger of mistrust, 64. *See also* Abrasive/abusive conduct of managers

KATHLEEN D. RYAN is a principal of The Orion Partnership, a consulting firm located in Issaquah, Washington, near Seattle. She received her B.A. degree (1969) in English from the University of California at Berkeley and her M.P.A. degree (1978) from the University of Southern California.

Yuen Lui

Ryan is known for her work with organizational culture, turning fear-based organizations into ones characterized by trust and collaboration. She has been described as "one of a handful of pioneering thinkers who are shaping the new world of quality . . . an organizational consultant with an instinct for translating complex human behavior into practical concepts." Ryan maintains an extensive national consulting practice, often working with her husband and business partner, George Orr. She has served as both a member and director of the Organization Development Professional Practice Area for the American Society for Training and Development. In 1980, she coproduced the award-winning training film *The Workplace Hustle*. Her second book, *The Courageous Messenger: How to Successfully Speak Up at Work* (Jossey-Bass, 1996), was coauthored with Daniel Oestreich and George Orr.

DANIEL K. OESTREICH is principal of Oestreich Associates, an organization development consulting firm based in Redmond, Washington. He received his B.A. degree (1973) from Yale University in history and his M.A. degree (1975) from the University of Colorado at Boulder in guidance and counseling.

Oestreich works creatively with leaders to help them hear feedback that will improve trust levels and systems performance and build strong workplace communities. He is respected as an effective, articulate coach, able to sensitively help clients find their own best paths of change and personal growth. He is coauthor, with Kathleen Ryan and George Orr, of *The Courageous Messenger* and has spoken nationally and internationally on a wide variety of leadership topics. His clients include health care, manufacturing, utilities, government, and nonprofit agencies and schools.

Oestreich's professional background includes many years as a personnel generalist for the City of Bellevue, Washington. He is a former board member of the Eastside Quality Council and a former member of the advisory board of *HR Newsletter*, a publication of the International City/County Management Association. He has written elsewhere on employee development and conflict management themes.

Michael Walmsley Photography

p. 35, 61, 81, 92, 101, 110-111

Also Available from Jossey-Bass

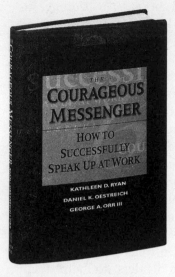

The Courageous Messenger
How to Successfully Speak Up at Work

Kathleen D. Ryan
Daniel K. Oestreich
George A. Orr III

Inspired by a pivotal chapter in *Driving Fear Out of the Workplace*, this book relates the finer points of communicating tough news, voicing strong opinions, and discussing difficult issues at work without compromising your position—or your job. Filled with tips, illuminating stories, and a wealth of practical exercises, *The Courageous Messenger* gives you the means to assess the benefits, risks, and motivations of communicating difficult messages. It helps you become a skilled messenger. And it teaches you how to speak with courage, clarity, and diplomacy, whether you're addressing peers, bosses, or employees.

The Courageous Messenger
Kathleen D. Ryan, Daniel K. Oestreich, George A. Orr III
Hardcover
ISBN 0–7879–0268–3
287 pages, $25.00